The War Lords
of Washington

THE WAR LORDS OF WASHINGTON

by

BRUCE CATTON

GREENWOOD PRESS, PUBLISHERS
NEW YORK

Contents

To My Son Bill

CHAPTER ONE

Handwriting on the Wall

THEY were often admitted to be the ablest men in the nation and they were very high up in the Defense Effort, and the best was none too good for them. If, collectively, they were neither as beautiful nor as terrible as an army with banners, individually they were very impressive. Their faces had that indefinable but unmistakable gloss which comes to faces that are photographed a great deal (good food, right living, and the proper kind of publicity can do much for a man) and if the North Lounge of the Carlton had been set aside for the party it was only fitting and proper.

For this was a rather special evening. Mr. Donald Nelson was giving a dinner in honor of the Vice-President, and of all the people in Washington only some two dozen had been invited. It was a little strange, when you stopped to think about it; this particular group of two dozen people, no more and no less, had never been segregated like this before and never would be again, and to bring them together—to make precisely these men and no others the select, obvious, inescapably chosen twenty-four— had taken signs and portents in the sky and a compelling breath on the face of the waters. Something momentous had had to happen, to the world at large and to the republic in particular, to bring this about. It had happened, and no one present knew quite what it was, but even the dullest knew vaguely that it had not yet stopped happening. It was the evening of Thursday, December 4, 1941.

On that particular evening there was nothing much to show that the calendar was moving on to one of those crucial, turning-point dates which say: Hereafter, nothing is ever going to be quite the same again. It was just a Thursday evening, and if the situation had grown a bit tense, why, then, it had been tense for a year and more and no one's appetite had been spoiled thereby. The paneled walls were lost in a haze of dim lights and cigar smoke before they reached the high ceiling, and any shadow which a Coming Event might be casting was effectively lost in the expensive dusk. It touched the high spirits and good nature of none of the assembled guests.

Except, perhaps, for Frank Knox. The Secretary of the Navy was grave as he joined the others at the bar before dinner, preoccupied with his own thoughts as he took his place at the dinner table on the left hand of his host. As a life-long Republican he had joined an objectionably Democratic cabinet because he felt that a time of emergency had arrived, and he had lately been confirmed in this opinion by confidential reports from the far side of the Pacific. He was no better fitted than the next man to appraise and interpret the shape of things to come, but he did know physical trouble when he saw it, and he saw it coming now quite clearly. Also, as a simple man who had been one of Teddy Roosevelt's Rough Riders, he knew a responsibility when he saw one, and the weight of the responsibility which he, as Secretary of the Navy, was carrying around right now was oppressive. The buzz and chatter of two dozen men enjoying the before-dinner cocktail eddied around him without quite touching him.

Then, too, there was the Vice-President, Mr. Henry Wallace. He was fitted to see what was coming; fitted to understand it, even to go out and meet it head-on, if people would only let him. But he had been touched, somehow, with a kind of Cassandra curse, so that any warning he uttered was apt to go unheeded. Tonight he stood in the group by the bar, nursing a soft drink which he did not especially want, and made small talk with men who—as no one knew better than himself—were unalterably opposed to that shifting one-tenth of him which they were able to see and understand. The heir-apparent to the New Deal dynasty was mingling socially with blue-chip industrialists tonight, and nobody felt quite natural about it.

Nobody, of course, except Nelson. Nelson felt natural anywhere. He was big, jovial, and self-possessed, and his round red face beamed through the cigar smoke like a harvest moon through the September haze. This dinner party might look like a shotgun wedding between industry and the administration—indeed, in a sense Nelson was the man holding the shotgun—but all the decencies were being observed, and in any case it had seemed to Nelson that some such meeting as this was necessary. The defense program was in a bad way. It had brought together, out on the open stage of public life in Washington, all of the unsolved contradictions, the unhealed antagonisms, and the poorly formulated aspirations of a country which had just been through a very hard and perplexing decade, and nothing was working quite right. Nelson clung firmly to a simple faith: that the country's groups and parties were not really divided by anything deep and fundamental, and that men of diverse backgrounds and viewpoints could work together admirably if they just sat down with each other, got thoroughly acquainted, and recognized their agreement on a common objective. This dinner party was a step toward that end: to make big business and Henry Wallace mutually familiar, leading each to see that the other did not have cloven hoofs. It would be a good trick if it worked, and Nelson was going to make it work if there was any virtue in relaxation, good food and drink, and the social graces.

He was courteously deferential to his guest of honor, the Vice-President, and to Mr. William Knudsen, the head man of the Office of Production Management. It was part of Nelson's genius that he could understand, and like, both of these utterly dissimilar men: Wallace, who could talk on any subject so long as it was strictly of an intellectual cast, and Knudsen, who could talk on any subject so long as it was purely mechanical. Between Nelson and Knudsen there was a faint sense of strain. Their stars had come into collision, somewhere. Washington is a city whose very air is flavored by the subtle shiftings of the beliefs, the hopes, and the desires of men who undertake to forecast and to analyze trends and coming events; and it was beginning to be the conclusion of such men that Nelson and Knudsen could not long go on as coequals in the defense program. This conclusion was not a private matter. It got into men's relationships and affected men's plans. Knudsen and Nelson were both conscious of it. One of the two, said the word in the air, was Wrong. Sooner or later things would come to a head. A latter-day Viking minus his helmet, Knudsen stood immobile among the others, a glass cupped in his heavy hand, small eyes twinkling out of a florid, impassive face. Physically, he was about the only man present who matched Nelson.

But if everyone relaxed and made friendly talk, there was a queer feeling of tension in the air. This particular grouping of men was incongruous. The lion was lying down with the lamb,

5

and both parties were quite aware that the time wasn't really ripe for it. A centrifugal force had been balanced by a force from the outside, but the balance was temporary and unstable and everybody concerned was keeping his eyes open and his fingers crossed. A dozen hostilities had been buried but burial had not been the sequel to death. After years of struggle, oddly matched rivals had made a truce, but it was only a truce and not a treaty of enduring peace. This was the century of progress and it was likewise the century of the common man, but what the common man and his progress were going to look like when the dust finally settled had not yet been disclosed. In unstable equilibrium a carefully contrived edifice had been set up, a house of irrational and wishful dreams, built on the shifting sands; for better or for worse they were going to try to make it endure through whatever howling storm the gods might be sending.

In any case, it was a fine evening and a fine party. After a time the men got around the long table for dinner. Dim light on the high walls, ruddy faces over white shirt fronts, deft waiters serving from silver dishes, a sharp-visaged *maître* hovering unobtrusively in the background, a hum of talk dotted with occasional bursts of masculine laughter; this is as it was in the beginning, is now and forever shall be, Washington without end, and the Carlton is a very fine hotel indeed. We are insulated, here. There is a war going on but it is a long way off, and nothing is going to happen that will really force us to grapple with the fundamentals. . . .

And finally the plates were taken away and the cigars were lighted, and Nelson got up to enfold the diners in the soft arms of after-dinner talk. On the surface, Nelson sounded just like a Rotarian: There is no difference among us as to aims, just differences over methods, which are unimportant. We are men of good will and we are working together, and behold there is no clash or disharmony that good fellowship and understanding will not cure. I have known our Vice-President and I have found him to be a great man and a regular fellow, who has contributed much to the defense effort; Mr. Knudsen is a great man and a regular fellow, likewise, and his contributions also have been immense. I have the utmost confidence in and so forth. . . . But underneath, nearly inaudible beneath the pat good-fellow phrases and the beaming smile, there was a note of almost desperate pleading

6

and anxiety: This government and private industry *can* make a go of it; we *can* sink our differences of opinion; there is *not* any basic, soul-compelling conflict here except the one that is coming on us from the outside, and for God's sake let's forget our doubts and mistrusts and realize what we're really up against and do something about it, because this is our last chance. . . . And so, after a while, Nelson presented the Vice-President, and sat down.

Now picture Henry Wallace, standing at the head of a long table looking down at a double row of faces, a double row of masks, groping for the thing to say that would bridge the gap between himself, and what he stood for, and the dominant majority. He stood there, his untidy hair straying down over one eye, head bent forward a little, smiling an uncertain smile, and he reached for the right word and did not find it. His long suit was to be himself—tenacious, uncompromising, building after the pattern that had been shown him on the mount—and this was not the night for it. He was capable of many things, but to adopt the Nelson touch and move lightly over things that could not be said —that, of all conceivable gambits, just was not in him, not on this night and before this audience. He was an alien in this room, and everybody knew it. Most of the men present felt toward him a mixture of condescension and resentment. He had nothing to say to them, nothing that they could understand, nothing that he could put into their kind of talk. So he was reminded of a story, and he told it. It was just a story, neither very good nor very bad, and it drew a round of polite laughter. The Vice-President sat down, to the relief of himself and his listeners.

Then Knudsen. He stood up, solid, honest, peering out from under his blond eyebrows, massive shoulders slightly stooped, talking in the quaint, stage-dialect Scandinavian brogue that never quite left him. He was at home here, and he talked on a level that his audience could understand. . . . We've had a big job to do here, and it has been tough, but all things considered it is being done pretty well. And this war overseas is simply a neighborhood disturbance of the peace on a big scale. We, the peace-loving people, had been trying to go our own way and mind our own business; now, because of this brawl, we have had to forget our ordinary work and take steps to restore order. We are the neighbors, getting together to stop an intolerably noisy gin party in the corner apartment. Pretty soon we'll have it squelched, and then we'll all go home and pick up exactly where we left off.

Thus Knudsen, and the world revolution as he saw it.

Then rose to his feet Edward R. Stettinius, Jr., incredibly handsome, with florid, youthful face under silvery hair, faultlessly groomed, giving out the easy, smiling good fellowship of a Y.M.C.A. secretary. It was this good man's misfortune that unofficial Washington knew him, from first to last, under the irreverent nickname of Junior. Just Junior. He carried with him the aura of a noble past; son of a Morgan partner, chairman of the board of U. S. Steel, amiable host at a vast estate in the horse country of Virginia, he had been one of the first great names of the business world to be brought into the rearmament program. Striking failures had occurred, in the defense effort, and the record trailed at his heels; a record, when all was said and done, of trusting that everything would come out all right if only people could be induced to believe that it would. Like Knudsen, he was a handsome ornament in the New Deal's collection of eminent reputations; also like Knudsen, he had suffered because the reputation had been given prolonged exposure to very foul weather. . . . Tonight, he said, he had good tidings of great joy for the assembled guests.

"I've just heard from Harry," he said, in the manner of one who refers to the best-loved of all the well-loved intimates of his friends. "Harry is better—lots better. He'll be able to leave the hospital soon, and he'll be back with us before long."

Now this was all very fine, except that the Harry of these remarks was Harry Hopkins, recently hospitalized with the stomach ulcers that were his constant torment. Things had come, then, thus far: a chairman-in-absentia of the board of U. S. Steel, standing in a roomful of his peers, could refer to Hopkins' impending recovery and to his return to a seat at the right hand of the President as to a bit of good news at which all present would rejoice. Harry Hopkins: we'll tax and tax and spend and spend, and look at all those men leaning on their shovels; and here is U. S. Steel, in silvery-haired person, welcoming him to our bosom. Unquestionably, every valley shall be exalted. Mr. Stettinius sat down, all aglow, and the guests patted their palms together politely, and there were no snide remarks.

Upon invitation of the host, Frank Knox stood up. The Secre-

8

tary of the Navy was in no mood for light banter. Not for him were the funny stories of the Vice-President, the quizzical parables of Knudsen, or the soft good fellowship of Stettinius. Knox performed his social duty by paying his respects to his host, remarking that he thought this kind of get-together was a good idea, and mentioning that he was glad to be present. Then, darkly serious, he looked down the long table for a moment in silence.

"I feel that I can speak very frankly, within these four walls," he said. "I want you to know that our situation tonight is very serious—more serious, probably, than most of us realize. We are very close to war. War may begin in the Pacific at any moment. Literally, at any moment. It may even be beginning tonight, while we're sitting here, for all we know. We are that close to it."

He paused, and the silence was impressive. Then he went on, his voice rising confidently.

"But I want you all to know that no matter what happens, the United States Navy is ready! Every man is at his post, every ship is at its station. The Navy is ready. Whatever happens, the Navy is not going to be caught napping."

He sat down, and there was a hum of comment. Nelson leaned over toward him.

"Are things really as bad as that, Frank?" he asked quietly.

"Every bit as bad," said Knox, nodding vigorously. "It can start at any minute."

Nelson meditated for a moment.

"You know," he said, "if we do have to fight the Japs, I can't see that there'd be much for our Army to do. Won't it be pretty much a Navy show?"

Knox nodded again.

"Oh, yes, of course. We're all ready for them, you know. We've had our plans worked out for twenty years. Once it starts, our submarines will go in to blockade them, and sooner or later our battle fleet will be able to force an action. It won't take too long. Say about a six months' war."

But there is always somebody around to spoil a good effect. Belshazzar gave a big dinner in Babylon once, and right at the height of the festivities a mysterious hand appeared and traced some words upon the wall, the general purport being that the dam had busted and that good men should take to the hills.

Tonight the spoil-sport, or moving finger, was a black-haired, bullet-headed man named Robert Wyman Horton, who rejoiced in the cumbersome title of Director of Information in the Office for Emergency Management of the Executive Office of the President.

Horton was a misfit at this party. He was the official mouthpiece, so to speak, for the defense program—for OPM, SPAB, and all the rest of it—and he had watched the entire process at close range ever since the formation of the original Defense Commission at the time of the fall of France, and he was not impressed by what he had seen. He was a Vermonter, exemplifying to a marked degree every characteristic of that rugged state; at all times and places he believed in saying exactly what he thought, and what he thought was usually rather acrid. He had thoughts, now, for which he craved utterance, and he passed up to Nelson a note which said, in effect, "How about calling on me for a few remarks next?"

Fortified by the all-is-well assurances of the Secretary of the Navy, Nelson glanced at the note, rose to his feet, and remarked that they would now hear from Mr. Horton, the Director of Information. He sat down, not without a faint misgiving or two about what might be coming next, and Horton got up. It was not long before Nelson realized that his faint misgiving was amply justified.

"I have been very interested," said Horton, "in the little talk which the Secretary of the Navy has just made. It has been very encouraging to be assured that the Navy is ready for whatever may happen. But somehow, some of the things I've seen recently make me wonder if the Secretary of the Navy may not be mistaken."

He fixed his cold blue eyes on Knox's face and went on.

"The other afternoon," he said, "I had to go over to the Navy Department to attend a conference. It was a little before four o'clock when I got over there. I was almost trampled underfoot in the lobby by captains and admirals, rushing out with golf bags over their shoulders. It seemed to me that the high-ranking people in the Department were knocking off work rather early, if we're so close to a war."

(Knox leaned over to Nelson and whispered savagely, behind his hand: "Who *is* this son of a bitch?")

"But the thing that really bothers me," Horton went on, "is something that happened last week. I had occasion to take a little trip down Chesapeake Bay on a little Coast Guard patrol boat. We were down around Norfolk, and late in the day the skipper of the boat—a chief petty officer—decided it might be interesting to cruise up to the navy yard and see what we could see. So up we went. We not only cruised up to the yard, but we cruised all through it. Nobody challenged us, nobody stopped us, nobody did anything to find out if we were really in a Coast Guard boat or just in a cabin cruiser painted gray.

"Now I've heard a lot about Navy security measures lately. Some of the news we've tried to get out, over at OPM, has been held up because the Navy objected that it would violate security. Okay; if we're close to war we have to be careful about giving away military information. But as I understand it, one of the top military secrets right now is the fact that the British aircraft carrier *Illustrious* is in the yard at Norfolk for repairs. Well, we cruised right by her dock. There she was, standing up like a ten-story building, with an enormous Union Jack flying over her. If we could cruise in like that and see her, I should think any German agent who wanted to could do the same.

"Anyhow, we left the yard after a while and went out through Hampton Roads, and pretty soon it got dark and we wanted to tie up somewhere and make a phone call. So we headed into the nearest place, which happened to be one of those big new navy installations—I think it was a mine base. We came in, after dark, and tied up at a pier where there were three or four minesweepers tied up. Nobody challenged us. Nobody tried to find out whether we were really in a Coast Guard boat, or whether we had any business in there. Nobody paid any attention to us at all. We got off the boat and walked along the pier, looking for some place where we could find a telephone. We didn't find any, so we walked on to dry land and pretty soon we came to a guard house or sentry box of some kind. We hammered on the door, and by and by a sailor stuck his head out, and we asked him where there was a public telephone. He pointed vaguely up the road and said it was about half a mile. So we walked up there. The guard didn't pay any attention to us. He didn't know who we were, but he didn't ask for a pass and he didn't want to see any credentials. For all he knew we might have been Hitler's grandsons.

"Sure, the CPO I was with had a uniform on. But there are at least thirty places in Norfolk where you can walk in and buy a CPO's uniform. All it takes is a little money. We could have been spies, saboteurs, anything—but the Navy, which is so touchy about the press releases that come out of OPM, let us wander all over that base, after dark, for upwards of half an hour, without once bothering to find out who we were or what our business was. We could have blown the whole place to pieces, for all the obstacles the Navy put in our way."

Horton paused, and looked coldly at Knox, who by now was painfully close to apoplexy.

"Mister Secretary," he said, "I don't think your Navy *is* ready."

This was the night of December 4, 1941.

CHAPTER TWO

The Readiness Is All

IT WAS very rude to spoil Nelson's dinner party, of course. It was all washed off, before the evening ended, chiefly on the ground that Horton was just a newspaperman by trade (to say nothing of being a New Dealer by preference) and couldn't be expected to know any better. But the rudeness looked rather different three days later; and, indeed, from the present distance, the whole evening stands out as one of the most significant and revealing little incidents of the whole war period.

Not just because Horton in his role as Belshazzar's finger had called attention to the Navy's unreadiness. Seventy-two hours later the Japanese themselves underlined that point with grim finality. That dinner party—the tone of it, the guest list, the things that were said, the attitudes that were made clear—would stand as a symbol and a symptom even if Horton had not been there at all.

For that evening emphasizes and illuminates two things— America's essential unreadiness for the war which had been so long foreseen, and the reasons for this unreadiness.

The Second World War was the only war in our history which we actually saw coming and undertook to get ready for. Eighteen months ahead of time the nation began to mobilize for war. The machinery creaked and groaned a good deal, there was much rushing around in all directions at once, and the job of preparation could have been done ever so much better; nevertheless, the fact does remain that this was the one time in American history when something fairly effective was done about getting ready for an impending fight.

But tied in with that is the astounding fact that when this war which had been anticipated and prepared for so elaborately finally arrived, it caught the country with its guard down as the country had never been caught before. The one time when we really tried to get ready we were most dramatically caught unready. Eighteen months of careful preparation led up to a dawn attack that caught us flat-footed. A bare three days before the attack the Secretary of the Navy—who was a limited man, perhaps, but who was also as completely honest, patriotic, and devoted a mortal as the government ever called into its service—served notice on Nelson's group that the war could begin at any minute. He knew what was coming. The Navy knew, the administration knew, the country knew. And yet what we got was the most stunning, humiliating surprise in American military history.

Why?

Without trying to stretch a point too far, it is suggested that the dinner party offers a useful clue.

The mere fact that that dinner party was held at all is significant. That party, given for the particular list of two dozen people who were its guests, was an attempt to bridge a gap. The gap existed because the effort to get the country ready for war had, of necessity, ignored one of the most profound and basic problems involved in the whole emergency that made war inevitable. Because the gap existed our effort to prepare for war was bound to be incomplete; until the underlying problem was met squarely, nothing that we could do could get us genuinely ready for the future—either then or later.

Now that ignored problem was simply the matter of finding an adequate answer for this question: Exactly, specifically, and in every-day terms, what are we fighting for?

The answer was not found before the war, during the war, or after the war. That was not because nobody knew what was at stake. Both the people and their elected leaders knew quite well what all the shooting was about. But the thing had to be formulated, not merely in words, but in actions as well, and that was what never happened; and the fact that it never happened has been progressively more costly ever since Pearl Harbor.

A dinner party to bridge a gap, the gap being symbolized by the fact that top New Dealers and top industrialists were sitting down together in an uneasy truce, with both sides conscious that the arrangement was only temporary and that its final fruits were quite unpredictable, and with nobody (except for the irrepressible Horton) quite ready to come out and say what he really thought on that or any other subject.

Back of the dinner party there had been several years of the most expert political manipulation America ever saw, performed by that expert manipulator, Franklin D. Roosevelt.

The story really begins, perhaps, on October 5, 1937, when Roosevelt made a speech in Chicago proposing a quarantine for aggressor nations.

"The will for peace on the part of peace-loving nations must express itself to the end that nations which may be tempted to violate their agreements and the rights of others will desist from such a course," said Mr. Roosevelt.

"America hates war. America hopes for peace. Therefore, America actively engages in the search for peace."

From this distance that sounds mild enough, perhaps, but at the moment it was rather shocking; shocking, particularly, to the very people who were Roosevelt's most ardent supporters. The nation then was still living in the disillusioning aftermath of the First World War. The evils of the treaty of Versailles and the greed of the Merchants of Death were much on people's minds; what the war had accomplished was far from clear, and the one thing that seemed most evident was that America had done neither herself nor the world at large any good by getting into it. These points of view were held, especially, by liberals; along with a belief in social security, collective bargaining, and government responsibility for the cure and prevention of economic depressions went a growing conviction that war was the supreme evil which must be avoided under every circumstance and at any cost whatever. Even preparation for war was bad, and a belief in the need for adequate preparation was the hallmark of a conservative, a backward-looker, one who lived in the twilight of an outworn era; the great defect in Roosevelt (from the liberal viewpoint) was his insistence on rebuilding the American Navy —he had even channeled a good deal of public works money into naval building, early in his first term, which was a scandal among the faithful. Furthermore, he was known to have a rather unsound leaning toward meddling in the affairs of Europe. A close friend and supporter had remarked (and the remark had been printed) that Roosevelt would go down in history as one of the greatest of presidents if he could just "keep out of Europe."

But here he was, boldly proposing a course which clearly carried great risks of war. Talk of a quarantine for aggressors was all very well—but suppose the aggressors refused to be bluffed? Wouldn't we then have to fight? And wouldn't that, in turn, mean useless tragedy, loss, and the destruction of everything liberals believed in? It was a commonplace of liberal argument, in those days, that neither our democracy nor any other could survive another war. What believers in democracy had to do, therefore—obviously—was to avoid war and all risks of war, and to "engage actively in the search for peace" the way Roosevelt described it looked very risky indeed.

The quarantine speech, consequently, evoked dismay in the very groups on which Roosevelt most relied. Sent up as a trial balloon, it brought back a highly adverse report. This medicine was altogether too strong. Roosevelt, who was never a man to get too far out in front of the public opinion which supported him, perceived the fact and pulled in his horns. No more was heard about quarantines.

But the world situation which had provoked the quarantine speech kept on getting worse, and during the next year it became very clear to the President—as to anyone who bothered to study the matter—that an exceedingly real and pressing threat to democracy was taking shape overseas. It was a threat that grew by what it fed upon, and what it fed upon was democracy's reluctance either to believe in its reality or to face up to the hard and dangerous things which had to be done to check it. The world situation was, in fact, a revolutionary situation which was absolutely certain to burst out in smoke and flame eventually, and the American democracy could no more ignore it than a Florida sponge fisherman could ignore the approach of a hurricane. As a man who had undertaken to give democracy a new meaning and a new vitality, Roosevelt had to get the country ready to meet the storm. But how?

The country had to be united to meet the danger, and the country was not united. It was split two ways, as a matter of fact, and the fissures ran across each other.

First of all, there was the split between liberals and conservatives, between New Dealers and old dealers; a deep split, symbolized by an almost hysterical Roosevelt-worship at one extreme and an equally psychotic Roosevelt-hatred at the other. The New Deal administration had formalized this division, so to speak. As Roosevelt's second term approached its end, it was beginning to be evident that nothing much had been finally settled. The underbrush had been cleared away and the ground had been prepared but the building hadn't gone up. The New

Deal had been a time of preparation rather than a time of final determinations; democracy could go ahead from the New Deal or it could recede, but it could not well stay just where it was—not for very long, anyway.

The second great split in the country was the one between the isolationists and the people who believed that isolation was no longer wise or, indeed, possible. This division had no relationship to the first one; there were Democrats among the isolationists and Republicans among the interventionists; devout liberals who believed in "staying out of Europe" at all costs, and solid conservatives who believed in doing whatever had to be done to stop the Axis. But there was a very real danger that these two fissures might ultimately become one fissure—that saving democracy from the Axis might (if FDR got too far out in front on it) come to look like a straight party measure, with most of the New Dealers and liberals lined up in favor of it and all of the conservatives lined up against it. If the country was to be aroused to meet the danger, the job would have to be done in such a way that the conservatives were not driven into the isolationist camp; for, by fate and ill-chance, the most strongly anti-Roosevelt conservatives in the land included the people who owned and operated the factories, the mines, the transportation lines, and the other facilities which would have to be put to work in democracy's defense.

Therefore there was no sense in going ahead with quarantine speeches. The job had to be done one step at a time, the country had to be nursed along most deftly, the President at all costs had to keep from getting too far ahead of the procession. This meant, among other things, that it was the *military* danger in the world situation which had to be emphasized. The Axis represented a supreme threat to democracy, true enough; but to dwell on that threat—to make it clear exactly why democracy was threatened, to trace the kinship between what the Axis stood for and what the New Deal had fought against at home, to demonstrate that the Axis must ultimately be stopped by force of arms because democracy's doom was certain and final if continued appeasement enabled the Axis to get its way without fighting—to do this, with the country still at peace, was to risk turning the vast and powerful conservative group into avowed and active allies of the isolationists. So it was the threat to national security that had to be talked about. The Axis menaced our national existence; our democratic way of life, to be sure, but above all our military and strategic security. The danger from overseas was first and foremost a military danger. The one thing everybody would go along with was defense; what we got, therefore, in capital letters, was a Defense Program.

But even that had to be done with extreme care. There was also the matter of the third term.

Laying aside all question as to Roosevelt's desire, or lack of desire, to perpetuate himself in office just for the sake of being president longer than anyone had been president before, it is perfectly evident that he had to run for a third term as part of his effort to beat the Axis. It took no very profound political augurs to forecast that no other Democrat had the least chance to be elected in 1940. If no Democrat, then a Republican; apparently (looking at it a year and more before election-time) either Senator Taft, who dwelt with the isolationists in see-no-evil land, or Governor Dewey, about whose policies no one at that moment knew anything at all. Q.E.D.; we must win a third term, and do it at the same time that we are preparing the country emotionally and physically for war with Germany and Japan, and yet do the two things in such a way that we don't get them all tangled up with each other.

No politician in America ever set himself quite so delicate a job. It meant being frank and not-frank at the same time; it meant calling on the last ounce of that skill at improvisation which had taken the administration so successfully through the first years of the New Deal; it meant delaying the settlement of all issues whose settlement could be delayed; and it meant compromises. It meant, in other words, that a vast load of unsolved problems would be carried over for handling *after* there had been a decision on the immediate question: Do we use all of our resources to stop the Axis?

Step by step, the task was done.

Early winter of 1939: Munich some months in the background, and "Peace for our time" already wearing shabby; no war yet, but increasing signs of war, with the thunderheads piled high beyond the ramparts; Roosevelt met with members of the Senate Military Affairs Committee for a confidential talk, asserted that a German invasion of France would fracture the frontiers of democracy, saw a garbled version of this get into print as the statement that "our frontier is on the Rhine"; denied he said it, found the remark nevertheless remaining in circulation, useful as a means of calling attention to the danger. . . . In January the House of Representatives refused to vote money for extensive harbor improvements, prelude to fortification, in Guam, partly because many members felt this would look like warlike provocation and partly because the measure's sponsor, Congressman Andy May of Kentucky, made a ridiculous spread-eagle speech about it, declaring that the vote on this bill would determine whether Congressmen were pro-American or pro-Japanese. (The House simply laughed at him; up from the floor of the chamber floated the strains of "The Stars and Stripes Forever," derisively hummed by some dozens of members in spontaneous harmony.)

April, 1939: Roosevelt finished a vacation at Warm Springs, told a good-bye crowd on the station platform, "I'll be back in the fall if we do not have a war." . . . Later in the same month he dispatched (and made public) notes to Hitler and Mussolini, proposing an international conference to head off the danger of war and suggesting that the dictators pledge themselves not to invade a list of some two dozen nations. Hitler made no direct reply, but ridiculed the entire proposition in a Reichstag speech a few days later.

In July the President tried a bigger step, sending a special message to Congress urging repeal of the arms embargo. This law, which required the government to prevent the shipment of weapons or munitions to any nations which were at war, was the product of the disillusionment of the mid-thirties, when the thorough work of the Nye committee had shown how closely our involvement in the First World War had been tied in with our extensive sales of munitions to England and France. It had come to appear that we got into that war because we first began selling arms to the belligerents, a business in which we had meant to be neutral, but which had turned out to be one-sided because the British blockade made shipments to Germany impossible. The arms embargo—support of which had almost come to be looked upon as a true test of liberalism—looked like a logical answer: stay out of the munitions business and at least we won't have *that* current moving to get us into a new war. It expressed the mood of the times perfectly. True enough, by making the

19

shipment of munitions impossible we might withhold aid from our friends and witness the triumph of hostile forces—but we had renounced war as an instrument of national policy, war was the greatest of all evils, war settled nothing, better to let the very worst happen in Europe than to take any chance on getting involved ourselves.

Now Roosevelt was demanding that this safeguard be dropped, and he called a group of senators to the White House for a talk about the urgency of the situation. His official sources, he explained, indicated that war in Europe was very close, could begin at any time, would almost certainly start before the end of the year: when it comes (he argued) it will be to our self-interest to give aid to one side; don't let us have our hands tied in advance. Up spoke Senator Borah, fading lion of an earlier day, to remark that he had his own sources about the drift of events abroad—unofficial sources, to be sure, but free of professional war-mongers, and hence reliable, more reliable than the President's sources; and these sources, he said contemptuously, indicated that there probably would *not* be a war. All of which, in due course, leaked out and was printed. Roosevelt, it seemed, was a war-monger. Congress was not yet ready to drop the arms embargo, and the attempt to get the law repealed was given up.

Then came the Russian-German treaty, and, a fortnight later, the invasion of Poland. The war had come in spite of Senator Borah, and affairs wore a different face. The President proclaimed a limited national emergency, instituted a neutrality patrol along the Atlantic coast, and in November persuaded Congress to modify the neutrality act with the famous Cash-and-Carry amendment—any nation which could pay cash and could provide its own transportation might buy munitions in America.

Concerning all of which there are two points to notice. First, the off-shore patrol was a *neutrality* patrol. A blind man could see whom it was aimed at, but the word was important. The habit of calling things by the wrong name was beginning to take hold; what we were doing was being done so that we might keep out of war and for no other reason, if the labels we were using meant anything. Second, passage of the Cash-and-Carry amendment was followed by the long period of the "phony war." The aggressor nations seemed to be oddly peace loving, and the nations which had gone to war to prevent aggression did not seem anxious to become actively belligerent. To assert that this was just the lull before the storm was, obviously, war-mongering. It was argued that the war would presently end in a negotiated peace, moderately just to all concerned and infinitely preferable to a finish fight, if Roosevelt would only stop interfering. The attempt to arouse the country to the danger, and to get something effective done about it, languished for some months.

It languished, in fact, until May of 1940, when the war came to furious life and the Nazis went crashing through France and the Low Countries.

Up to this point, a great deal of the nervousness and uncertainty which were so apparent in Washington seemed to have been created by the President himself. Hitler was obviously up to no good, and the general trend overseas was undeniably bad, but it was still possible to argue that the new war must ultimately drag on into a stalemate from which all parties would emerge with a minimum of damage, if the President could just relax a bit and not try to save the world before the world was in need of it. . . . But all of a sudden the old world, and the old pattern of thought, ceased to exist. The Maginot Line, which had been basic to the argument that this war could not be fought out to a decision, was swept away and became no more germane to the point at issue than the Macedonian phalanx. The war *was* going to a decision and it was going with unbelievable speed, and the decision looked as if it would be one we could not live with; and liberalism, so eager to take the most optimistic view of things, was compelled to realize that even a peace-loving democracy might presently have to decide whether it valued peace more than democracy, no matter how many fine words would have to be swallowed. Roosevelt went before Congress to demand an air force of 50,000 planes, plus a billion dollars for the Army and Navy.

This was a stunner, and it took the breath away; most notice-ably, the breath of the Army Air Force, nothing in the Air Force's dreams having foreshadowed anything like this. For days thereafter, reporters who went to see the Army press relations people were told that of course we needed an expanded air force, and we ought to have a good many more planes, and all that, but still—well, it wouldn't do to come right out and say so, but figure it out for yourself, this idea really was pretty wild: 50,000 planes would mean a ground force, for the Air Corps alone, of upwards of a million men, and everybody knew that was just out of the question, and anyhow where on earth would all of those pilots come from? . . . But France was falling out of the war and perhaps even out of history; if England could be saved no one was prepared to say just how, and the threat to American security had suddenly become very real and pressing and was no longer just something that an overardent president had dreamed up. Roosevelt followed his plea for 50,000 planes by demanding four billion dollars for a two-ocean navy; characterizing Mussolini's declaration of war on France as "a stab in the back"—a highly unneutral remark which nevertheless won pretty general approval—he went on to declare that "we will extend to the opponents of force the material resources of this nation."

To the opponents of *force*. The aggressor nations were to be opposed because they were aggressors, and the democracies were to be supported, not because they were democracies, but because as democracies they were inherently peace-loving; the country was being roused to meet a threat to its physical security, and whatever the infinite complexities and perils of the world situation might be, we were going to talk about the chance of invasion and the menace inherent in armies, navies, and bombing planes; freedom and democracy could be taken for granted, they could be talked of later, there was a presidential campaign coming up and the conservatives must not be scared over into the camp of the isolationists. For the "material resources of this nation," in so far as they could be catalogued and weighed, consisted of tangible assets owned and operated by men who distrusted Roosevelt profoundly and passionately and had a fiercely jealous regard for their own independence of action. Those men had to be brought along as willing partners. The economic royalists, denounced and derided through two terms of the administration, had a part to play now and it was a part they themselves had to accept.

Therefore: give them a piece of the performance. June of 1940, and a Republican convention coming up, and some far-reaching action by the President. Two old-school Republicans were named to the cabinet—Henry L. Stimson, who had been Hoover's Secretary of State, was named Secretary of War, and Frank Knox, who had been Landon's running mate in 1936, and one of the most unbridled of New Deal critics, became Secretary of the Navy. (Sheer coincidence, or impish Roosevelt delight in dumb-founding the political opposition, to make these appointments right on the eve of the Republican convention?) The nominations were read off, without advance warning, to a drowsy Senate chamber on a quiet afternoon, galvanizing the senators to startled attention; burly, red-faced Bennett Clark, Democratic isolationist from Missouri, sprang to his feet unbelieving, bellowing out *"What?"* in unparliamentary astonishment. The Senate confirmed the nominations, there being no good reason to do anything else, but the shock was great.

Along with this the President named an Advisory Commission to the Council of National Defense—a strangely mixed grill of industrialists and New Dealers—and instructed it to begin mobilizing the nation's industrial resources for rearmament. The Defense Program was formally launched, the great experiment had begun, and a carefully balanced team with the most vaguely defined powers and responsibilities got to work.

Almost by open definition, this venture was experimental. The members of the Defense Commission (as it immediately became known) were, technically, advisors and nothing more. E. R. Stettinius, Jr., was advisor on industrial materials; William S. Knudsen was advisor on industrial production; Ralph Budd was advisor on transportation. Balancing them, Leon Henderson and Sidney Hillman were, respectively, advisors on price stabilization and on unemployment. Miss Harriett Elliott, Dean of Women at the University of North Carolina, was advisor on "consumer protection," and Chester C. Davis was advisor on farm products. Each advisor proceeded to set up a staff to perform the "investigation, research, and co-ordination" required in his particular field, quarters were found in the white marble Federal Reserve Bank Building on Constitution Avenue, the forthright Horton was brought in as press man and general mouthpiece, and the operation got under way, not without creaking and lost motion.

For better or for worse, some sort of industrial mobilization was going to be attempted, and if it seemed obvious that the Defense Commission could not long exist in its headless and amorphous form, at least a start was being made. More important, this oddly assorted combination of men was the visible evidence of a truce between the New Deal and big business. The truce might be short or it might be long, it might work out this way or it might work out that way, but it was at least a bit of assurance that the defense effort was not to be a straight New Deal program, with all opponents of the New Deal lined up against it. The appointments of Stimson and Knox showed that some sort of olive branch was being extended in the field of straight politics; the Defense Commission, revolving painfully amid organizational defects which it was quite unable to remedy, indicated that the program to repel aggressors did not, necessarily, have anything to do with the controversial struggle for the more abundant life. The defense effort, in fact, was rather like a brand new baby, which—for all anybody could predict—might grow up to be either a horse thief or a clergyman. Its heredity was strangely mixed and somewhat impromptu, and its early environment promised to be rather difficult, but nobody could tell, all sorts of things might happen, future developments were for the future to determine; at least the program had been begun.

After the summer of 1940 the tempo became much faster. The overage destroyers were swapped for island bases. In a fireside chat the famous expression, "Arsenal of Democracy," was given to the world. The amazing venture of the Lend-Lease law was proposed, passed, and put into effect. The four freedoms were enunciated. The Defense Commission was replaced by the Office of Production Management—a two-headed operation under the joint direction of Knudsen and Hillman, a better organization endowed with more powers but still an experiment, still a makeshift, with the reins still held by the President. The new organization grew in size and in authority, reaching out over the economy with controls far more stringent and extensive than any the New Deal itself had ever proposed; but there was not any feeling of unity, any clear-cut sense that the men at the top knew precisely where they were going or how they were going to get there. The presidential election had passed, the third term had begun, Hitler had attacked Russia, America by now was very obviously committed to *something;* yet that something remained undefined, except to the extent that a determination to perfect the nation's defenses could define it, and if the nation was riding rapidly to Armageddon it was still riding two very different horses. The marriage between the New Deal and big industry was clearly an uneasy one, with both parties meditating extensive infidelities—but it was still a marriage, and most of the amenities were being observed.

For the President was succeeding in his difficult political maneuver, at the cost of being unable to undertake any other maneuvers of consequence. He had got over the big hurdle, by the fall of 1941; isolationism—seemingly bred into the bone, fundamental to any calculation of America's future course—had been overleaped. Politically, the people had made an amazing about-face. In September of 1939 the one certainty had seemed to be that America would resolutely shun involvement in this war no matter what happened; but now, two years later, it was perfectly obvious that the nation had taken sides and was going to back its choice with everything it had.

But that was the only decision that had been made. We were committed to the defeat of the Axis but to nothing else. So carefully and painstakingly had we been led to this commitment that it still could not really be talked about; we were still arming purely for defense and for nothing else, and while the defense was beginning to be rather aggressive, nevertheless the ultimate nightmare in most minds was a picture of Hitler finally defeating England and then assailing America much as he had assailed Norway. We were going to be ready for that, in any case; what else we were going to be ready for, what else we might have to get ready for, what problems the act of getting ready might raise, what the whole business was really all about—all of this was still something for future determination.

And yet consideration of these points could not very well be postponed. One of the top officials in OPM once remarked that the defense effort was so vast that in the mere doing of it we might, if we were not extremely careful, destroy the very values we were trying to defend. That was true enough, in the fall of 1941, and it was getting truer every day; but because the job of getting ready to meet the military threat posed by Hitler had taken such careful handling, the exact nature of the things we were trying to defend had not been defined or realized. What was being overlooked was the fact that *if* anything more was involved than just the beating-off of a military threat—if, in other words, we were trying to do anything more than just perfect

25

our continental defenses—then the way in which democracy armed was of supreme importance.

Far-reaching decisions would be made, even though they might not be recognized as such; the goals we would achieve by winning the war would, to a large extent, be determined by the way in which we set about winning it. Our once-unshakable determination to stay out of Europe's war at all costs had finally been overridden because Europe was not just having another war: it was being torn by a world revolution, in which we were bound to be involved simply because we were part of the world. Whether we would cope with this world revolution would depend very largely on how we met the war; on how we brought the strange, contradictory, infinitely various elements of America's physical and spiritual power together into one unified display of strength. All of the unsolved problems of the New Deal period were going to come up for decision as part of the process of beating the Axis, but at the time of Pearl Harbor nothing had been settled except that we *were* going to beat the Axis.

. . . We often remark that the President of the United States has the biggest job in the world. Perfectly true, too—and in time of war, actual or undeclared, the job gets unimaginably bigger; too big, indeed, for any one man to carry. Authority has to be delegated, the President can set only the most important policies, other men must take care of the operations and set the lesser policies incident thereto; there simply is no other way to do it. Thus, for instance, when a vast defense program is being set up, it would be absurd to expect the President himself to decide whether it is both feasible and desirable to create combinations of small manufacturing enterprises which can, by pooling their resources, handle large contracts for the production of munitions. He may or may not think that desirable, in the abstract sense, but in the very nature of things he cannot make the determination himself; he must, of necessity, leave that decision to the men he has appointed to mobilize industry. But suppose that just that decision turns out to be basic to the entire task of determining what democracy is fighting for, of bringing democracy through the war ready to face an unpredictable future. What happens then?

What happens then is that the very ideals the President is working for may speedily become unattainable, unless the organization he has created shares his ideals and is able to make its desires effective. But the organization to which all such matters were being entrusted in 1941 met neither of these two requirements. It was a compromise group, deliberately so created because of the apparent necessities of the political situation; it had to set a pattern as it went along, in the course of making operating decisions, because no pattern had been set for it; and Nelson's dinner party on the eve of Pearl Harbor symbolized the situation perfectly. We had warships and guns and airplanes enough, at Pearl Harbor, to have beaten off the Japanese; yet we did not do it, we were not really prepared, we were not ready because the means we used to get ready could not conceivably have succeeded. For the readiness we lacked was an emotional and intellectual readiness to meet the unforeseeable: a matter of determining exactly what it was that we were trying to do and then translating that into an action program for democracy. We had done a great deal, by the end of 1941, but we had not done that. We still have not done it.

CHAPTER THREE

The Stars in Their Courses

THE LORD made man upright, and man sought out many inventions; and, seeking them, became exceedingly articulate, with a way of placing a high value on the spoken word, so that what is said very often has a determining effect on what is done. Which is one way of accounting for many of the odd things that happened in the eighteen months which followed the appointment of the Advisory Commission to the Council of National Defense.

For the Nelson dinner party just before Pearl Harbor was, among other things, the product of a year and a half of government by double talk. Ever since June of 1940 the administration had been busy doing one thing and saying that it was doing another. This was a matter of necessity, or at least it seemed to be so, the general idea being that what was going on represented such a profound reversal of public sentiment that it couldn't be done at all if it were defined too bluntly. The word "defense" thus became a sort of carryall; it conveyed everything that anyone might want it to, from a simple desire to keep Hitler outside of the three-mile limit to a determination to rebuild the nation's whole social and economic system. Everything was being done for defense, and since that meant so many different things to so many different people, it had to be done most delicately; which meant that much of it was done badly, most of the operators in question lacking the precise and definite touch. Yet it would not do to become too vocal about the matters that were being mishandled, because to do so might force a redefinition of the whole job—which, as a matter of practical politics, was inadmissible. Wherefore: double talk.

Government, in other words, was being run on a public relations basis, using that expression in its least complimentary sense. With honorable exceptions, the prevailing thesis in Washington for many months had been: make people think that everything is going to come out all right. If we just say that we're united, and say it long enough, maybe we'll find that we actually are united; gloss over all inconsistencies, pretend that the unresolved conflicts are in fact resolving themselves, act as if the problems we never quite got down to cases with in the last eight years have all been solved; ride it out on all the assorted high reputations we can collect, and if something still is lacking we can always fall back on the golden voice that carries conviction.

Harsh words, not justified by facts? Well, look at the record.

Since June of 1940 the country had been doing a strange and a mighty job. It was preparing for war as it had never prepared before, and it was doing so under very odd circumstances. Completely disillusioned about the munitions makers, it was shoving at them more money than the munitions makers had ever dreamed of. Deeply cynical about armies and military men, it had resorted to peacetime conscription. It had put all kinds of raw materials under controls which, by the fall of 1941, had become fairly strict and irksome. It had interfered with the conduct of innumerable peacetime businesses and it had begun to cut down on the flow of goods to consumers. All of this it had done, and—which is important—all of it had been accepted by the people with remarkably little complaint, because the people knew perfectly well what was at stake.

But all of this was going on under a protective coating of double talk. We were not going to get into a foreign war. No American boy was going to die on foreign soil. (Cassino, Iwo Jima, Okinawa, Tarawa, St. Lo: just names in an atlas, not yet crowned with the blood and stars to put them beside Bunker Hill and Chickamauga.) We were not preparing to make an end to fascism, unless by good fortune we could denounce it to death; we were simply preparing to defend the continental United States against invasion, and that was all there was to it. We were going to get ready to play our part in a drama which, according to our most solemn pledges, could not take place. We were going to do drastic things, but nothing was going to be changed and nobody need worry too much.

Nothing was going to be changed. That was both the enabling clause and the statute of limitations for the whole business. A key point in the adroit leadership which was lining America up as the ultimate foe of the Axis was the necessity to bring into the defense effort, as active co-operators, the proprietors of the nation's chief physical assets. The job couldn't be done without them, but their fears and suspicions—which, where Franklin Roosevelt was concerned, were deep and beyond number—had to be allayed. For the duration of the prewar defense period, therefore, the game had to be played their way; whatever preparations the nation made had to be made within the bounds of territory that was familiar to these men. This meant that the rules of the game were not to be changed.

This might have been all very well if, as everyone was insisting, America faced nothing more than a simple military threat—a hostile army on the loose which might ravage city and countryside, exact reparations, destroy naval bases, and inflict the other damages which hostile armies inflict under the codes of conventional warfare. The big catch in it was that what the country faced was infinitely more than a simple military threat. Miracles might indeed be possible, but to make adequate preparation for the tremendous challenge of a world revolution without making any substantial changes in the status quo at home—this, under the circumstances, was the one miracle that was not possible; yet it was precisely this which seemed to the men in charge of the defense effort to be required of them. Far-reaching change (plus the boldness which is needed to meet change) was the basic necessity of the situation. Yet the men to whom the President had given the job knew better than to talk about it—or were themselves, by predisposition, by self-interest, or by the weight of vast possessions, constitutionally unable to see it.

As a result, the defense effort as a whole became a venture about which it was not humanly possible for the administration to be frank.

There are, as a matter of fact, few more instructive or melancholy tasks open to a patient researcher nowadays than a study of some of the speeches made by leaders in the defense effort in the months before Pearl Harbor. The two who came closest to speaking out were Donald Nelson and William L. Batt, in private life president of SKF Industries in Philadelphia. Over and over again these two men, with sincere eloquence, warned of the vastness of the job we had undertaken, of the existing threats to freedom, of the need for devoting everything we had to the task before us; but it was not possible for either of them to go all the way, to lay the facts right on the line and say: "Good people, here it is. This is the score. You can see what we're really up against and what we have to do." Always there was a skirting of the edges, and an approach by indirection—not because Batt and Nelson were double-talkers by nature, but simply because the very conditions under which they were working made it impossible for them to be entirely frank and say exactly what they were up to.

All of which is depressing enough; but not especially damaging, maybe, since the one hundred and thirty million Americans really knew what was going on and gave it their support? The damaging part of all of this was the effect that it had right in Washington. The government tried to kid the people but what it succeeded in doing was to kid itself. The habit of double talk was a profoundly limiting factor in our preparation for the emergency.

Some very high-priced business and industrial talent had been assembled in Washington. These men had been told to do a job; had, in fact, received elaborate instructions, set forth in public addresses and in executive orders from the White House. Press and public had taken these orders seriously, and results were being awaited. But the trouble was that everything that these men had been told to do was based on the official theory that it was all for passive defense. Instructions, grants of authority, blurbs in the daily press—all pointed in the same direction: Get ready to defend our shores; we're not going to get into the war unless somebody brings it over here; take drastic action fearlessly, but whatever happens, don't really upset anybody.

Which meant that the top men in the Defense Commission and, later, in the Office of Production Management had been put on a spot. The cruelest of requirements had been placed on them: they had to transcend both their explicit instructions and their own built-in limitations. Told to do one thing, they were actually supposed to do another. This put a terrific obstacle in the way of men like Batt, Nelson, and Leon Henderson, who knew perfectly well what the score was and were determined to do something about it. Even worse, however, was the latitude it gave to the men who were not Batts, Nelsons, or Hendersons—to the holder-backers, to the men who were confused or timid, to the men who believed above all things in business as usual, who shrank from any step that would "upset established patterns in industry," and were deeply committed to the task of getting all the new wine stowed away in the old familiar bottles.

An illuminating case in point is provided by the experience of Mr. Floyd Odlum, the financial genius of Atlas Corporation, who burst into view early in September, 1941, as Director of the Division of Contract Distribution in the Office of Production Management.

As Odlum himself remarked, shortly after he took office, "the most important duty of this new division is to bring about as quickly as possible a wider distribution of defense orders among small business and small communities, and to speed the defense effort." This sounds prosaic enough, but what it actually meant was that Odlum had been tapped for Skull and Bones, and that he had been given a green light to revitalize the whole operation.

For some queer things had been happening, as the defense program kept on expanding in 1941. Not only were the military supply contracts being heavily concentrated in the hands of the industrial giants, on a to-him-that-hath-shall-be-given sort of basis —an official release from OPM early that summer pointed out that fifty-six corporations held three-fourths of the total dollar value of all contracts thus far awarded—but a nation which was beginning to see that it would need every ounce of productive capacity it could muster was also beginning to see that it had a great deal of productive capacity which, unaccountably, was not in use at all. Specifically, a considerable number of factories had been shut down, their workers made idle. These were the little fellows, for the most part, the plants the Army procurement officers had never heard of and didn't want to hear of, the companies whose capital and whose connections were too weak to arouse any especial interest in the land of one dollar a year. Embattled and purposeful, the War Department was displaying an unalterable reluctance to comprehend that military goods might be made satisfactorily by a concern several degrees smaller than, say, the Ford Motor Company or General Electric, and OPM was doing nothing whatever to call the point to the Department's attention. And the small producers who could not get contracts were, in steadily increasing numbers, being caught in the mounting shortages of raw materials and hence were unable to continue their normal peacetime production.

As a matter of fact, the problem went even farther than that.

The giants themselves had all manner of machinery that was not turning out a dime's worth of production for the Army or Navy. Heavy contracts had, for instance, gone to the automobile industry; but most of these involved the building of new plants and the purchase of new tools. The great bulk of the plant and machinery already existing in the industry was doing nothing whatever for defense production. It was the nation's greatest single industrial resource, and only the fringes of it had been put to work for defense. For the automobile makers, like any other reasonable men, refused to throw all of their facilities into production for the Army and Navy until the Army and Navy asked them to do so; and the Army and Navy, who were doing all of the buying, simply weren't asking them.

What was needed, obviously, was a program with some drive and breadth, backed by a genuine realization of what the country was up against. If the country was to use more than just its left hand in getting ready for war, it needed above all things a really vigorous procurement program, a means of broadening the base of production, a real survey of the country's entire industrial plant and a determination to use that plant effectively. And Odlum was the man who had been anointed for this task.

Odlum was given an executive order—an executive order, under Washington operations, being both a presidential directive and a grant of authority. The order Odlum got was both sweeping and vague; which is to say that it instructed him to do practically everything but did not quite come to the point of saying just how he was to do it. It began by asserting that its purpose was "to provide for the most effective utilization of existing plant facilities for defense purposes; the conversion into defense production of civilian industries affected by priorities and raw material shortages; the alleviation of unemployment caused by the effects of such priorities and shortages; the local pooling of facilities and equipment; subcontracting; and the wider diffusion of defense contracts among the small business enterprises in every part of the nation."

Note particularly those final clauses. They point directly to one of the great lost opportunities of the entire war program; a lost opportunity whose effect, being cumulative, we are still feeling; an opportunity that was consistently ignored, although it was pointed out unmistakably before OPM even came into being. This opportunity—not to make too many words about it—was the one presented by the words "pooling" and "farming out."

In the fall of 1940 a number of communities had reached down to the grass roots to see what they could do about supporting the defense program. The case of Beaver County, Pennsylvania, is typical.

The people of Beaver County got together to see what resources their county had which might be used for defense production. They set up a county committee, made up of business leaders, labor leaders, city and county officials, pastors of various churches, representatives of luncheon clubs—a committee representative of all groups and classes in the community. This committee made a careful survey of all the manufacturing capacity in the county, found out exactly what factories and machines were idle, listed the kinds and quantities of labor that were available, and came to definite, well-founded conclusions about the type and volume of defense material which the idle facilities might produce. Then the committee tried to interest someone in Washington in what had been found, word having gone out that Washington was interested in trying to find idle resources that might be put to work.

The Beaver County people succeeded in interesting practically nobody except for a man named Morris L. Cooke, a consulting engineer from Philadelphia, who was then serving in Sidney Hillman's Labor Division of the Defense Commission. Cooke had been studying the possibility of pooling community resources so as to create a defense production potential which would not exist if the resources were taken separately—this being one of the cases where the whole is greater than the sum of its parts—and the Beaver County idea was right down his alley. But Cooke was in the Defense Commission's *labor* division. He had nothing at all to do with the placing of contracts, and since he represented Sidney Hillman's outfit he was automatically suspect when he tried to talk to the men who did have something to do with it. All he could do was plan and exhort. He did both vigorously, but to no effect. The pooling and farming-out program, urged by Cooke, brilliantly exemplified by the Beaver County committee, and taken up by several dozen other communities before all hands came to realize that the boys at the top just weren't going to play it that way, offered a direct and effective means to tap the nation's unsuspected sources of strength. Put into full effect, all across the country, it would have been democracy in action. It could have shown, in day-to-day operation, what OPM pretended to show: all elements of the community working together for a common cause, capital and labor and government united on their own terms and doing a job they all wanted to do. It would have been the apotheosis of the free enterprise system, brought down from the National Association of Manufacturers' cloudy level to something that the ordinary American could understand and have a piece of.

But it all came to nothing. Cooke was sidetracked, and so was the idea he stood for. But the idea was remembered, here and there, and Odlum's charter of authority was a direct invitation for him to pick up the idea and go places with it. Furthermore, generalized though it was, the charter did promise Odlum just about all the authority he needed. It authorized him to formulate and promote specific programs for the purchase of munitions and supplies by the armed services from smaller units of industry; to make such changes as he desired in government procurement practices and procedures; to develop and activate plans for the conversion to war production of peacetime industries; to organize and use community "pools" after the Beaver County model; to provide both financial and engineering aid for small manufacturers, needed in defense production—and, in general, to get things moving all along the line by just about any means he found advisable.

Now what all of this really meant, when interpreted in the light of How Things Get Done in Washington, was that Odlum was empowered to shoot the works. There was not in Washington at that time the shadow of a doubt that under this order Odlum could have made himself a Minister of Supply with complete authority over the Army and Navy procurement system and over the direction of the Nation's industrial potential. In Washington, under FDR, an official was rarely given a clear-cut directive right at the start. What he got, usually, was an indication of the President's desire and a chance to spread himself. A man like Leon Henderson, like Harold Ickes, or like William Jeffers—to name three highly dissimilar functionaries—would proceed to interpret his basic document on a broad plane. That is, he would

35

act as if all of the hazy authorities which it seemed to confer were in fact solid, clear-cut, and unmistakably legal, and he would yell to high heaven whenever anyone got in his way. So doing, he would presently find that his own interpretations of the document were accepted throughout the government, and his as-if legality would become legality in fact.

This unquestionably would have been so in Odlum's case. The President—who tended to know more about how the government was really operating than some of the men who worked for him often supposed—would have backed him; for that directive gave about as clear an indication of what Roosevelt really wanted as was usually vouchsafed to anyone. Congress, which had been plagued for months by the complaints of small and middle-sized businessmen, and which had been looking with more and more suspicion on the way the War Department and OPM were mishandling the defense program, would have given Odlum any legislation he needed the moment he showed that he had an intelligent program and meant to do something about it. Odlum had come up to a loose ball on a confused and broken field; all he needed to do was pick it up and run with it.

It turned out to be utterly beyond him. The mountain that labored and brought forth a mouse would have had to take second place to the Division of Contract Distribution operating under the Odlum charter. In addition to a rather large number of speeches, Odlum produced principally two things to make memorable his tenure of office—a headache for Donald Nelson and a brief but gaudy feast for the eyes.

The feast for the eyes consisted of three red-white-and-blue railroad trains. Their formation was announced to the public in a press release issued from OPM on October 21, 1941:

"To make sure that no qualified manufacturer—no matter where he is—misses an opportunity to get a defense contract for lack of information, officers of the Army, Navy, Maritime Commission, and the OPM will tour the country beginning November 10 in three special exhibit trains, painted red, white and blue. The specials will carry exhibits consisting of samples of defense equipment and parts needed by the services to give prospective defense manufacturers a clear idea as to the type of articles needed."

A subsequent release explained that each train would be on the road about a month, and that each was to be made up of six cars carrying the samples and two cars carrying the government men.

The headache for Nelson was produced at about the same time. Lacking the eye-appeal of the fancy railway cars, it was subtler but fully as provocative. Briefly, it was a proposal that there be set up, for the use of small manufacturers who could not "get into war work," a pool, or kitty, of 2 per cent of the nation's available supply of critical materials. The materials thus segregated would be doled out to the little fellows so that they could stay in operation until such time as better arrangements could be made —or until the emergency ended.

This hit Nelson late in November, just when the shortage of everything from zinc to aluminum was becoming most acute. As executive director of the Supply, Priorities, and Allocations Board, Nelson had been working all fall to take these critical materials out of nondefense production, to set up an effective priorities system, to arrange a means of directly allocating the most critical materials to the places where they were needed most. Just when he was beginning to see daylight ahead, along came the 2 per cent plan (as he wrathfully dubbed it) and threatened to upset the whole works. It not only would have wrecked the system of controls which was being erected; it reflected a complete misconception of the entire situation. The big idea at the moment was not to "do something for the little fellow"; it was to do something for the country, of which the little fellow was a basic part, and to which in its hour of desperate need the little fellow had something useful to contribute. . . . Nelson devoted a good part of the Saturday before Pearl Harbor to the preparation of a brief attacking the 2 per cent plan, for use at a meeting of the priorities board the following Monday. As it happened, however, the news from Honolulu Sunday afternoon automatically sent the 2 per cent plan deep into limbo.

These two achievements, then, chiefly marked Odlum's exercise of his opportunity. Their significance lies in the way they reflect the fatal weakness of the entire OPM period—the weakness for doing things at half stroke, for dodging the fundamental issues, for making performance *look* good rather than making it good in fact. The red-white-and-blue trains represented, in essence, an effort—not to solve the problem of the small manufacturer, but to create the impression that the problem was being

37

solved. They had the true circus touch. They were an attempt to gloss over a failure to come to grips with a problem; a failure, in fact, even to understand what the problem was.

For the problem (to repeat) on the eve of Pearl Harbor was not the plight of the small businessman, the unemployed worker, and the small community; the real problem was the plight of America itself. Complex, varied, infinitely intricate, the nation possessed thousands of sources of strength. It had never recognized them all; some of them it had never really used, others it had used without knowing that it was using them. It desperately needed to discover them, to make the fullest use of them, to call forth a maximum effort that would not only beat down external enemies but that would give to each man and each element in the society a deep and lasting realization of what democracy really is and of the matchless strength and vigor which a free society possesses.

That kind of effort we never got, which is one reason why we are where we are today. To a considerable extent (though *only* to an extent, when all is said and done) the evasions, the fumbling, and the empty talk of the OPM period are *why* we never got it; and of these, the patriotically tinted railroad cars, clanking across a land that was demanding to be put fully to work, stand out as the living sign and symbol.

For this failure, on the part of the men to whom the big job was entrusted, to recognize the problem, tied in with a failure to recognize the nature of the world crisis itself, which is another point that is illustrated by the Nelson dinner party.

Genial, ruddy-faced Knudsen had made his little talk, and in it he had likened the whole situation overseas—the rise of fascism, the channeling-off into oppression and bloodshed of the fears and despairs of bewildered millions, the whole deadly threat to everything America stands for and lives by—to a neighborhood gin party that had become an intolerable public nuisance. To be sure, Knudsen was not at the moment trying to express any profound thoughts about the war. He wasn't making a speech; he was just letting loose a few after-dinner remarks. But he expressed, nevertheless, unconsciously but effectively, the prevailing viewpoint among the men who were supposed to see to it that we got fully prepared for what was coming. This was just another war. We had wanted to stay out but it looked as if we couldn't, so we'd get it settled as quickly and smoothly as we could and then we would go back to the old familiar ways.

It would have been a good trick if we could have done it, but the stars in their courses were all lined up on the other side. . . . France crushed, the British Empire dissolving, Russia rising to a new dominance, all the guidelines erased in Asia, the outward forms and patterns by which Europe, whose heirs we are, has lived by for a thousand years visibly gone forever: and we are going to *go back* to the old familiar days and ways? . . . There was abroad in the land, in those days, a considerable realization of what it was that we were up against. The administration knew, the people themselves knew—would Americans, otherwise, have consented to conscription in time of peace? The world revolution was not going unrecognized, back there in 1941, except around the council table of OPM and the War Department—the one place of all places where myopia was sure to have disastrous consequences.

And this myopia—this soothing, it's-only-a-noisy-gin-party frame of mind—did not exist by accident. You can't ride out a world revolution very well unless you can summon a revolutionary force to your own aid. We had at our disposal the strongest revolutionary force of all—unadulterated democracy, played all across the board. But how are you going to summon up a revolutionary force when your burning, moving, underlying desire is to preserve and protect the status quo?

You aren't. You can't. And they didn't. It was easier and more comfortable to send red-white-and-blue trains across the land. The only trouble is that we are still paying for them.

CHAPTER FOUR

Sixty-four Dollar Questions

LIKE the Christian faith of Paul the Apostle, Donald Nelson in the fall of 1941 was the substance of things hoped for and the evidence of things not seen.

Both the substance and the evidence were badly needed, that fall, and they had to be embodied in someone. That they should come to rest in the stout and jovial person of the former executive vice-chairman of Sears, Roebuck and Company was partly a matter of his own personal fitness and partly a matter of sheer desperation on the part of the elements. For the whole defense effort, from the moment of its creation in mid-1940, was the living embodiment of a pathetic but tenacious confidence in the endurance of Things as They Have Been, leaving much to be hoped for and much to be looked for. The guiding light that shone in the Social Security Building in Washington was a flame that burned in the hearts of men who had taken (so to speak) the country as they found it and had done very well for themselves thereby, and their program expressed a deep complacency. Do what must be done, but above all things do it without rocking the boat or changing the old familiar rules of the game: that was all the law and all the prophets.

All very well and very natural, as a guide for the chairmen of boards of directors; all very inadequate, as a leading string for a people entering the fiery furnace. The inadequacy had been growing more and more obvious, by the time of Pearl Harbor. Yet there was not, up to the moment of that catastrophe, any visible and compelling reason why matters should not continue as they were. An intricate, delicately poised structure had been erected, and while there was nothing in particular to keep it from collapsing there was also nothing in particular to bring it down. In the Office for Emergency Management of the Executive Office of the President there had been set up an Office of Production Management, empowered and instructed to look wise, to issue statements, to make studies and give advice, and even to take certain definite and concrete actions. Along with this, partly over it and partly underneath, there was a Supply, Priorities, and Allocations Board, which had the dual function of carrying out OPM's wishes and seeing to it that what OPM wished was somewhere near adequate. A step removed was the Army and Navy Munitions Board, vested with ancient authorities and busy about their exercise. Above and beyond all of these, and openly contemptuous of the civilians who tried to hustle the military, were the War and Navy Departments. All of these maintained a state of equilibrium. They could do quite a number of useful things. Given a decade or two of unbroken peace, they might even get the nation ready for war. But, in any case, their interlocked edifice was *there*. After a manner of speaking, it worked. It was not going to fall down unless somebody shoved.

Fortunately, there were people around who were beginning to shove. Nelson came to represent them—to typify the effort to stop the floundering and get down to cases. He had been called in under the old Defense Commission, as one of the business experts whom the New Deal was rather frantically summoning to its aid. His specialty was purchasing. The government was beginning to spend money at a rate that went far beyond anything even the New Deal had previously imagined, and it seemed logical to have someone around who knew how to spend large sums of money intelligently. But it was not long before people began to see that Nelson was not just another business big shot. Probably the first symptom he displayed which helped people come to this conclusion was his ability—almost unique, among the dollar-a-year tribe—to realize that Leon Henderson neither carried a lighted bomb in his pocket nor conducted human sacrifices by the light of the moon. As far as most of the dollar-a-year men were concerned, Henderson was the undying reminder that the New Deal was dangerous and hateful. I remember going into the office of one such, somewhere along in the middle of 1941, and finding the occupant full of a kind of somber triumph—like a man who, against the will of his bitter enemies, has succeeded in confirming his darkest suspicions.

"Say," said this man, a successful middle-western manufacturer of I forget just what, "did you come by the OPACS Building this morning?"

OPACS, in case you have forgotten, was the Office of Price Administration and Civilian Supply, headed by Henderson. It had just moved into a temporary building near the OPM's Social Security Building.

"Yes, I guess I did. Why?"

"Did you notice the big flagpole, out in front of it?"

"Not especially."

"Well, I did. It's just been painted. *And it's been painted red.*" He leaned back, gazing up triumphantly to appraise the effect of this horrid revelation. Then he added, "And don't tell me that's just a coincidence!"

That was pretty much the way Henderson affected most of the industrialists who found themselves his coworkers. But Nelson was different. To begin with, it was easy for Nelson to like people, and he liked Henderson. For another thing, Nelson had sense enough to see that Henderson was not a dangerous radical. Most important of all, he found that he and Henderson thought alike on the overriding need for a genuinely all-out program to beat the Axis. So he and Henderson, in addition to becoming good friends, became a team, a nucleus around which those who were shoving against the wobbly OPM edifice could, ultimately, unite their efforts.

There were not very many of these shovers, at the top level. Nelson, Henderson, Batt, Vice-President Wallace—that is just about the list. But there were more of them down on the second and third layers, where the professional New Dealers—i.e., the government career boys, the Bright Young Men of fact and legend—had been placed to be idea-men and action-provokers for the big shots. Of these, by far the most important was Robert Nathan.

Nathan, in fact, was one of the most important men in Washington in those days, by any standard. The fact that this country was able, shortly after Pearl Harbor, to lay out a production program big enough and broad enough to win the war was due to Nathan as much as to any other single person. It was Nathan, more than anyone else, who supplied Nelson and Wallace with the ammunition they used, in December of 1941, to convince the President that the country could and should do ever so much more than either OPM or the War Department had any notion of asking it to do. He was a huge, burly, broad-shouldered man who looked rather like a tackle for the Chicago Bears, or like a professional wrestler—looked, as a matter of fact, just the

42

least bit like a highly intellectual Primo Carnera—and the higher echelon in the War Department learned to hate him with a sleepless and vindictive fury. They finally got him, too, upwards of a year after Pearl Harbor; had him drafted into the Army, thus turning one of wartime Washington's few irreplaceables into a buck private doing basic training. The country didn't even get another buck private out of the deal, as it turned out, since Nathan presently had to be invalided out of the service because of a sciatic condition; but the War Department was relieved of a man who had been bothering it, so maybe the deal was worth it.

A sample of the exchange between Nathan and the military which helped to create the War Department's *delenda-est-Nathan* frame of mind can be glimpsed in correspondence Nathan had with Lieutenant General Brehon B. Somervell, Commanding General of the Army Service Forces, in the fall of 1942. The background of this correspondence is illuminating. After spending a year or more, prior to Pearl Harbor, prodding the War Department to raise its sights and embark on a really adequate production program, Nathan had had to spend most of his time after Pearl Harbor trying to convince the War Department that there really was a limit, after all, and that the war effort would be ruinously handicapped if the Department insisted on a program substantially bigger than could be handled. He submitted to Somervell, accordingly, a set of documents designed to show that there was an upper limit to the nation's productive capacity and that the entire production program would be botched up if that limit were exceeded. Somervell sent him a reply which denied everything and which concluded with these words:

"I am not impressed with either the character or the basis of the judgments expressed in the reports and recommend that they be carefully hidden from the eyes of thoughtful men."

In return, Nathan wrote the General that "in view of the gravity of the problem discussed in these documents, I hesitate to take your memorandum seriously," and wound up with the remark: "I appreciate your frankness in stating that you are not impressed by the character or the basis of judgments expressed in this report. Your conclusion from it, however, that these judgments be carefully hidden from the eyes of thoughtful men, is a *non sequitur*."

Neatly put, of course, and all that; but even a civilian can't talk that way forever to a three-star general in time of war without paying for it, and Nathan finally paid.

Nathan's drafts on the bank of brass-hat ill will had not yet come up for payment, however, in the fall of 1941. He was hard at work in those days as chief architect of the program which the all-outers were finally able to use as a basis for action. This program came to be known, unofficially, as the Victory Program, although that name somehow got lost in the shuffle after Pearl Harbor. The actual war production program, on which the war was fought and won, was erected upon it; it was the job which—as far as production was concerned—made ultimate victory possible.

In its essentials the Victory Program was extremely simple. It consisted principally of the answers to two questions: "What do we need to make in order to beat the Axis?" and "Can we do it?"

The really odd part about it all is that these two questions did not get answered until the very eve of Pearl Harbor. And if getting the answers was a tough job, it wasn't nearly as tough as getting the questions asked in the first place. For the queer, fog-like air of unreality that hung over the defense program through most of its first eighteen months was given its most characteristic and amazing flavor by the fact that the people in charge never at any time knew precisely what they were setting out to do or made any effort to find out. The real fight that Nelson and the other all-outers had to wage all through 1941 was basically a fight to try to get them to find out.

There were obstacles in the way of finding out. First and foremost was the very framework of the job itself. Nobody had ever said, right out in the open, that we were mobilizing our forces to beat the Axis even if we had to cross all of the seven seas to do it—that there was no point to anything that was being done unless it was the kind of showdown that would wind up with either Hitler or Uncle Sam being carried out on a shutter. What we were doing, remember, was preparing for self-defense. The North American continent was going to be held inviolate. "Measures short of war" was a chilling, crippling phrase, especially when the only people who took it seriously were the very people who were supposed not to. If you stayed on the surface—and that was by all odds the most comfortable place to stay, in

1941—you could not put your finger on any single failing in the defense effort and say, objectively and conclusively, "This is insufficient." Insufficient for what? No time schedule had been set, and there was no quantitative program. Henderson might break his teeth trying to get the auto industry to make fewer passenger cars and more munitions; the unanswerable argument could always be that he had no real yardstick by which he could prove that what was currently being done was going to fall short. Industry was doing all the War Department asked it to do; how could you go beyond that?

For the War Department didn't know the answers either, and if it did it could see no good reason for telling them to civilians. It had been given no clearer directive than the OPM had been given, and in matters of this kind the War Department is the last organization in the world to go beyond the limits of its directives. It had been told to raise, arm, equip, and drill an army of two million men, and to make various additional items of munitions. Lend-Lease was at its elbow, with a list of goods the British wished to have. But these did not add up to a program. It might well be—as Nathan pointed out in October—that some twenty billion dollars in defense appropriations had not yet been translated into actual contracts; but there was nothing in the books, anywhere, to prove that this meant somebody was not moving fast enough. It was impossible to define "fast enough," just as it was impossible to define "big enough," in terms that would stick.

This meant, obviously, that OPM was fatally handicapped because it did not know exactly what was expected of it. But it faced an even bigger handicap in an intangible: a deep, cautious, instinctive reluctance on its own part to get the answers it needed.

For those answers were practically certain to be upsetting. The men who ran the defense program were men from big industry. They were honest and they were patriotic, but they were also men who were thoroughly conditioned by background and by environment. Suppose they had admitted, to themselves and in public, that the defense program was not really just an extra bit of fire insurance but was actually the first long and irrevocable step toward a final showdown with the Axis and everything the Axis stood for; their comfortable reliance on the status quo would instantly have gone up in smoke. The desire to have a defense program that would not really change anything

45

very much would have been doomed; for it would at once have become inescapably obvious that nothing would do but a program which would change everything a great deal, much of it permanently. The attempt to show that we really had enough steel, enough aluminum, enough rubber, enough of this, that, and the other thing, would have fallen on its face—as, in fact, it was then in the process of falling, only it wasn't necessary to admit it.

A grim specter haunted these men's minds in those days; the specter of going back, some day, to ordinary peacetime pursuits and finding the nation equipped with more productive capacity than could profitably be employed. This specter was back of the resistance to the expansion of basic capacity, back of the resistance to a defense program determination that would make such expansion unavoidable. The nation had just come through a decade in which men were painfully confused and irritated by the fact that the mere ability to produce more than was needed somehow seemed to mean that they had to get along with less than was needed. A too-ardent defense program—a program based on realities, which expanded productive capacity all along the line, with no concern whatever for the way it might have to be used after the war—was not to be embraced lightly. Genuine abundance can be the most horrifying of all concepts.

Therefore the basic questions had gone not only unanswered but unasked, these many months. The man who started the chain reaction which finally got them asked and answered was not a member of OPM. He was, in fact, a foreigner—Jean Monnet, who had begun his war service in 1939 as a member of the French Purchasing Commission, and who had gone over to the British after the fall of France, eventually coming to Washington as a representative of the British Supply and Munitions Board. For it was Monnet, early in 1941, who began preaching the gospel which in the end was to find expression in the "arsenal of democracy" phrase: the idea that the Axis could never be whipped unless the enormous productive resources of the United States were put to work, to the fullest possible extent, to produce the goods which Hitler's enemies needed. Monnet had no public forum from which to expound this gospel, but he talked it up vigorously at dinners, at parties, and at conferences, and he made converts. The all-outers in OPM listened and found that Monnet's idea was their idea; and out of it all, at last, grew a definite project, with White House blessing, to get the sixty-four dollar questions asked and answered.

Nathan's immediate boss was Stacy May, head of OPM's Bureau of Research and Statistics. May went to London to get a tabulation of British needs. Batt went to Russia with the Harriman mission and got a tolerably adequate picture of what the Russians needed; not a full breakdown, the Russians being reticent, but enough to come and go on. And President Roosevelt, early in the fall of 1941, ordered the War and Navy Departments to make a survey of the good and chattels they would have to have to win an all-out fight with the Axis.

Simultaneously, the President gave the all-outers their first real break by setting up the Supply, Priorities, and Allocations Board with Vice-President Wallace as chairman and Nelson as executive director. SPAB was an organizational nightmare to any administrator with a taste for orderly arrangements and clear-cut lines of authority; it was half in OPM and half out of it, it was both OPM's servant and master, and it fell just far enough short of being the long-awaited "super agency" to make the irreverent wonder what on earth FDR thought he was doing now; but it did serve a good purpose, in a left-handed sort of way. For one thing, it got Nelson out from under the OPM Sanhedrin. This made it possible for him to grapple with the problems of such basic raw materials as aluminum, copper, and steel, and resulted in some straightforward programs for expansion of productive capacity at the same time that it permitted an approach to an effective job of putting scarce raw materials in the hands of the producers who needed them most. For another thing, it brought Nelson and Wallace together.

They made a good team, even if the team did not actually last very long. Each man complemented the other, had the qualities the other lacked; if it had been possible, somehow, to combine the two into one man the result would have been a world-beater. Nelson was hale and hearty, a mixer, a salesman, outwardly a complete extrovert but inwardly moved by currents which no one could trace or understand, himself least of all; a man who fought by enduring rather than by slugging, capable of vast loyalty and self-abnegation, with a mind that worked far under the surface, a mind that got excellent results but seemed to get them by some subconscious process that could not be traced. He had a way of making you feel, after you had talked to him

47

for five minutes, that you had known him all your life; but after you had known him for a long time you began to realize that most of him was far out of sight where you could never really see or touch it. I believe he was, at bottom, the loneliest man I have ever known.

Wallace, of course, was in many ways the opposite of all of this. If Nelson looked like the complete extrovert, Wallace looked like the complete introvert, although the outward seeming was just as deceptive in his case as in Nelson's. He had a genuinely first-rate mind, and he always knew exactly where it was and what it was up to; but he lacked Nelson's ability to suffer fools gladly, and he tended to grow uneasy, even tongue-tied, when he felt that he was with people who did not talk his language—which, of course, was just where he was, a good deal of the time. He was not in the least the vague and impractical dreamer he was popularly supposed to be; his mind was scientific, direct, and orderly, and he was really a better, tougher, and more realistic administrator than Nelson. But if his mind was scientifically direct and accurate, it was also scientifically inquisitive. Abstractions interested him, especially abstractions which, if studied earnestly, might be turned into practicalities; he had, at times, a way of thinking out loud, when some new idea came to him, turning the thing over and looking at all angles of it verbally, and now and then it happened that he did this while making a public talk of one kind or another, which usually led to a little misunderstanding of what he was really talking about. He was a much more articulate person than Nelson, but at the same time he was much more likely to say things that were bound to be misinterpreted, if only because of his tendency to assume that any man of good sense could easily see what his words meant even though they were strung together imperfectly. Wallace was a harder man to get acquainted with than Nelson, but much easier to understand; and the two men reacted quite differently under pressure. Nelson's instinct was to fix his eye on the desired goal and take whatever belaboring came his way, in the feeling that if the goal was only reached the incidental pummeling didn't really matter much; Wallace was equally steadfast in going for the goal, but was much readier to slug back if someone tried to stop him. Nelson would never have been capable of Wallace's savage public attack on Jesse Jones—the incident that resulted in Wallace's being blown out of the Board of Economic Warfare;

48

Wallace, on the other hand, could never have taken what Nelson quietly took from Under-Secretary Patterson and General Somervell.

Unlike as they were, these two men nevertheless found plenty of common ground to work on, and their mutual effort in that fall of 1941 was the best thing that happened to America all year. They spearheaded the fight to get the unthinkable questions asked and answered, and when they succeeded they took the result where it would do the most good—namely, to the White House.

On September 17, 1941, Nelson wrote to the War Department, the Navy Department, the Maritime Commission, and the Lend-Lease Administrator, asking for "estimates of requirements over the next two years based on military objectives as determined by the reporting agencies." What finally came back was turned into the Victory Program by May and Nathan.

In brief, what Nathan got to work with—as a result of May's visit to London and Batt's visit to Moscow, the President's directive to the armed services, and Nelson's request for estimates—was a detailed tabulation of the new military equipment, from tanks to dungaree jumpers to airplanes to machine guns to deck swabs to battleships, that would have to be produced in this country by September 30, 1943, if by that date a sustained and successful offensive were to be launched against the Axis. Here, at last, was the answer to the first of those two key questions: "How much have we got to make to beat the enemy?" It was not a final answer, for the goals were changed many times before the war ended; but it was the completely indispensable, long-awaited first answer. It was *an* answer; and because it had finally been obtained, it was at last possible to find out just what sort of load the American economy was going to have to carry during the next two years.

It was now Nathan's job to find the answer to Question Number Two: "Can we do it?"

This meant taking the statements of requirements and translating them into terms of raw materials, component parts, man-hours, energy, and dollars, and then matching all of these against the nation's known potentials. It meant making all of these translations with one eye on the clock, for the time factor was vital. (We can make 50,000 airplanes, beyond question, given time enough; but can we make them by a year from next Thursday,

49

and if we do what will that mean to our ability to make machine guns?) This involved setting up an almost infinitely elaborate algebraic formula. Twenty thousand tanks in twelve months equals so many tons of steel plate, and x number of heavy bombers means y quantities of aluminum extrusions, which does so-and-so to the press capacity at Pittsburgh and Cleveland; cargo ships and destroyers are valves and pumps and blowers and ball bearings, but they are also copper wire and steel plates and heavy forgings as well, and if we need this many rounds of antiaircraft ammunition we must have that many thousand tons of sheet brass, which will do such-and-such to our ability to produce field telephones . . . and so on, for page after page, and please make it all come out in weighted dollars so that we'll be able to stack it up against the figures on national income. . . . It meant, all in all, matching what we at last knew we *had* to do with the best possible estimates of what a completely energized nation *could* do—and figuring, therefrom, whether what we were at the moment doing was anything we dared be content with.

This was the Victory Program; unwelcomed by either OPM or the War Department when it finally emerged, but altogether about as useful a set of tabulations as America ever obtained in an hour of dire need. For the point that needs emphasizing, over and over again, is that America was confronted in the fall of 1941 not only by a military challenge but by a moral challenge as well. It not only had to win the war; it had to win it in a way that would show what democracy could do when it was doing its absolute best. A military victory by itself was not going to be enough. Through the victory, and beyond it, democracy somehow had to find its strength—and, finding it, had to know that it had found it, had to know *how* it had found it, so that what democracy *is* could speak all across the world with a clear and confident voice that all men would want to listen to.

All of that was tied up with the formulation of the Victory Program. That we didn't quite make it, finally—that we got over the first hurdle and flunked the second, that we won the war but failed to achieve a triumphant democracy—wasn't the fault of the men who put the program together and made it mean something. They at least made sure that we could get the military victory.

CHAPTER FIVE

What Will People Think?

THERE is good reason to suspect that the man who cared not who made the nation's laws so long as he could make its songs must have worked either for big industry or for the United States Government. It can be shown, at least, that this preoccupation with what is said rather than with what is done tends to be characteristic of both groups. Between a business big shot planning a public relations campaign and a government bureaucrat meditating the announcement of a new action program there is a profound similarity. "What will people think?" is the gnat that buzzes in each set of ears.

When industry and government, then, warily and with suppressed misgivings, joined hands to create the Defense Commission early in June of 1940, almost their first official act was to hire a press agent. In industry he would have been called a public relations advisor; actually, in government, he was called a Director of Information; the job, minus trimmings, was the same. The new venture had to have a mouthpiece.

Both sides, apparently, lived to regret their choice. For the man appointed—named by the President, and suggested to him by Lowell Mellett—was the same Robert Horton who, eighteen months later, was to spoil Nelson's dinner party; an unmalleable character, notably devoid of tact and possessed of a fixed idea which at times cut squarely across the desires of both businessmen and bureaucrats. In the end they unloaded him, but not before he had managed to plant his fixed idea where it would keep bobbing up to annoy people.

This fixed idea was quite simple. It was a conviction that the sole job of the mouthpiece for a government agency was to tell the people the plain, unvarnished truth about the things that agency was doing. To an extent, this conviction had been evolved during the years Horton worked as Washington correspondent for the Scripps-Howard newspaper chain—a final reincarnation, no doubt, of that chain's ancient masthead motto: "Give light and the people will find their own way." To an extent, too, it

51

derived from his more recent experience as information director for the U. S. Maritime Commission, the spot from which Mellett plucked him. But beneath both of these things—beneath the reporter's ingrained impatience with double talk, and the government man's awareness of the ineffectiveness of the cover-up—there was a sturdy, old-fashioned Vermont belief in democracy taken straight; a conviction that in the end the people have enough sense and enough decency to come up with the right answers if they are just given all of the facts.

Now the New Deal had entrusted the defense program to a number of men who possessed glittering reputations: of all earthly possessions, the one which men are most apt to wish to retain and also, unluckily, the one most subject to rust and tarnish. But the first revelation which these men received was that their public relations man conceived it to be no part of his job to protect any reputations whatever. They discerned that he was a man in whose simple creed a fact had to speak for itself without any aid from the prompter's box. They were saddled with a propagandist who did not believe in propaganda; stuck, apparently for the duration, with an unbridled democrat. It is only fair to add that this association was trying to all concerned.

And there wasn't much of anything they could do about it. For when the President replaced the Defense Commission with OPM, at the beginning of 1941, he took Horton and his informational organization entirely out from under OPM's control. Horton's Division of Information, technically, was a completely separate organization, the coequal of OPM itself; on paper, it was a part of the Office for Emergency Management, that presidential holding company for so many war agencies. Horton's boss was not William S. Knudsen but William H. McReynolds, administrative assistant to the President, and over him there was nothing but the White House. As the defense program expanded and OPM became a large and complicated organization, its separate parts were served, publicity-wise, by information men whom Horton had hired and whose loyalty stemmed through him to the administration as a whole and to the idea which Horton embodied, rather than to the particular functionaries with whom they happened to be working. OPM did not have full control over its own publicity. The channels through which that publicity had to flow were controlled by Horton, and Horton did not work for OPM. He worked for the President.

Horton built up a rather large organization, as such outfits go in Washington, and he staffed it mainly with former newspapermen; a few advertising men and industrial public relations men were hired, but they were taken on as technicians, not as policymakers or policy-interpreters. Furthermore, Horton saw to it that his staff was thoroughly indoctrinated. That indoctrination ran about like this: We are working for the people. They are footing the bill for this defense program, and if it comes to fighting they are the ones who will have to carry the guns, and they have a right to know exactly what is being done, how it's being done, and why it's being done. It's up to us to enable them to find out. We are not supposed to cover up any mistakes that may be made, we're not supposed to build or to protect anybody's reputation, we're not supposed to try to make something look good when it isn't good. That's not what we're being paid for; we are neither salesmen nor promoters. As far as OPM is concerned, we tell what it is doing rather than what some official may want people to think it is doing. If what it is doing makes sense, then OPM will have what they call good public relations, and that'll be just dandy; if it doesn't, then OPM won't have good public relations, and that will be no concern of ours because we aren't a public relations organization. The people have a right to know either way, and that's all we are concerned with.

This did not mean that the top officials of OPM were unable to say to the public anything that they chose to say. If they ordered a press release issued, it was issued; if they wanted to speak their minds—at a press conference, in an interview, in a public speech—they did so. In that sense, and to that extent, they had full control over their publicity mechanism. The catch is that "to that extent" is only a minor part of the publicity operation of a government agency.

For the information man in government doesn't speak to the people directly. Leave the radio and the movies out of consideration, for the moment, and concentrate on the press—the wire services, the daily papers, the trade press and the weekly and monthly magazines. These are represented in Washington by large numbers of reporters who are eminently capable of looking out for themselves. The reporters will accept press releases and speech handouts, and they will attend press conferences, and if they get genuine news thereby they will print it; but they move strictly under their own steam, and what they want mostly is access to the news in its native and unedited state. They want to get at someone who can answer questions; someone whom they can rely on to give them a straight answer. If a government agency is doing something, or is about to do something, or is suspected of being about to get ready to do something, the reporters will accept a press release as a formal statement of action taken or of intentions made manifest; but what they really insist on getting—what they will get in one way or another, in spite of hell or high water—is someone in that agency who knows what the score really is and is willing to tell the truth about it. That required truth may be an elaboration of a formal press release, it may be a series of facts behind the press release, it may be material which was very carefully left out of the press release, or it may simply be a down-to-earth answer to such questions as "What's cooking?" or "What's this all about, anyhow?" The point is that in the long run the bulk of the Washington news which the public reads is obtained in that way and not from mimeographed handouts.

That is where the government information man comes in, if he comes in at all. The reporter who is hunting question-answerers would naturally like to go all the way to the top, but that is physically impossible most of the time. A Donald Nelson, for instance, running a War Production Board, cannot, with the best will in the world, see a score of reporters every day. (As a matter of fact, Nelson was unusually accessible to reporters, but even so he could not grant more than a small fraction of the requests for interviews.) As a day-in-and-day-out arrangement, the press has to find someone below the top level. But the operating men below the top level are usually very busy men, too, and what the press needs is someone who is always accessible as well as communicative. All of which puts it up to the information man, who was put there to meet that need.

If he knows what is really going on in his agency, and if he is at all times ready to give a straight answer to any question a reporter may ask—especially to the embarrassing questions—he serves a useful purpose and becomes worth the money the taxpayers are paying him. He can be useful in a variety of ways:

54

by answering questions himself, by producing requested facts, statistics, or documents which the reporter can't find unaided, by making it possible for the reporter to talk to some operating official; but first, last, and all the time he has to play it straight, avoiding special pleading and remembering that he is being paid by the people, and that the people have a right to know what their government is doing. He is useful to his agency, in short, only to the extent that he is useful to the inquisitive public— meaning, primarily, the press. For if he is not genuinely useful to the press, the press quickly learns to ignore him altogether, and then he is useful to no one.

All of this was part of the Horton indoctrination. What it meant was that neither OPM nor its successor, WPB, was at any time equipped with a public relations staff, as that term is commonly understood. There was no such thing as covering up mistakes or putting stuffing into an empty shirt. The record had to speak for itself. If Horton was a public relations man he was one who believed in democracy with the bark on.

This was not unimportant, as the country moved down through the slow stages of the defense effort to the crisis of actual war. From the very start, there was a strong tendency in Washington to assure all and sundry that everything that was needed was in fact being done and that no one had cause for worry. The men who embodied this tendency were completely honest about it; they believed this themselves, and it was only natural for them to want the nation as a whole to believe it also.

Thus the Defense Commission was barely six weeks old when Stettinius, who was responsible at that time for the supply of raw materials, was issuing a progress report stating that "we may expect to have available as needed in defense industries adequate supplies of critical and strategic materials," and adding that "the situation generally is more hopeful than we anticipated six weeks ago." He spread himself slightly, covering all the metals from aluminum to tin, and touching on the problem of rubber supply by stating that "it is expected that before this month is over a plan of synthetic rubber production will have been worked out which in the future could eliminate our dependence upon imports."

Simultaneously his chief oil advisor, Dr. Robert E. Wilson, was issuing a statement saying that "so far as the petroleum industry generally is concerned its growth since the last war has been so tremendous that even satisfying the enormous demands of a mechanized army presents no serious problem."

By the end of November, 1940, Stettinius was announcing that the anticipated production of ingot aluminum during the next two years appeared ample to take care of all military and civilian requirements, with a margin to spare. He reinforced this one a month later with further assurances, and concluded acidly (the aluminum program by now being under some public criticism) that "it is unfortunate that public anxiety over our national defense preparations should be based upon reports of shortages which do not exist." (Two months later he was putting all aluminum producers under mandatory priorities because the shortages were so pressing.) And at the end of February, 1941, Gano Dunn, a consultant to Stettinius, was issuing his famous report asserting that no expansion in steel capacity was needed—that there was, in fact, something of a surplus.

This Dunn report is worth dwelling on briefly. Dunn, an estimable and upright gentleman who in private life was president of the J. G. White Engineering Corporation, prepared his report at Stettinius's direction at a time when the existence, or otherwise, of a shortage in steel capacity had become a burning issue. The report was transmitted to the White House by OPM and was released by the President himself; even more, it bore the official presidential blessing, inspiring Roosevelt to assert that talk of a steel shortage was a deliberate lie. All in all, this ought to have settled the question of a steel shortage and restored confidence. But it didn't, somehow. On the contrary, the echoes of the Roosevelt voice had hardly died away before stories were being printed making new predictions of an imminent steel shortage, questioning Dunn's estimates of requirements, and citing figures about military, civilian, and overseas demands which indicated that steel was going to be very tight indeed. As things turned out, inside of three months Dunn had to issue a second report in which he took a much less optimistic view of the situation; and when SPAB, early in the fall, ordered a ten-million-ton expansion in steel capacity there was pretty general agreement that the action was slightly overdue.

The interesting part about this is not that Dunn made a bad guess on steel requirements, or that the President sounded off with words which he would gladly have eaten whole a bit later on; Washington being what it was, those points were routine. What is worth recalling is that the doubting Thomases on the press, who printed detailed refutations of OPM's report on steel, got the figures, the estimates, and the forecasts which they used to break down Dunn's report from OPM itself.

For OPM was not a unit, blessed with singleness of mind and heart, then or at any other time. It contained holder-backers and all-outers, optimists and pessimists, business-as-usual advocates and everything-for-defense men—and it never succeeded in muzzling any of them. The Stettinius all-is-well chorus never had the slightest chance to become an official OPM party line, rigorously observed by one and all—even when, as in the case of the first Dunn report on steel, it had the President's backing—for the simple reason that the reporters never had any trouble getting at the people in OPM who knew that all was very far from well and who could cite facts and figures to prove it. Horton's informational organization was not a fence to keep out unwelcome inquiries. There were times when it was much more like an open gate.

Events then proceeded to compound the felony. In mid-April of 1941 the President took the old price, consumer, and agricultural divisions of the faintly surviving Defense Commission and fused them into a brand new agency, the Office of Price Administration and Civilian Supply. He directed this agency to prevent profiteering and undue price rises, to make sure that the civilian economy got the goods and materials it needed, and in general to look out for consumer interests; he put Leon Henderson, the fire-breather, in charge of it; and he located the agency in the Office for Emergency Management, separate from OPM and of equal status to it.

The interesting part about this was that Horton's Division of Information was also in OEM, specifically instructed to act for any and all OEM agencies in the matter of publicity. As a result, while it continued to serve OPM with one hand, the Horton organization also had to serve OPACS with the other; and OPM and OPACS at once began feuding.

The feud involved no mere point of bureaucratic rivalry; it grew directly out of the basic and thorny question of how far and how fast the nation ought to get ready to fight an all-out war, and it speedily created as strange a situation as the Washington bureaucracy ever saw. OPM, the war agency par excellence—the organization that was supposed to be channeling all available resources into war preparations—stood for a moderate effort. It represented the idea that the defense program could somehow be put on top of the normal peacetime economy; in effect, it stood for a guns *and* butter concept, offering a safe refuge for those who thought the war probably wouldn't happen and didn't want to see anything disturbed very much even if it did. The War Department found itself in full accord with OPM on this program; it was prepared to ask of the nation no more than the nation could provide without giving up its delightful new boom in consumer goods. But OPACS, whose job it was to protect the civilian economy, was lined up from the start in favor of a Spartan life, with everything that the civilian didn't actually have to have, thrown into the scales against Hitler. Henderson took the view that an agency instructed to protect civilians ought to begin by finding out how much protection the civilians really needed. The conclusion his boys quickly reached was that the civilian didn't need anything like the amount of protection he was getting. Therefore: cut down, cut fast and sharply, and turn the savings into war goods.

This feud was not long in coming out into the open. It got there in connection with the argument over what ought to be done about the automobile industry.

No industry in the country is as directly and immediately interesting to the average citizen as the auto industry. It is the miracle-worker, the pride and joy of the mass-production era, the living image of the triumph of the machine; also, it produces the cars without which the modern American cannot go to work, take a proper vacation, or in general get any fun out of life. Touch the auto industry sharply and the nation immediately becomes aroused.

All of which was perfectly obvious to everyone in OPM and OPACS, in the spring of 1941. Two other factors were equally apparent. The first was that the industry was incomparably the greatest consumer of steel and other critical metals in the entire country; the second, that Director General Knudsen of OPM was, so to speak, the auto industry incarnate.

Shaken together and brought to high temperature, these three factors produced an unstable mixture, likely to explode at any time. It began to pop in the spring of 1941.

The first warning that America could not have an adequate defense program and an unrestrained boom in auto manufacturing at the same time came from Knudsen himself. On April 17 he issued the following statement:

"I have just concluded a meeting with the leaders of the entire automobile- and truck-producing industry, which I called to consider the growing defense production job that faces us.

"The entire industry willingly accepted an initial 20 per cent reduction in the production of motor vehicles for the model year beginning August 1 this year, in order to make available more manpower, materials, facilities and management for the defense load now being made ready.

"The reduction will amount to approximately one million units."

This was followed, some weeks later, by formal notification from OPM to the motor manufacturers of the individual allotments of cars to be made during the year beginning August 1. These allotments totaled 4,224,152 vehicles, and OPM added:

"The allotments to individual companies gave due regard to the necessity of maintaining the relative position of the different companies in the industry, their size, field organization, employment, and their relative position in regard to passenger vehicles and trucks."

A reduction had been ordered, therefore, but it still left the industry facing an exceptionally good year, for the reduction just about equaled the anticipated increase over the previous year's production. The action was just a wee mite misleading, too; the reduction hadn't been made in order to free skilled men and machines for defense production, but because the materials for unlimited automobile production had just naturally ceased to be available. Henderson's men began to meditate on all of this —especially his chief deputy, Joseph L. Weiner, a tough little lawyer who had been named assistant administrator in charge of civilian allocations—and shortly thereafter OPACS took the ball away from OPM and began to run with it.

Late in June, OPM called a meeting of the automobile manufacturers to nominate a defense industry advisory committee, the idea being that this committee would help the government work out a further curtailment of automobile production if such were necessary. The meeting was duly held, on July 2, and a committee was organized. Henderson, meanwhile, had announced that OPACS was going to hold a series of conferences with the consumer durable goods industries, to discuss allocation of scarce materials among competing civilian claimants; and a fortnight after the OPM meeting he called the auto makers into session with his deputy, Weiner. This was not a happy meeting; the auto makers felt that Weiner was both unreasonable and vindictive, and Weiner felt that the auto makers were excessively deficient in co-operative spirit; but in any case, a week after this meeting OPACS announced that automobile production for the twelve months beginning August 1 was going to be slashed by 50 per cent.

Naturally, this caused an explosion. OPACS had acted without benefit of OPM and without consultation with Knudsen—had acted, in fact, at the very moment when Knudsen was conferring with the auto people about "an orderly curtailment program," had acted in a field which OPM felt was none of Henderson's business, and had used authorities which OPM supposed were reserved exclusively for OPM. Even more important was the matter of the underlying approach. OPM was curtailing auto production simply because materials were getting so short that auto production was going to have to come down anyway and the coming-down might as well be done in an orderly manner with due regard for everyone's competitive position; OPACS was frankly knocking off auto production in the hope that the resulting pressure would compel all of the reluctant parties involved—auto makers, OPM, and War Department—to turn men and machines which had been making autos to the manufacture of war goods. There were stormy scenes, followed by peace conferences; ultimately, late in August, something of a compromise was worked out, OPM agreed to go along with the 50 per cent cut for the twelve-month period, and OPACS agreed that the cut should begin at a slower rate during the first three months of the production year, so that the reduction in the level of operations would be more gradual. But in the process OPM had taken a shot well below the waterline—or, as the OPM people felt, below the belt.

There was a reorganization. SPAB was invented, to serve as a sort of superboard on priorities and allocations. OPACS was, by presidential ukase, split in two, the Office of Price Administration remaining as a separate entity, and the Weiner operation becoming part of OPM entitled the Division of Civilian Supply. In a way, this was a victory for OPM; the separate outfit, using powers which OPM had thought belonged solely to OPM, was abolished. The victory was made rather hollow, however, by the fact that the obstreperous Henderson remained in a dual capacity, price administrator outside of OPM and director of civilian supply inside of it. Furthermore, he kept Weiner on, in OPM, as operating head of the Civilian Supply Division. He was wholly unrepentant, and his wings had not been clipped in the least. As a footnote it might be observed that Stettinius, the chief apostle of optimism, was promoted up and out. He became lend-lease administrator, and went on later to become, successively, Secretary of State and rector of the University of Virginia; which, in a way, doubtless added up to a steadily ascending progression. . . .

What all of this meant, of course, was that the deep, fundamental split in the government—or at least in that part of the government which was getting the country ready for war—had come out into the open in such a way that nobody could fail to notice it or to think about it. Which gets us back, rather round about, to Horton and his organization.

For there developed in the administration, while this was going on, an increasing and quite understandable feeling that the government really ought not to be talking with so many different and contradictory voices. The people might be getting confused. These interagency rows ought not to be carried on in public, even though the public good was thereby served. Government's public relations, in short, were bad. Horton was the director of information, as far as the defense program was concerned; where to point the finger, unless at him?

Knudsen spoke through Horton; so did Henderson. The reporters who dug up the material with which they demonstrated confusion, cross purposes, and inadequacy in the defense program went to Horton and his organization to get the material; or at least, if they didn't get it there, Horton steered them on to it; or, in any case, he didn't keep them from getting it. And the speeches Horton permitted the OPM dissidents to make! Here

61

was Henderson, for instance, telling a trade association convention: "There has been far too much concern within industry over the dangers of expansion, too much willingness to accept shortages of raw materials, of plant capacity, of power, of freight cars, as an inevitable concomitant of all-out production in this country. We have been too prone to think of vested interests, of friends in industry who might be embarrassed when the emergency is over by more plant capacity than it was thought could be used, on the basis of past experience." Here was Stacy May, chief of OPM's Bureau of Research and Statistics, asserting in a radio address that "we have tried to meet our armament loads by placing them on top of the normal business-as-usual procedure. . . . It is not unfair to say, I think, that to a great extent we have kept our best managerial skill, our best machinery, and our most highly skilled labor upon civilian production."

Also, there was this sort of thing: by May of 1941 electric power had begun to run short and OPM was trying to remedy matters. While it was trying, one of OPM's most distinguished consultants, Mr. C. W. Kellogg, who in private life was president of the Edison Electric Institute, chose to make a speech at Buffalo declaring that no shortage in electric power was to be expected. As soon as press reports of this speech came in, Horton saw to it that OPM released an official statement saying that "OPM is not in agreement with the views on this subject which the press has ascribed to Mr. Kellogg," and adding sharply: "On the contrary, representatives of the OPM have been actively engaged with other agencies of the government in developing a program to provide the additional power needed for the expanding defense requirements, particularly in the fields of aluminum and magnesium production." To be sure, this statement was issued with Knudsen's full approval; but Horton had instigated it. Couldn't he have glossed it over, somehow?

Consequently, Horton began to come under fire from two sides: from the New Dealers, who after all hated to see the administration looking as if it couldn't run a defense program, and from the corporation presidents in OPM who hated to see industry looking as if *it* couldn't either. It was not Horton as an individual who was under fire so much as it was the idea that he stood for; the idea that the people's business is something the people have a right to know all about, whether it is being done well or badly; the unwavering conviction that "public reaction" will take care of itself if the job which the public reacts to is done properly. As long as he had charge of the publicity channel for the defense program there was no chance to kid the public. Yet the only alternatives were (a) to stand by helplessly and watch good men lose prestige, or (b) to do something fairly drastic about the causes for this loss of prestige. Either one was painful to contemplate. The whole defense effort, from the very start, had been based upon a deep unwillingness to be frank about what was being done.

Broadly speaking, there were two ways to remedy matters, assuming that the whole trouble was in fact a public relations problem.

One way involved putting careful controls on everything that was said by everyone in all of the war agencies, so that there could be created a picture of a unified, harmonious, far-sighted, and efficient administration that saw its problems ahead of time, grappled with them masterfully, and in general handled the people's business the way it ought to be handled. This would mean assaying every bit of news that emerged from the war agencies—speeches, interviews, off-the-record revelations, every-thing—to see whether it helped to create the desired picture, and suppressing everything that didn't.

There is a lunatic fringe to everything, of course, and the reductio ad absurdum of this approach is best illustrated by what happened one day to Stephen Fitzgerald, who succeeded Horton as Director of Information for the War Production Board some months after Pearl Harbor. A dollar-a-year man called Fitzgerald into his office one day and said that he had been worrying about the unpleasant publicity WPB had been getting.

"What we ought to do," he told Fitzgerald, "is to get out a simple press release whenever WPB does anything and require all of the papers just to print that press release exactly the way we write it, without adding anything of their own or leaving any of it out. Then we wouldn't have all this confusion and people's minds wouldn't get so upset."

The other approach to the publicity problem attacked it other-end-to. It called for the erection of something like a propaganda agency—something just exactly like one, come to think of it—to "sell the war" to the American people; an outfit that would undertake to arouse enthusiasm for democracy, for the free-enterprise system, for forty acres and a mule or a chicken in every pot, or whatever the chosen slogan might be. The business-men in OPM and WPB tended to favor the first approach, and the dissatisfied New Dealers inclined toward the second.

First port of call for all New Dealers who wanted a change was Lowell Mellett, who had picked Horton for the job in the first place and who still sat at the right hand of the father in the White House as far as questions of government publicity were concerned. Mellett, a soft-voiced, slender chap with graying hair and a quaint habit of sitting on one ankle and smiling quizzically at nothing at all when the arguments got hot, was besieged all through the months before Pearl Harbor by well-meaning folk who pleaded for a vast propaganda effort. Oddly enough, Mellett found that these earnest people, who were devoted to the job of beating Hitler, almost always wound up by saying that what the country needed was someone who could do the kind of job Goebbels was doing in Germany. . . . Well, of course, not exactly like Goebbels, but the same kind of thing, and just as effective. . . . One day Mellett got tired of merely replying that the government in a democracy had no business propagandizing its own people, and let loose with a mild explosion.

"Look," he said, "it would be easy to do a Goebbels job here. Horton could do it, I could do it, anybody could do it—if you could give us Goebbels' advantages."

"Meaning what?" asked the delegation of the moment (including, incidentally, a cabinet minister).

"Meaning," said Mellett, "two things. First, complete indoctrination of the American people for the preceding one hundred and fifty years. Second, complete, air-tight control over anything that is said anywhere in America—on the air, in the press, in Congress, from the pulpit, in the movies, or on the corner soap box. That's all it would take to do a Goebbels job. But it *would* take that much."

. . . It's not unimportant, this question of government publicity in the war effort. On the contrary, it goes to the heart of the whole question of what we went to war for and what our victory would mean after we had won it. What *does* the government of a democracy say to its own people in time of crisis? The President, members of Congress, cabinet ministers—individually, they obviously have a responsibility for exhorting, for interpreting, for summoning up emotional and intellectual support. But what does the government, as such, do about it? Does it simply let the facts speak for themselves, or does it suppress some facts and color other facts in order to create a desired impression?

Hide-bound businessmen had one approach and doctrinaire New Dealers had another. Different as they were, both groups shared one controlling emotion: a distrust of the naked processes of democracy. Back of the businessman, demanding that the press print about WPB only what WPB wished to have printed, and the government official, urging Mellett to find a home-grown Goebbels, there stands the same unexpressed feeling: the shadowy, lurking conviction that the people, when you get right down to cases, are the faceless multitude after all, requiring to be cajoled and nursed along and led by the hand. Just give the facts and let the people make up their own minds? But suppose they don't come to the right conclusions? To what *we think* are the right conclusions?

It leads, inevitably, to an overpowering concern with what is said; which, in its own turn, is in itself a refusal to face real issues, a symptom of the belief that it will be easier to make people think that the right things are being done than it will be to go out and do them. It's the red-white-and-blue train all over again: we won't actually slug our way through this problem by making full use of the potentialities of the little fellow, but we sure will go all the way across hell's half acre to make people think we are doing it.

And if, in the end, when the shooting is all over, the little fellow has not really been used, if he hasn't been given a self-respecting part of the job, if he has never been given reason to feel that it really was his job and that he was all-important in it, if he has just been someone to placate rather than one of the folks who make the wheels go round . . . and if he is fully aware of the fact, by sober experience . . . and if there just happen to be an awful lot of him . . . do you, by that time, begin to have a little trouble demonstrating that democracy means an irresistible action program of, by, and for the people?

CHAPTER SIX

Philosophy of the Salesman

H AVE a look, first of all, at the attitude of mind which led
to the demand for manipulation of day-to-day news about
the defense effort and the war program.

One morning in the spring of 1941, William S. Knudsen,
Director General of the Office for Production Management,
called Horton into his office and· handed him a fat memorandum.
"Read that," he said. Horton looked at Knudsen and saw the
faintest echo of a twinkle under the sandy eyebrows. Then he
read the memo.

Unsigned, it was entitled "Memorandum on Defense Publicity."
It had been prepared (as far as anyone could learn) by a Detroit
advertising agency and had been submitted to Knudsen through
channels. It undertook to make clear that neither Knudsen nor
businessmen in general were getting a fair shake out of the
government's publicity set-up, which had been devised by scheming New Dealers to give all the breaks to labor and to the
administration.

It began by reciting the obvious fact—that Horton and his
organization were answerable to the President rather than to
Knudsen. Then it went on to a detailed analysis, headed "Indications of Bias in Press Releases." These indications, the memo said,
were many. More press releases had been issued for Sidney
Hillman, it pointed out, than for Knudsen; the score, by actual
count, was fifty-six for Hillman as against thirty for Knudsen.
Furthermore, Hillman had been allowed to propagandize shame-
lessly. On February 7, he had stated that "harmony prevails in
the employer-employee relationship," and Horton had distributed
this statement as a press release. A fortnight later Hillman had
come out with an eleven-page statement about the "remarkable
record" of labor unions in the defense program. This performance
had been capped, in March, by the distribution of a Hillman-
inspired pamphlet boldly headed, "Labor Speeds Defense."
During all of this period, the report pointed out, "there was not
a single press release giving Mr. Knudsen's side of the picture";

and when Knudsen gave the House Judiciary Committee a memorandum suggesting legislation "to ameliorate the strike situation," the Horton office had failed to issue his memo as a regular press release, even though it did mimeograph it and make it available on request. Further, it was complained, Horton had issued a release stating that manufacturers could get certificates of necessity to enable them to take advantage of tax amortization provisions of the Internal Revenue Code, without explaining that these provisions were a matter of simple justice to the manufacturer; the impression was left that "great favors were being granted in order to get plants built to produce defense goods."

There was a great deal more along this line, and the report also complained that Horton was giving altogether too much publicity to Henderson's attempt to keep prices down and not nearly enough to the solid achievements of industry. The report wound up by lamenting: "Even industrial representatives in government agencies have not shown that the very industries which they represent are making definite and unusual contributions. It is uncertain to what extent this is caused by direct or indirect censorship, or by the absence of insistence from industrial representatives that their stories must be told."

Horton read the memo through to the end and laid it down on the desk.

"Give me three guesses where that came from?" he asked.

"I give you *no* guesses," said Knudsen.

"Okay," said Horton. "What are you going to do with it?"

"Do with it? I'm going to file it," said Knudsen, tossing the memo into a basket. And that was the last anyone ever heard of it.

This is as good a way as any of pointing out that Knudsen himself never had any part in the general demand for more carefully regulated publicity. He could of course have had all the sound-effects men in Detroit at his elbow, just by hinting that he wanted them, but he never gave the hint. His one preoccupation was his job, and it was his tragedy that he had been given a job he didn't fit. He was a production man, and being director general of OPM was not a production man's job. It called for the combined talents of a conciliator, a politician, a seer, and an economic statesman, perhaps, but it was a blind alley for a man whose genius lay in the shop.

. . . One evening, late in 1941, a university professor who was serving as an OPM consultant happened to leave the Social Security Building just as Knudsen was leaving. Knudsen recognized him and offered to give him a ride uptown. They got into Knudsen's chauffeur-driven Cadillac and started off.

Slightly impressed and flattered—his acquaintance with Knudsen was of the slightest—the professor felt that the least he could do was promote a little casual conversation during the ride, so he made the effort. Tentatively, he raised various current topics of interest—the fighting in Russia, Japan's possible intentions in the southwest Pacific, the proposed two-price system for copper—but none of them registered. Knudsen was friendly enough, but his conversation was strictly limited to "yes" and "no." The professor finally gave up and they rode on in silence. Presently the car went around a corner at rather high speed, and the professor remarked that it performed well on curves . . . and found that he had hit the jackpot. Knudsen came to life. He explained just how the rear end of the car had been built so that it would take curves well. He went into detail about matters of design, balance, and construction. He had the chauffeur drive around the block a couple of times, taking some curves fast and others slowly, to illustrate the matter. From that moment the conversation was lively. Knudsen had found a subject he could talk about.

As a matter of fact, Knudsen had a right to call for some special publicity handling if anyone in Washington ever did. Because he took the OPM job his reputation suffered in a way he didn't deserve—which is to say that he was blamed for things that were not altogether his fault; was blamed, really, for not being an entirely different sort of person than he actually was. But he never offered an alibi. The advisors who urged him to get rid of Horton and call on the limitless publicity resources which the automobile industry could so quickly bring to his service could never get him to listen. He treated their pleas just as he treated the memo which he showed to Horton: he filed them, without comment.

Knudsen was a story-book character, and his loyalty to the President was something which a great many professed New Dealers could profitably have studied and copied. Knudsen was the immigrant boy who made good, the lad from Europe who had found America to be exactly the land of unlimited promise

68

that the legends said it was; and he retained something of the Old World idea of the place of the ordinary citizen in relation to the head of the state. He was devoted to Roosevelt, not just because Roosevelt had charmed him, although Roosevelt had done that; there was in his loyalty a tinge of the duty and respect a Danish peasant might owe to his king.

This came out where Horton, at least, could see it, during the fall of 1940, when the third-term presidential campaign was at its hottest. Most of the men in Knudsen's own circle, naturally, were very much anti-Roosevelt, and as the campaign wore on they made repeated efforts to get Knudsen to declare himself publicly for Willkie. Since it was obviously impossible for him to do this while remaining as the chief pillar of Roosevelt's defense agency, these efforts took the form of circulating stories that Knudsen was going to resign—to resign, of course, because as a solid leader of business he found it quite impossible to continue to work for the New Deal. (This, by the way, was a typical Washington way of putting oblique pressure on Knudsen. The best way to make a rumor come true, in Washington, is to get it into print a few times. The subject of the rumor sees it, and in the end may come to believe it himself and act accordingly.) Anyhow, some of these resignation stories at last got into print, and the reporters began to bombard Horton with queries: Is Knudsen going to quit? So one morning Horton went to see Knudsen about it.

"I understand you're resigning," Horton said.

Knudsen looked up blankly.

"Who? Me?"

"Yes. It says here in the morning paper you're going to quit."

"*Me?*" repeated Knudsen, honestly bewildered.

"Yes. The story says you don't want the President re-elected so you're resigning. If you are, we can get a release out on it, if you like."

"Me resign?" said Knudsen. "Me quit the President? Why— why, *he calls me Bill!*"

Calming a little, Knudsen asked why such stories should be printed in the first place when he had no intention of resigning, and Horton explained the ways in which election campaign currents were swirling around the Defense Commission. Knudsen

69

rejected the whole idea indignantly, and in his indignation his quaint brogue thickened.

"Dis job—dis is not politics!" he said angrily. "Dis is *defense!*"

The particular flavor that was attached to Knudsen's career in government is illustrated by an encounter he had with a Senate committee during the early part of the Defense Commission period. Shortages of various raw materials were beginning to be irksome and a priorities system was being set up. Nobody liked priorities and the system wasn't working too well; and there grew up, in Congress, a feeling that it might be best to take the priorities power out of the hands of the Defense Commission and set up a wholly separate agency, answerable strictly to Congress, to handle priorities and nothing else. The administration learned of this with deep misgivings; the priorities power was the very heart of the defense program, and to set up a separate priorities agency would immediately wreck the Defense Commission and hamstring the whole defense program; so Wayne Coy, one of the President's most trusted confidential aides, called a meeting of the top men in the Defense Commission to discuss how this new project could best be defeated.

The Defense Commissioners promptly agreed that the proposed legislation must be headed off, and agreed further that Knudsen —as the Commissioner whose word carried the most weight— should be the spokesman who would go to the legislators and show them why the bill must not pass. All of the arguments against the proposal were carefully rehearsed; and a few days later Knudsen, all primed, appeared before a Senate committee that was holding hearings on the matter. He was put into the witness chair and was duly sworn.

"Mr. Knudsen," said the committee chairman, "I understand you wish to be heard on this proposed legislation?"

"I do, sir," said Knudsen, nodding vigorously.

"Will you give us your thoughts about it?"

"Well, sir," said Knudsen, "I'm against it. It just won't work."

"Why won't it work?" asked the Senator.

Knudsen fixed his glasses—pince nez, at the end of a long black ribbon—more firmly on his nose, and looked gravely from one Senator to another.

"Gentlemen," he finally said impressively, "where I come from, when I say a thing won't work—*it don't work.*"

And that, in effect, was all of Knudsen's testimony. So high was his reputation, so great was the respect which was felt for him at that time on Capitol Hill, that the offending legislation was killed forthwith.

A couple of nights later Coy went to a cocktail party. As he entered the room he saw Knudsen, chatting with friends; and at sight of him Knudsen waved genially and began making his way through the crowd to get over to him. When the two men were face to face Knudsen clapped Coy on the shoulder, rumbling deep chuckles, his face aglow with mirth.

"I know what you're wondering," said Knudsen. "You're wondering: Why didn't he use all those fine arguments we worked up for him, when he talked to the senators? And you know what I'm telling you? I'm telling you: *I forgot 'em!*"

. . . The President let Knudsen down with a cruel bump, in the end. When the War Production Board was suddenly created, with Nelson as its chairman—unmistakably an official ruling from the White House that OPM had failed—Knudsen got no advance warning whatever. He first heard of the change when an office associate laid the news ticker announcement on his desk, early one January evening. Nelson, coming back from the White House where the laying-on-of-hands ceremony had been performed, hurried to Knudsen's office for a conversation that was difficult and embarrassing for both men. Knudsen was crushed; the man who called him Bill hadn't even bothered to put a cushion under him when he dropped him. There had been a very elegant cushion for Stettinius, but there wasn't any for Knudsen —just as, two and one-half years later, there wasn't to be any for Nelson, neither. . . . As far as Nelson had been able to find out, the White House had no plans for making any further use of Knudsen's services; Nelson finally sold the President on the idea of offering Knudsen a high commission in the Army and a job as production trouble-shooter for the War Department—a role, incidentally, which finally gave Knudsen a chance to use his talents effectively.

In the end, Knudsen quietly swallowed his hurt and accepted the new job. It took him a couple of days to make up his mind about it, and during that time the story began to go around that he would return to Detroit and publicly denounce the President. After Knudsen blew these stories up by quietly letting it be known that he would stay on, Horton went around to see him. He walked up to Knudsen and stuck out his hand.

"Mr. Knudsen," he said, "I'd like to shake hands with you."

Knudsen shook hands and asked, "Why?"

"Because I know what you've had to take, these last few days, and I want you to know that I admire you for the way you've taken it."

Knudsen looked at him for a moment, then walked over to the window and stared out over the open, brown-grass space of the mall. When he spoke the inevitable brogue was a little stronger than usual.

"You know," he said slowly, "the President—he is my boss. He is the Commander-in-Chief. I do whatever he wants me to do. If he tells me to take a gun and walk back and forth in front of those doors"—he gestured toward the sidewalk five floors below, where during the early stages of the war uniformed sentries with bayoneted rifles paced their beats—"if he tells me to do that, I do it. He is the Commander-in-Chief."

. . . Knudsen, in other words, never bought any part of the idea that what the defense effort and the men in it needed was better handling of publicity. Neither did Nelson, who succeeded him. Quite early in the game, Nelson expressed his views on the subject by saying that he believed the American people would do anything that was asked of them if they were convinced that it was necessary and knew that everybody was being treated fairly, and he felt that the government's part in convincing them was pretty much limited to displaying the facts and letting the people judge for themselves. At his first press conference after he became chairman of WPB, Nelson told the reporters that he wanted to do his job "in a goldfish bowl," and he stuck to this idea much longer than anyone expected. It was not an easy decision to stick to, either. During the first few months after Pearl Harbor, a large number of highly skeptical reporters were watching WPB with hawk's eyes, to see whether it moved fast and courageously on the all-important job of converting civilian industry to war production. OPM's fatal weakness had been a paralyzing reluctance to approach that job; when OPM was replaced by WPB, most of the OPM officials were retained to fill the same roles in the new organization that they had filled in the old; and no one who was familiar with the record was at all sure that they would do much better in WPB than they had done in OPM. Furthermore, WPB was no more a completely harmonious body than OPM had been. It always contained plenty of men who were perfectly ready to provide reporters with inside dope designed to prove that this, that, or the other thing was not being done as well as the war emergency demanded. The Horton information division had never operated to keep reporters away from those men; on the contrary, it usually functioned so as to bring them together.

As a result, Nelson never quite knew when he picked up his morning paper just what kind of stories he was going to read about the operation he had in charge. He got plenty of criticism, in those first few months, from people who felt that WPB was not moving fast enough or going far enough. There wasn't, really, any standard by which the job could be measured; Nelson himself used to remark that it would be several years before he would know whether WPB had been too slow or too fast in the conversion program. So there were bound to be ardent souls in WPB who, at any given stage in the proceedings, felt that WPB was being as timorous and as laggard as OPM, and who would talk to reporters about it.

The point is that Nelson never tried to gag them. There were differences of opinion, the fate of the country depended on getting the job done right, and—as he saw it—it was entirely proper for people to know that differences of opinion existed. Instead of trying to control the flow of publicity so that people would be bound to think WPB was doing the job right, Nelson simply did the job as well as he knew how to do it and waited for the performance to speak for itself. He never tried to have the words set to music.

Neither Knudsen nor Nelson, then, had much use for the theory that a government official ought to be able to make everybody else look at things with the same pair of glasses he himself used. But it does seem, sometimes, as if they were almost unique. Neither among the businessmen nor among the bureaucrats in Washington were there very many who shared their view. The woods were full of people who believed in democracy but. The longer the war lasted the more they were heard from. In the end they became dominant. Less and less, as Pearl Harbor receded into the background, did Nelson and his successors

73

operate in a goldfish bowl; more and more, as the war progressed, did the public officials who kept asking, "What will the people think?" add the second question, the pay-off question—"And how can we keep them from thinking it?"

This was partly because the administration itself abandoned its original idea in regard to public information and came to look upon the entire war program as something that had to be "sold," as if it were a deodorant or a new gargle. It was partly because the war agencies got so big and so loose-jointed that no power on earth could keep their several big-wigs from tucking private public relations advisors away on their staffs in one disguise or another, the net result being an unco-ordinated but almost universal attempt to prevent the leakage of "unfavorable" news. And, last but never least, it was partly because the War Department finally muscled into a territory where it did not belong, and conducted an incredible campaign of psychological warfare against the American people.

An accurate reflection of the attitude which ultimately prevailed is to be found in a quaint memorandum entitled "Public Relations," which was written by a dollar-a-year consultant on Nelson's staff for the guidance of the topside late in November, 1942. Nelson never adopted its recommendations; indeed, he treated it precisely as Knudsen treated the earlier memo from Detroit—by filing it. But the general idea back of the memorandum did, in the end, prevail; for which reason the document is worth a little study.

The memo began by suggesting that WPB ought to set up a small, highly skilled group to shape and handle its public relations politics. This group, it suggested, should consist of four people: a boss-man, designated, for convenience, The Chief; an assistant to The Chief; one of the operating officials of WPB, presumably to lend weight and substance to the operation, and a newspaperman.

The memo warned that the man appointed to be The Chief would have to be quite an operator—"this job requires psychological planning," and The Chief must have deep knowledge of the tides and currents of public emotion. If possible, he should be an advertising man, and when appointed he must be given a title that would be ornate enough to command the respect of the other dollar-a-year men. It would of course be necessary to have

74

the newspaperman in the setup to handle the press releases, but he must at all times be firmly controlled by The Chief, the expert opinion-manipulator; for, unhappily, the average newspaper chap, even when elevated to a public relations role, "is too sympathetic with the demands of the press to have a story at any cost."

Following this discussion, the memorandum went on to the broad question of public opinion. It asserted:

"WPB is already thoroughly publicized, therefore all releases of information should be reviewed in the light of their contribution, not to more publicity, but to the attainment of public favor. The same thing is true in respect to public statements by officials of WPB.

"The deficiencies of WPB are naturally seized upon by press and radio with more glee than its successful achievements. Methods must be found, therefore, to give true value to WPB's really significant results.

"Whenever possible, predictions and quotas should be avoided, except when understatement is used in full confidence that figures will be exceeded. Predicting 60,000 of something and making 50,000 is a failure. Predicting 45,000 and making 50,000 is a success. The public has no way of knowing whether the original quota is adequate or not. (In fact, most public officials also are at sea.)"

On its progress from the author to the desk of the WPB chairman, this memo passed through the ken of another of Nelson's assistants who read it, found it good, and added his own thoughts in a covering memo. A noteworthy paragraph from this attachment reads:

"The whole direction of the public relations activities under the new setup will be changed to one of pre-testing the public reaction and planning the whole public relations program, not to satisfy the newspapers and the radio, but to get a more favorable reaction toward the War Production Board and to eliminate so far as possible the controversies of one kind and another which emanate from this agency in the form of news stories. Rather than be forced to make explanations for announcements which have reached the press, it is estimated that the policies established will, to a large extent, eliminate stories of a controversial nature unless an analysis of the public reaction before the release is made makes it clear that the reception will be what is desired."

75

Now it may be that all of the above adds up to an excellent strategic plan for an organization preparing an attack on five o'clock shadow, tattle-tale gray, or some similar menace to the public welfare, but as a bill of particulars for a government agency charged with harnessing the energies of the people in wartime it is fantastic beyond belief. From start to finish, the program is based on the idea of manipulating public opinion, and its assumptions are explicit: never mind about telling the people what they want to know, just tell them what will make them think well of us. Falsify statistics and predictions if necessary—nobody will know the difference, and it will make the record look good. Edit everything that we say or that we allow other people to say so that we can build the right kind of success story. Ye shall know the truth and the truth will make you good and cagy about what you say to the reporters.

The simple and unalterable fact, of course, is that no government agency whatever, at any time or under any circumstances, has any business even having a public relations program—except for the unadorned policy of making just as many of the facts public as the good Lord will permit. Our whole form of government is based on the idea that the people call the shots. In the long run a public agency gets good public relations only by deserving them, and if it even tries to get them in any other way it is attempting to commit a fraud upon democracy. You can put it down as Rule One: Whenever you find a government department, bureau, or commission beginning to shape its words or its deeds so as to create a desired public reaction, you have found an agency which is right on the verge of stepping on its own tail feathers.

Rule Two, unfortunately, reads out of Rule One, viz.: When the heat is on, the temptation to *try* to create a desired public reaction becomes almost irresistible. The people may be a faceless multitude, but in the end what the people say goes. The very fact that their reaction can't be ignored is what sets up the tendency to monkey with it. The more important that reaction is, the greater the desire to get it under control. And besides, it is so much easier to lay out a propaganda campaign than it is to do the hard, uninspiring work that will eventually win public support on its own merits.

And the whole situation that confronted the American government as the war wore along presented a temptation that was, probably, too great for any imaginable collective human resistance. This war was for keeps, and it seemed that it couldn't be won unless a large number of bitter discords were turned into harmonies. The original policy of calling a spade a spade, even if you tripped over it and barked your shins, was just too good to be true—for sticking to it would have meant, finally, finding the strength either to remove the discords altogether or to ignore them. There had to be a retreat, and there was; a retreat from democracy, born of an unwillingness to put ultimate faith and confidence in the processes of democracy.

This does not mean that the administration ever formally adopted a "public relations" program like the one set forth in the memo to Nelson. It didn't have to; it simply let its guard down, and let the men who agreed with the memo do their stuff. It gave up the centralized control which was the only solid defense against that memo's viewpoint; and at the same time it groped for, and finally established, another kind of control which actually rested on the memo's underlying idea—the idea that plain facts were too rough a diet for a people at war, the idea that the presentation of these facts had to be "programmed," somehow, so as to create the desired effect. It all seemed very reasonable. Washington was hammering out a war program as it went along, building not to a thought-out pattern but according to the necessities of improvisation. There wasn't any central theme to its effort, except the desire to win the war. Because there wasn't a central theme, Washington talked with varied and discordant voices. This made the people confused. Confusion in wartime is obviously bad. *Ergo:* We must have no more confusion, and we will avoid it by making sure that everyone in the orchestra is playing the same tune.

This called for an orchestra leader of uncommon talents. The first conclusion that leaped to the mind was that Horton just wouldn't do. He wasn't interested in harmony, and anyway some of his players were getting ready to mutiny. By the time of Pearl Harbor, the administration was pretty well committed to the thesis that there had to be a new information policy, a new kind of information control, and a new man to run it.

The first man to be mentioned in this connection was the late Fiorello LaGuardia, the Mayor of New York. LaGuardia was

77

brought down to Washington on a part-time basis to run the Office of Civilian Defense, which had been established in the early summer of 1941. OCD was supposed to rally the energies of the people in behalf of the defense effort, and it was a natural spot for a propaganda agency since a good part of its work was propagandistic in nature anyway. At his first press conference, LaGuardia mentioned that his office would be a new source for authentic facts and figures about the whole program; then he threw all his abundant energies into the first job that came to hand—the campaign to collect scrap aluminum, which gave him a good chance to show what he could do in the way of haranguing the multitude. Unfortunately, the people were exhorted to contribute old aluminum on the plea that this would help make bombers, and after the stuff had all been piled up the Army's production men coldly pointed out that scrap aluminum was no good for airplanes—they had to have the virgin metal. The let-down was bad, especially since no arrangements had been made for getting the scrap to the smelters after it had been collected, and the search for a propaganda agency turned definitely away from the Office of Civilian Defense.

This trial balloon having collapsed, the administration tried a new approach. In the fall of 1941 it set up the Office of Facts and Figures with the distinguished poet, Archibald MacLeish, as its head. (It was sheer hard luck that Washington's habit of referring to every agency by its initials, and then making a word out of the initials if possible, caused this organization to be known as "OFF.")

As the name implied, the Office of Facts and Figures—strange echo of LaGuardia's words at his first press conference—was supposed to be a central, authoritative source for figures, statistics, and other cold facts about the defense effort. To become such a source, OFF had to exert considerable authority over the agencies which were already issuing such figures. To do that effectively it needed either a definite charter of sweeping authority or a driving force at the top which could impose its will with or without such a charter. As it happened, OFF didn't have either; its charter was sadly defective, and MacLeish simply wasn't a slugger. OFF lingered on for some months, but it made no great impact on the situation. It is noteworthy for just one reason: its establishment was a definite step toward a conscious attempt to shape and manipulate public opinion, and a step away from the original Mellett-Horton idea.

The next step was designed to go farther, and did, for it resulted in the establishment of the Office of War Information.

All through the first months of 1942 the Bureau of the Budget —that little-known agency which sometimes has more to say about how the government operates than anyone outside of the White House—had been making an elaborate study of the informational activities that were being carried on in connection with the war program. It entrusted this study to a highly capable government career man, Milton Eisenhower, for a number of years an influential official in the Department of Agriculture, and at that time much better known in Washington than his brother Dwight, an army officer. Eisenhower for some time had felt that the government needed a central information agency— not one that was limited to the agencies that had been set up in OEM, but one that would embrace all activities that were in any way connected with the war effort. What his report to the Bureau of the Budget called for—and what we finally got—was a mechanism whereby the government would speak with just one voice about its war program. Whether it was reporting on the number of airplanes built, stirring up the people to collect scrap rubber, explaining the need for fat conservation, or telling the people of occupied lands that democracy was coming to the rescue, the government would use a single mouthpiece.

Two forces made the administration receptive to this proposal.

One was the increasing pressure by the dollar-a-year men for an end to Horton and all his works. Hearty co-operation by business with government was essential; it would come a lot easier if the chief business agency in government felt that it was getting a little understanding and sympathy from its own press section. Horton was openly contemptuous of the good faith and even of the innate ability of some of the nation's leading industrialists. In a radio program designed to explain the aluminum shortage, he had bluntly listed "the aluminum monopoly" as one reason for the shortage. Taken to task for this, afterward, he had used the words "damned Jesuitical hogwash" to characterize the argument that there was no monopoly, that if there was it had helped rather than hurt, and that in any case it was damaging to the war effort to talk about it.

79

The other factor was the growing feeling that the government had to give the people a picture of unity and harmony in Washington. The fact that such unity and harmony did not exist was beside the point; the picture had to be created, and the only way to create it was through the top information agency. Reduce the confusion of tongues by setting up one man to supervise all of the talking, give him the authority and the organization to make his control effective, and see if the people could not then be told about unity and harmony in the war effort in words they might believe; it seemed worth a try.

But above and beyond these two factors was another consideration, which was never talked about but which was actually the most important of all.

A government information policy is not shaped in a vacuum. What is to be said is determined, in the end, by what is to be done. Now the categorical imperative of the situation in 1941 demanded that America recognize the world revolution and act accordingly. But how do you meet a world revolution under the guidance of dollar-a-year men? Just how far can the formulas of the status quo be stretched? Don't you reach their breaking point before you get to the scene of action?

That was the whole trouble. Every time that breaking point was reached we shied away. The things that would have to be *done* to bring an emotionally integrated people through the years of fire were not done; therefore, it was necessary to fall back on words. This whole concern over what was to be said and who was to say it is important only because it reflects a fundamental failure in the field of action. The story of the government's informational activities during the war is really the story of that failure. Fighting for its life, democracy drew its war cries from the philosophy of the salesman.

CHAPTER SEVEN

Comes the Showdown

BECAUSE of the telephone, Mr. George Lyon was having an unquiet Sunday. An old-time Scripps-Howard editor with battle scars all over his ample frame, Lyon had recently come to Washington to serve as purveyor of public information for Mayor Fiorello LaGuardia in the Office of Civilian Defense. This was a job that made even the editing of a newspaper for Roy Howard look like a quiet and carefree way to make a living. The Little Flower was given to odd quirks and tangents; furthermore, nobody knew quite what the Office of Civilian Defense was really supposed to do, and the Mayor's insistence that it do it vigorously, without ceasing, and in the full light of all attainable publicity was occasionally a bit trying.

So here it was Sunday afternoon, and Lyon was taking his ease at home, free for the week end from the frantic unpredictabilities of the Mayor and the OCD. But the telephone kept ringing.

First the Associated Press.

"Hey, George, do you know where the Mayor is today?"

"Up in New York, as far as I know."

"Well, is he going to be issuing any statement today on air raid precautions?"

"Statement on air raid precautions? No, we've got nothing new on air raid precautions. The Mayor'll be back in town Tuesday, most likely."

A little later, the Washington *Post;* similar question, similar answer. Then the United Press; then someone else; then somebody from Horton's office, asking rather urgently how the Mayor could be reached. The whole town seemed to be filled with a desire to learn the views of Mayor LaGuardia—ordinarily no difficult task—and Lyon, trying to drowse his way through an uneventful Sunday afternoon, began to get irritated.

Finally, around dusk, Horton himself got on the telephone.

"Look, George, we've just got to get hold of LaGuardia somehow and get a statement from him about air raid precautions."

A long-suffering man, Lyon was at last moved to protest.

"Bob, will you tell me why in the hell everybody on earth wants to know what LaGuardia thinks about air raid precautions? On Sunday afternoon? Good God, he's said all he's got to say about that. There's nothing new on it. What's got so hot all of a sudden about LaGuardia and air raids?"

There was a silence at the other end of the wire, followed by a chuckle.

"Oh. I take it you haven't had your radio on this afternoon?"

"I have not. I was trying," said Lyon, with dignity, "to get a little sleep."

"Well, the Japs have just attacked Pearl Harbor and we're in the war."

That was about the way it went in Washington on the afternoon of December 7, 1941. People kept getting the news inadvertently, so to speak; by sunset, most of the top officials of OPM and SPAB had gone down to the Social Security Building, where for some reason they drifted into Bill Batt's office. It was a funny sort of gathering. Nobody had much to say; everyone was weighted down with the feeling that something drastic and spectacular ought to be done—now, right away, tonight—but when they got right down to it they realized that there wasn't anything they could do—nothing that could be done right away, before Monday morning. Held back for so many months by its own fears and hesitations, OPM found itself standing on the threshold of the long-expected war, possessing neither a plan for action nor the authority to put such a plan into effect. In the end, all that could be done that evening was to whip up a brief speech, stating that all of the country's resources would now be mobilized quickly and with ruthless determination. A spot was obtained on a radio network, Nelson hurried off to the station to deliver the speech, and everybody went home. . . . Out Massachusetts Avenue a crowd of several thousand people had gathered in front of the Japanese embassy—gripped, apparently, by the same desire to do something that had seized the OPM officials, and thwarted by the unhappy fact that there just didn't seem to be anything that could be done.

As a matter of fact, while there was nothing that OPM could do on the night of December 7, it was still not altogether too late for the agency to redeem itself. It was to get two more chances to show that it could handle the war production job in time of war. The first chance came to a head on Tuesday, two days after Pearl Harbor.

On that day OPM drafted and submitted to SPAB, for transmission to the President, its estimate of the maximum volume of war production that could be had during the next two years. (Just before the meeting Nelson encountered Under-Secretary of the Navy Forrestal, looking glum. "Cheer up, Jim," said Nelson heartily. "That news from Pearl Harbor was a terrible blow, but in a way it was a good thing. It'll unify the country, and now we'll really get the war production you need." Forrestal, who knew more than it was pleasant to know about the amount of damage the American fleet had suffered, rubbed his chin reflectively. "Yeah," he said, "but the price was too goddam high.")

The Victory Program had already been formulated, but it was still unofficial—a creation of Stacy May and Bob Nathan, carefully nurtured by Wallace and Nelson but not yet sent on to the President, and not yet accepted by either OPM or the War Department. May and Nathan had concluded that it would be physically possible for America to produce forty-five billion dollars' worth of war goods in 1942 and sixty-five billions in 1943—estimates which turned out to be amazingly close to what was actually accomplished—but as of the day after Pearl Harbor they were having a very hard time getting anyone to believe it. The War Department, speaking for the Army, still had a modest view of what it was going to need; OPM, speaking for industry, had an equally modest view of what industry could do.

So what happened, on that Tuesday afternoon, was that OPM handed in a set of figures and estimates showing that during 1942 American war production could be increased to a possible maximum of thirty-three billions, and that in 1943 it could go as high as forty-four billions. Even these figures, although they fell far short of the Victory Program estimates, represented a sharp upward revision over anything OPM had previously admitted to be possible. Late in November the most optimistic OPM guess about maximum 1942 production was twenty-seven billions—a bare three billions above the rate that was actually reached in December, with the boom in civilian goods production still going strong.

83

These estimates by OPM were duly forwarded to the President, who knew that a much bigger job would have to be done if the Axis were to be beaten. OPM had muffed the first of its two remaining chances.

A couple of days after that, Nathan wrote a note to Nelson, heading it simply, "Random Thoughts." In it, he remarked that the atmosphere in OPM since Pearl Harbor had been deeply discouraging.

"All along the line," said Nathan, "there appears to be a complete lack of realization that we must *now*, if not before, go all out for munitions production. The original figures on potential production as submitted by OPM, and even those boosted up as a result of Tuesday morning's meeting, were completely disheartening. Raising the 1942 production potential from the scheduled level of twenty-seven billion dollars to thirty billions, or even to thirty-three billions, makes no sense in terms of the tremendous industrial resources of America."

It was the captains of industry, right then, who were appraising America as a static economy. The concept of a dynamic America that could do ever so much more than it had ever done before seemed to be coming from the impractical theorists who, as FDR's critics in Congress were fond of saying, had never met a payroll.

Nathan continued:

"We all realize that an all-out effort is needed and we all talk in terms of such an effort, but frankly I see no evidence of action consistent with such philosophy. Under war there must be a changed set of principles, and a strict adherence to fundamental principles irrespective of personalities. Frankly, either SPAB must take hold of the situation firmly, immediately, or there must be another agency to do the job."

While Nathan was writing this letter, Vice-President Wallace was writing a letter of his own. Instead of writing to Nelson he was writing to the President, and he was taking pains to point out the "internal inconsistencies" of OPM's statement of its own case.

The OPM document, Wallace noted, estimated that a monthly peak production of three and one-half billions would be reached in October, 1942, and a monthly peak of four billion, seven hundred millions in October, 1943, which was all very well; but, the Vice-President continued, "any reasonable progression from the $3.5 rate to the $4.7 rate would give a 1943 total far above the forty-four billion dollars stated; if charted, in fact, would run the figure to about fifty-two billion dollars."

Further, Wallace said, "Mr. Knudsen's figure of forty-four billion dollars for the 1943 total presumes an average rate of three billion, six hundred seventy millions a month for that year —which is lower than the probable rate for any one month of 1943, if his other estimate of four billion, seven hundred millions for October 1943 is to be accepted."

In other words, OPM's own estimate of America's war job didn't hang together. What Wallace was telling the President was that OPM was not only far too pessimistic, but that it couldn't even cipher.

Washington is a loose-jointed place, which is frequently a great drawback but is sometimes its salvation. The dust-up over the size of the job that the nation ought to be called on to do is a good case in point.

Here was OPM, formally telling the President that the utmost the country could produce in the first year of the war was thirty-three billion dollars. Here, on the other hand, was the Victory Program, stating that the figure ought to be forty-five billions. The difference between the two programs might— probably would—be the difference between victory and defeat. But the Victory Program, which OPM disowned, had been put together by OPM's own Division of Research and Statistics; and the official OPM estimate, which was the one OPM sent to the White House, to stand on or to fall from, was being disowned and derided by OPM's own experts—for the statistical analysis Wallace used to blow up the OPM estimates had been given him by May and Nathan, who worked for OPM.

This deadlock, to say the least, was odd. In a tightly run, efficiently operated government, May and Nathan would have been sent to Coventry for this insubordination and their estimates would never have reached the White House, and in preparing his program for war the President would have had nothing solid to rely on except the gloomy forecast of OPM. But the loose-jointedness above mentioned came to the rescue.

For one thing, there was nothing to keep Wallace and Nelson from discarding normal channels. Wallace had access to the ear

85

of the President, and Nelson had the Victory Program in his pocket. What could be simpler than for the two of them to go to the White House and show the President that he need not tie himself down to the OPM estimates? Which, as a matter of fact, is just what happened.

For another thing—all in all, it was even more important, perhaps—there was the press.

There are stuffed shirts and lightweights in all trades and professions, no doubt, and the Washington press corps probably has its share, but there certainly were none in the group which covered the defense and war agencies. They were alert, preternaturally suspicious—the average war agencies reporter, it sometimes seemed, wouldn't embrace his own grandmother without first inspecting her reticule to see if there was a gimmick in it— and it was extremely hard to satisfy them with anything short of the exact truth. Furthermore, no one had ever put a protective screen around OPM to keep its dissensions and its conflicting viewpoints hidden. Horton's theory that everything that happened in the people's production agency was the people's business paid off in a huge way during the Pearl Harbor period.

For the reporters, who shared in that theory up to the hilt, had no trouble whatever in learning about the Victory Program. They knew how it had been put together and who had done it, they knew how it overshadowed the OPM-War Department notions about the size of the job to be done, they knew who was fighting for its adoption and who was resisting it; and they passed their knowledge on to all who cared to read the newspapers. Nothing official was ever said about it. The Victory Program was never discussed in a press release. But the reporters right then were not relying on official statements and press releases; they were circulating about, cultivating their news sources, relying on carefully selected "leaks" for the information with which they could tell the American people what the chances were for a war program that would beat Hitler.

The "leak," by the way, is one of the most important elements in our whole democratic system of government; one of those roundabout but effective devices by which the operation of the bureaucracy is kept in line. It is worth a moment's study, and here is how it works:

A "leak," in the reporter's language, is an official person who is willing to divulge, to a reporter he trusts, information which the agency he belongs to is either unwilling or unready to reveal. As far as the reporter is concerned, the essentials are that the official be far enough on the inside to know what his agency is up to, and that he be completely truthful in telling about it. The official's own requirement is, usually, that the reporter never reveal the source of his information. A very large part of the really important news that comes out of Washington originates in leaks, of one kind or another. Any news story which attributes its statements of fact to "a usually reliable source" or to "an official who would not permit his name to be used" is based on a leak, nine times out of ten.

And it is through the leak that the people are kept in touch with their government. It is the leak that gives them a look at high policy while it is still in the formative stage. It is the leak which enables them to know whether the fine boasts and pretensions of an appointed person are really justified. It is the leak —telling them what may happen, what is being planned, what the carefully hidden facts actually are—which makes it possible for them to react while there is still time and thus exert an influence on the handling of affairs. To be sure, the leak involves a good deal of lost motion. It is frequently misused by self-seekers and schemers, it makes for much confusion, and it sometimes drives hard-working cabinet ministers almost crazy; but our particular form of government wouldn't work without it.

The heads of all government agencies are bitterly opposed to leaks—except when they themselves indulge in leaking, which is another story. Nothing is more edifying than to see a cabinet minister or a board chairman earnestly huddling with a group of his aides, trying vainly to figure out just who in the organization gave out the story which this morning's *Times* is carrying. This attempt almost invariably fails. The head of an agency almost never knows where the leaks are; if he did know he could plug them and they would cease to be leaks. The agency's information division, however, if it is any good, does know where the leaks are, or, if it doesn't know, can quickly find out. If it is devoted to the cover-up theory it can usually get them plugged; if it isn't, it can see to it that they remain open and that the reporters have access to them.

There was no plugging of leaks during the Pearl Harbor period.

On the contrary . . . The whole network of civilian war agencies resembled a boiling cauldron. Officially, neither OPM nor the War Department believed that the nation could or should produce, in wartime, very much more than it was at the moment producing. Officially, neither agency had any plans for harnessing the resources of the giant automobile industry. Officially, neither saw much need to change the cumbersome procurement system. But the press wasn't limiting itself to official viewpoints. It was talking to the men who *knew* that the country would have to do much more than it had yet imagined it could do—men who *knew* that the war might well be lost unless the men at the top in Washington stopped being timorous and got together for an all-out effort.

The whole situation is beautifully illustrated by a series of articles which the Washington *Post* began printing on December 23, 1941, under the general heading, "Wanted: A Director of Supply." These stories were written by Alfred Friendly, one of the ablest reporters in Washington, and Nelson later credited them with having been largely responsible for bringing about the dissolution of OPM and the formation of the War Production Board. (Which was an overstatement; there were many other factors, including the representations which Nelson himself made to the President. But Friendly's stories unquestionably had immense influence.)

Friendly bluntly declared that "America's military potential is being wasted" and asserted that it was at the moment "left unorganized, unrealized, only one-third used." He discussed the Victory Program in detail, cited the reasons for believing that it could be accomplished, showed how far current production was falling short of the rate obviously needed for victory, and then showed why the existing setup was incapable of making the necessary improvement. In four front-page stories he pulled out facts that were being discussed behind the scenes and cited chapter and verse to show that what satisfied the War Department and OPM was disastrously short of being enough to satisfy the country.

The impact of these stories on official Washington was terrific. It may be true, as left-wing critics maintain, that the press has lost much of its influence with its readers, but its influence in official Washington is as great as it ever was, if not more so.

(Elected and appointed officials in Washington can even be swayed, and often are, by what the newspapers say in their editorial columns; a statement difficult to believe, but true.) At any rate, Friendly's articles could not be ignored. They were too obviously written by a man who knew exactly what he was talking about. And the interesting point is that they were based almost entirely on leaks. To prove his case Friendly had made very little use of official statements or formally released material. Instead, he had talked privately to the men who could not say publicly what they knew, as patriotic Americans, simply had to be said—specifically, to Nelson, to Batt, to Henderson, to Nathan, as well as to a host of others. As late as Christmas Day, for instance, Batt was privately revealing to him that the Army and OPM still did not believe that the Victory Program could be accomplished. Knowing that Batt knew what he was talking about, and knowing that he was completely truthful, Friendly thus could make the flat statement on his own recognizance, as it were, and the fact itself—highly important, with the nation in the state it was in—could be brought out into the open where it needed to be.

Great are the uses of the leak: a device the founding fathers never thought of, but essential to the operation of the democracy in these complex times. To a certain extent, at least, inefficiency in government is not, as we usually think, merely one of the incidental by-products of democracy; it is one of the things that make democracy possible.

However all of that may be, OPM had muffed its first big chance and had been publicly discredited. By the end of 1941 it was almost impossible for anyone to suppose that the administration would leave the industrial war effort in the hands of this particular agency. But OPM was to have one more chance. It still had to tangle with the conversion of the automobile industry to full war production.

The automobile makers were due to come to Washington on January 5, 1942, to discuss this question. Here, with all the spotlights turned on, OPM was to commit its final fumble. With its record of failure made complete, OPM retired from the scene shortly thereafter, to be replaced by the War Production Board with Nelson in the driver's seat. WPB took a new tack, the automobile industry was converted, and OPM was forgotten.

But as the story of how all of this happened unfolds it is important to bear in mind that there is a great deal more to it than the simple tale of a ninth-inning error with the bases full. What was to be lost—by OPM, by WPB, by the government itself—was an opportunity. For in its handling of the automobile conversion problem the government, once and for all, was to accept the world crisis of 1942 as a war and not as a revolutionary challenge. It was to lay its hand, very briefly, on a revolutionary weapon—and then it was to decide not to use it. The decision was automatic and distinctive, but its effects were far-reaching. Let's see how it all came about.

CHAPTER   EIGHT

For Full Partnership

A FEW days after Donald Nelson became chairman of the
War Production Board, someone brought Walter Reuther
into his office and introduced him. The boss of war
production and the mainspring of the United Auto Workers had
not met before; now, for perhaps twenty minutes, they sat together making get-acquainted talk, each one cautiously measuring
the other against the background of the war emergency. After
Reuther had left I asked Nelson what he thought of him.

Nelson grinned.

"He's quite a fellow," he said. It was characteristic of Nelson,
by the way, that he could use the word "fellow" without sound-
ing like a Y.M.C.A. secretary. "We had a nice talk."

Nelson meditated for a moment, then chuckled.

"Three-fourths of the dollar-a-year men around this place are
scared to death of that little fellow," he said. "And, you know,
they ought to be scared of him—because he's smarter than they
are."

Smarter or dumber, there is no question whatever that as 1942
opened Reuther had completely out-maneuvered the OPM big-
wigs and had given them the jitters. He symbolized the great
piece of unfinished business which they did not know how to
handle; the conversion to war production of the giant auto
industry, first item on the agenda if America were to win the
war, and the one item above all others which it was going to be
embarrassing to handle. Neither OPM nor the industry itself
had a plan for doing the job. Reuther, unfortunately, did have
one. It was a plan which both Detroit and Washington thoroughly detested, but it was A Plan—the only plan there was, in
fact, and this at a time when even a bad plan was obviously better
than no plan at all. One month after Pearl Harbor it seemed quite
possible that the Reuther plan might win by simple default.
And if it did . . .

For if Reuther symbolized the failure of the powers-that-were,
he also stood for something even more ominous. Labor had grown

up and had ideas. This wasn't going to be like the last war, with the trade associations running industry and Gompers exhorting the boys not to strike in return for management agreement to a temporary cessation of union-busting. Labor was coming up to the quarter deck just as if it had a right to be there, making suggestions about how the ship ought to be handled. It was hard to see where this sort of thing would stop, once it got started, although it wasn't at all hard to see some of the results it might lead to before it did get stopped.

What the labor boys had come up with was a proposal for a joint board—call it an industry council—to run the auto industry during the war. The council was to be a three-way affair, headed by a government man and containing equal numbers of industrialists and union men. It was not to be an advisory body, making suggestions to government or to management; it was to be *the* authority, empowered to make plans and commitments for the entire industry and to distribute production among the various corporations and plants within the industry according to the technical needs of conversion. It would operate mostly through three subcommittees.

One of these was to be a technical committee, composed of the best engineering personnel of the auto companies, plus representatives of the parts producers, plus representatives of labor. This committee was to plan the conversion of basic facilities and the distribution of production among them; to organize the engineering activities of the companies, in other words, eliminating duplication and wasted effort.

A second committee was to deal with the labor supply. Again, it was to be balanced as to management and labor representatives in its make-up; and it was to have authority to transfer workers to the most vital production points, to up-grade workers where necessary, and to supervise the retraining of workers who might be displaced during the transition period.

The third committee was to handle subcontracting. It was supposed to include the best purchasing agents of the auto companies, the best technical personnel of the parts producers, and —once more—representatives of the unions. Its job would be to insure that the facilities of the parts companies and of the other auto industry suppliers were used to the maximum, and that "the tens of thousands of small plants for which no provision has yet been made in the war effort" were effectively put to work.

So there it was, at last, out in the middle of the table for everyone to look at; something new under the sun, a complete departure from all conventional ideas about who runs industries vested with the public interest. This was not labor standing by the edge of the desk, hat in hand, gratefully accepting the opportunity to make a suggestion here and there; this was labor declaring that it had just as much responsibility for winning the war as management had and asserting that, on the whole, it possibly had just about as much to contribute. It was a revolutionary proposal— not fascism, not communism, nothing that could be put in any of the familiar pigeon-holes, but something breath-takingly new.

And the worst of it was that industry was by no means in good shape to repel a proposal of this kind.

It all went back to the early days of the defense effort. A cynic once remarked that wars are won by patriotism plus 8 per cent. Big business, personified in the Defense Commission and OPM, had gone that one better by setting out to make a defense program on the basis of better business than ever before *plus 40 per cent additional business in defense work*. Which is to say that the guiding thought, all through the formative period of the defense effort, was that the defense load could be put on top of ordinary peacetime production. But the production of civilian goods was soon stimulated to new heights, so that it became altogether extraordinary, by the spending of defense funds. Altogether, this meant a terrific drain on raw materials and on plant capacity. But adequate quantities of raw materials to meet this drain just weren't there, because of industry's overpowering reluctance to expand raw material capacity. And the plant capacity wasn't there, either, to all intents and purposes, because the defense production was supposed to come principally from brand-new factories and machines, the existing equipment being devoted to the peacetime boom; and it proved physically impossible to create nearly enough new capacity to do the job, although the effort to do so had in itself constituted an important additional drain on the supply of raw materials.

This had got things gummed up to a marked degree, by the time of Pearl Harbor, and the gumming-up was nowhere quite as obvious as in the auto industry. Early in the summer of 1941

OPM had decreed a cut in automobile production. But Knudsen had admitted at a press conference that this cut had been made, not because the government needed the auto factories for defense production, but because of the growing shortage of raw materials. In other words, although we relied on a policy of building new plants to do the war job so that the old plants could go on making peacetime goods, the old plants were being forced out of peacetime production because they couldn't get materials; but they were not being put to work making munitions, because the new plants were going to carry that load. Within the week following Pearl Harbor, notice was served on the auto industry that production of passenger cars would have to cease by mid-winter—but this, again, was simply a reflection of the increasing shortage of metals, and was not a part of a planned conversion program. There still was no plan to put war work into the soon-to-be-closed auto factories.

This was all very much on the record, as 1942 dawned. The Washington *Post* had carefully analyzed the entire situation as far back as the preceding August. Reuther had been vocal about it, before Congress. Shortly after Pearl Harbor, testifying before the House Committee Investigating National Defense Migration, he had underlined it:

"The thing that we pointed out a year ago was that the machine-tool industry was overtaxed, not because of the defense effort, but because of the fact that new plants were going up and the machine-tool industry was being called on to duplicate machinery that was going to be idle in our own industry."

OPM, meanwhile, had taken what now seem like unnecessarily elaborate pains to demonstrate that it didn't know what on earth to do with or about the auto industry. Two days before Christmas the same committee that had questioned Reuther questioned W. H. Harrison, OPM's Director of Production under Knudsen. Harrison was asked:

"If you had been able in August to foresee the curtailment order of the week following December 7, reducing auto production almost to zero, I presume that in order to maximize output you would have called in the auto manufacturers and given them larger contracts and asked them to undertake a bigger amount of defense work than you did at the time; is that correct?"

"No, sir," said Harrison stoutly. "I think that the decisions and conclusions made in August were reached on the basis of considerations then available and I haven't seen anything that has happened since August up to now to indicate that these considerations were wrong."

Congressman John H. Tolan of California, who was chairman of the committee and who was doing the questioning, went back for a retake on that one. Harrison might have argued that OPM could not be blamed too much for failing to foresee that Pearl Harbor was going to be bombed. Instead, however, he was saying that even if OPM had foreseen Pearl Harbor—even if it had known, in August, that war was going to start in earnest in December, so that the manufacture of pleasure cars would have to cease regardless—there would have been no reason to start loading the industry with war contracts. So the Congressman spelled it out, to make sure.

"You mean that if, on August 30, you had been able to foresee the necessity of complete curtailment of the auto industry, you would not have acted differently with respect to the orders let?"

"That is correct," said Harrison.

At the time of Harrison's appearance the Tolan committee also questioned Knudsen and Under-Secretary of War Patterson, each of whom testified that no plan for the conversion of the auto industry existed.

Commenting on all of this a couple of weeks later in a letter, Congressman Tolan remarked:

"To date the industry has received four billion dollars of war contracts. Aside from truck production, it is questionable whether as much as five per cent of the existing automotive facilities of the industry have been used on these contracts. Instead, many new plant facilities are still under construction, a number of which will not come into full production until a year from today. . . . In the stress of argument, both sides seem to have overlooked the fact that on December 7, 1941, this nation was dealt a stunning blow by a treacherous enemy."

The auto industry itself had supplied the one touch that might have been lacking. In the fall of 1941 it brought out its 1942 models dolled up with more bright work—principally chromium, one of the scarcest and most badly needed of critical materials—than any living man had previously seen moving along the highways on four wheels.

The stage was set, then, for some highly unusual proceedings, when OPM called the heads of the automobile industry and the heads of the auto unions into a conference on January 5, 1942. Out of the meeting, supposedly, was to come a master plan for putting the industry to work for war. Something of the kind had to emerge; the war couldn't be won without it, and, just incidentally, it was clear to one and all that OPM couldn't survive a fortnight.

But neither OPM nor the War Department had a plan to offer. The industry itself had no plan; indeed, for some time it had been explaining desperately that only an insignificant fraction of its tools and equipment could possibly be converted to war work under any circumstances whatever—a statement which was to be proved completely false before three months were up. But in this vacuum the workers themselves did have a plan. It was the only plan in existence, it had been thoroughly publicized, and the people who opposed it had been doing their human best to destroy all confidence in their own ability to cope with the situation. Something was due to crack.

Two things were immediately obvious, when the Reuther plan was laid on the table.

First, if this plan were adopted for the auto industry it would be adopted by many other industries—for, in its essence, this was the much-talked-of Murray plan, conceived by the CIO a year before and vigorously pushed ever since. The CIO at that very moment was backing an identical plan for the copper industry and seemed to be in a fair way to get it adopted, the copper supply just then being one of those appallingly critical problems which caused men to reach desperately for almost any kind of program which looked as if it might help. The other obvious point was that if a scheme like this were adopted in wartime, it would almost certainly be a long time evaporating, come peace again.

This, in other words, was *It*.

A thin and insubstantial ghost of this idea had been in the air ever since the defense program had begun. Sidney Hillman had been appointed to the original Defense Commission. Later, when OPM was established, a bow in the direction of joint labor-management responsibility had been made by installing Hillman as "Associate Director General" alongside of Knudsen—a step whose chief effect had been to infuriate the conservatives, although Knudsen himself stood up under it pretty well. OPM had set up industry advisory committees, and to an extent had balanced them with advisory committees representing labor. All along, there had been at least a degree of recognition of the fact that Labor, spelled with a capital L, had become a major element in American society: not just a collection of troublesome people who had to be placated with wage increases every so often, but one of the key pieces in the whole setup, a fundamental *resource* which had to be used.

But the bow had been little more than just a bow. OPM's Labor Division had a number of useful and effective achievements on its record, but it had never been able to give labor a share in the direction of the program as a whole. Hillman sat in the inner councils, and labor was supposed to be satisfied with that. The fact that most of the decisions which really affected the way men do their jobs and support their families and participate in the nation's destiny were not made in the inner councils at all, but were made in the day-to-day actions of the operating industry and commodity divisions of OPM, was not supposed to be relevant. If a union man could produce useful ideas in connection, say, with the problem of expanding copper production, well and good; chances were he would be listened to. But the mere idea that the head of the copper division—or of any other industry division in OPM—might conceivably be a union man, rather than a man from management, was utterly foreign to the prevailing habit of thought.

To the end of the war, labor was up against this attitude: a president of a corporation, taking leave of absence (with full pay) from his desk and being sworn in as a government official, immediately ceased to be a "representative of industry" and became, in fact and in substance, a government official, fit to be entrusted with the exercise of government authorities; a union man, similarly taking leave from his job and being sworn in as a government official, remained a "representative of labor" from start to finish.

The idea that a union man might stop acting like a spokesman for labor and begin acting like a sworn official of his own government, if his government would only consent to look on him in that light, literally never dawned on anyone except the labor

97

people. The mere notion that it might make sense (and bring about speedier war production) to install a Reuther as the top OPM production man in place of a Harrison was just too fantastic for serious consideration. To be sure, Reuther happened to be a man who, on the record, was anxious to bring about a speedy and effective conversion of industry, and had at least a few definite ideas about how it might be done, while the unfortunate Harrison was a man who could not see that Pearl Harbor had created any particular new incentive for getting war contracts into the industry. But Reuther was from labor and Harrison was from management—vice-president and chief engineer of the American Telephone and Telegraph Company, in private life—and that was definitely all there was to it.

Which is exactly what labor was driving at. For what the Murray plan and the Reuther plan really boiled down to was a demand for recognition of labor's own partnership in the nation. Above all, labor wanted to *belong*. The mental and emotional attitude which accepted the dollar-a-year man as an institution but insisted that labor could not be trusted with similar responsibilities obviously meant that labor did not belong. There was no partnership and it was bad form to suggest that there ought to be one. The status quo had never contemplated such a thing.

Actually, this proposition came much closer to adoption than anyone would have imagined. The opposition was powerful and it was prepared to fight to the death, but it was painfully demoralized. Something had to be done and it had to be done quickly, and this Murray-Reuther scheme was literally the only idea on the agenda. For about twenty-four hours the plan hung in the balance, not because the labor people had converted anybody in particular but simply because nobody else had anything whatever to offer.

. . . It ought to be noted, in passing, that Sidney Hillman was not the moving spirit in the fight for the Reuther plan. On the contrary. Some of the red-hots in his Labor Division were active in its support, but Hillman himself was definitely against it. The bit of folklore which depicts Hillman as a dangerous radical who tried to pervert the whole defense effort into a means of making labor dominant simply is not true. At the time of this meeting with the auto industry, Hillman favored nothing more than a mild extension of the work of the existing OPM labor and industry committees. These committees might in some cases be combined, he felt, but their work should be limited to finding facts and submitting recommendations; they should be strictly advisory, and should have none of the authority contemplated by Murray and Reuther. In mid-December Hillman put himself on record by writing, in respect to the Murray-Reuther proposals, that "one hundred thirty million people cannot delegate to any combination of private interests final decision on matters of basic policy."

What finally defeated the Reuther plan, as a matter of fact, was—by a supreme irony—a mechanism which the administration had originally set up to keep big business from gaining complete and permanent control over the American economy. It was a device intended to save the dollar-a-year man from himself, as you might say, and in the end it saved him from Philip Murray; a gun aimed at the philosophy of Bernard Baruch, which finally brought down that of Walter Reuther.

It is worth examining in some detail.

CHAPTER NINE

The Emperor Is Naked

IT ALL began even before the Defense Commission had been organized. The first question the administration had to consider, when it began to get the country ready for war, was a fundamental: Does industry run the show, or does government?

This was not just a question of whether or not top industrialists should be called into government, on a dollar-a-year basis or otherwise, to take charge of the machinery. It went much deeper than that. Getting the country ready for war meant, in the last analysis, preparing for and finally making the transition to a full war economy. That was an undertaking so vast that the mere doing of it—regardless of the outcome of the war itself—was going to have profound and lasting effects on the country. Nothing like it had ever happened in America before. Whether it wanted to or not, the country was going to be changed very greatly by what it did to win the war. The way in which it undertook the job could be every bit as important as the action itself.

For this was going to be a war of steel mills and copper mines, of assembly lines and machine tools, of power plants and laboratories, of mechanics and technicians; a mobilizing and using of the *total* strength of the country. Young men were going to die in battle, but their deaths would be unavailing if the power back of them were not harnessed right. Whatever was done, there had to be a degree of control over all phases of the country's industrial life greater than anything we had ever contemplated before. How was this going to be applied, and specifically who was going to do it?

The answer right at the start seemed likely to be: Industry will do it. Not individual industrialists, temporarily serving as government officials, but industry itself—its trade associations, its own boards and committees, using powers handed over by the government, and exerting complete control over the nation's economic life. That was the approach that had been made in the last war, under the War Industries Board. That was the theory on which the more recent NRA experiments had been conducted. That was the direction of the thinking of the War and Navy Departments; it was, indeed, embodied in the Army's industrial mobilization plan. Furthermore, that was the method Baruch advised, and Baruch was the nation's foremost elder statesman, an oracle and a pundit whose judgment few men cared to question.

The first step toward what later became the defense program was taken in the summer of 1939, before the European war got started, when the administration set up a War Resources Board— composed of a number of blue-chip industrialists with Stettinius as chairman—and told it to review and perfect existing plans for economic and industrial mobilization and in general to submit its own ideas about what ought to be done. The general understanding was that in the event of war or the imminent threat of war this board would remain on the job and would automatically become the war production agency.

The Stettinius board followed the established trend. In its final report it recommended use of the Baruch pattern—a central agency to transmit the government's requirements to industry, with industry's own organizations given the power to carry them out, and explicitly freed by special legislation from the danger that organizations or individuals might subsequently be prosecuted for infringement of the antitrust laws.

On the surface the idea looked highly reasonable. It would relieve the government of the necessity for creating an immense organization in Washington; the production job would be put into the hands of the producers themselves, and the incomparable resources of American industry would be directly enlisted, with both responsibility and authority explicitly given to industry. Government can't make airplanes, industry can; therefore industry gets the job, lock, stock, and barrel, and there is no nonsense about government telling industry what to do—government simply tells industry what is needed, and industry does all the rest. It *did* look reasonable; indeed, from one point of view, it was the most reasonable and logical proposition in the world, and it guaranteed that any defense program or war production program that might be undertaken would enjoy the complete and enthusiastic backing of industry's biggest muscles.

But there was a catch to it, as there is to so many good ideas. What lay ahead was a full war economy. Fitting the country into such an economy, and enabling it to operate thereafter, involves an almost infinite number of controls, and the controls go right to the heart of the nation's life. Priorities, allocations, price regulations, the endless ramifications of limitation orders and conservation orders; these tell a businessman what materials he can get, what he can make, what price he must pay and what price he may charge, they tell him what sort of business he is in, they determine how big the business is, in the end they tell him whether he is in business at all. As far as the businessman is concerned they are the supreme exercise of the police power of the state.

And what the Baruch system really rested on was the flat assumption that industry itself should have the right to determine these controls and, in large part, to administer them after they were determined. The work would be done by trade associations and by other groups chosen by industry. Inevitably, it would fall into the hands of the biggest units in industry. The big fellow would hold the power of life or death over the little fellow. Special legislation would remove any chance that a subsequent administration could use the antitrust laws to penalize over-enthusiastic exercise of that power. Never before had it been so baldly asserted that the public welfare was identical with the welfare of big industry; never before had there been such a thoroughgoing plan for turning full control of the nation's economic life over to the dominant groups in industry.

In short, this was the road to full, permanent cartelization of industry; a broad, straight highway which would unquestionably enable industry to mobilize for war but which, unless Providence should be unexpectedly kind, would also make possible the removal of the props from under the free enterprise system once and for all.

It proved altogether too much of a dose for President Roosevelt. The New Deal was prepared to co-operate with big business to obtain a defense program, but it wasn't going to hand over title to the old homestead. The War Resources Board turned in its report; the President thanked the members, filed the report many fathoms deep without breathing a word about its contents— Donald Nelson subsequently remarked that to the end of his days as war production boss he never so much as got a glimpse of it —and quietly abolished the board.

The first tentative approach to a defense program, then, had been scratched before post time. The next approach was more roundabout. Discarding the Baruch program, the President bethought himself of a forgotten law passed back in August, 1916, which had designated six cabinet members—the Secretaries of War, Navy, Agriculture, Interior, Commerce, and Labor—as a Council of National Defense, and had authorized the naming of a commission to advise them. Under this law he named an Advisory Commission to the Council of National Defense—the group which became known as the Defense Commission—and put it to work.

But although the War Resources Board had died, its memory lingered on, both in the Defense Commission and later in the Office of Production Management. If there was to be anything resembling an approach to industrial mobilization, government and industry had to co-operate; government had to consult with industry for a wide variety of reasons, and to do so it had to call on committees representing the different industries. As these committees began to be set up, the question of the exact use that was to be made of them became important; and the Baruch approach began to be used, if only because it seemed perfectly natural and logical to most of the dollar-a-year men who were dealing with the committees. After all, Stettinius, who had been chairman of the short-lived War Resources Board, was a key figure in the Defense Commission and later in OPM. Baruch's personal advice was continuing and persuasive. The War Department had not lost its faith in the idea that broad authorities should be delegated to industrial groups. All in all, as first the Defense Commission and then OPM painfully groped their way toward an effective program, the Baruch idea began to go into effect and the industry committees seemed quite likely to get and to exercise the powers that the War Resources Board had proposed that they should have. By the winter of 1941 the fight against turning full government authority over to big industry was in a fair way to be lost.

It was at this point—on February 7, 1941, to be exact—that the President made one of the most important appointments to a war agency in the entire history of the mobilization effort. He named John Lord O'Brian general counsel of OPM.

O'Brian was one of those little-known officials who never received very many headlines but who did work of immense significance. A Buffalo Republican, he had been head of the War Emergency Division of the Department of Justice in the First World War, and under President Hoover he had served as head of the Anti-Trust Division. He was a mild-mannered, solid little chap, bald as an egg, looking and acting a full twenty years younger than his age; he was firmly convinced that the general viewpoint expressed in the antitrust laws was vital to the preservation of America's democratic society, he was an immensely able lawyer with a knack for standing immovable as a block of granite when the occasion required . . . and, just incidentally, he was a close personal friend of Attorney General Robert Jackson.

It was O'Brian, more than anyone else, who saw to it that the Baruch formula was not finally adopted in the mobilization program.

As general counsel, first for OPM and later for WPB, O'Brian had to develop and put into effect a guiding policy governing the production agency's relations with industry. (This was a job for the general counsel because any such policy was bound to cut across existing legislation; formulating the policy was, first and foremost, a matter of legalistics. What do the laws *permit* us to do? Can we do what needs to be done under these laws, or must we ask for their modification?) O'Brian immediately rejected the idea that committees from industry should be set up as agencies of government, using government powers in the control and regulation of industry. His answer to the dollar-a-year man's plaintive question, "How do we get around the antitrust laws?" was, simply: "We don't." When the War Department, in March, 1941, formally proposed that suspension of antitrust laws be requested for the duration, O'Brian turned the proposal down flatly. Working with the Department of Justice, he evolved the policy that was to be followed throughout the war.

Boiled down, this policy was: Government delegates no powers to private agents. It must, of course, use industry committees, but these committees will be strictly advisory; they will set no policies and hand down no orders, and they will have nothing whatever to do with policing any regulations that may be issued. The distinction between government and representatives of private interests must always be clear-cut. When government wants concerted action from an industry, it will obtain advance approval from the Department of Justice, and its proposal will go to the industry committee in writing; the industry committee itself may not even propose such a plan. In return, the government will guarantee that members of industry committees will not be prosecuted under the antitrust laws for any actions which are taken at government's request.

Having worked out this policy, O'Brian promptly nailed it to the church door through an official exchange of letters with Attorney General Jackson. This meant that as far as OPM and any successor agency were concerned, the policy was as the laws of the Medes and the Persians. It wasn't just something that the OPM general counsel had cooked up, ready to be repealed by any general counsel who might take his place; it was a formulation of the official administration attitude, and Attorney General Jackson—flanked by the fearsome Thurman Arnold, who was then head of the Anti-Trust Division—was there to make it stick. Having done all of this, O'Brian then saw to it that the proper machinery was set up in OPM to make everybody toe the line. It took a little time to do this, since the old idea died hard. There were rumblings of discontent, and occasional complaints that the country would never get a real defense program unless it suspended its ridiculous, industry-crippling, antitrust laws, but by the end of 1941 the pattern had been firmly set and was being followed.

That was the background against which OPM, early in January, 1942, met with the leaders of the automobile industry and the leaders of the auto labor unions. The Murray-Reuther proposal for a joint committee exerting full control over the affairs of the industry drew bitter opposition from the industry men. C. E. Wilson, president of General Motors, declared that "to divide the responsibility for management would be to destroy the very foundation upon which America's unparalleled record of industrial accomplishment is built." What really mattered, however, was the fact that the proposal cut squarely across the O'Brian-Jackson policy. OPM was not finally called on to say whether responsibility for industrial management should be divided, in the manner complained of by Wilson, because of the prior decision—a decision of the administration itself—that government authority and responsibility could neither be divided nor delegated. Delegation of authority was delegation of authority, whether it was made to an unleavened committee of industrialists, or to a committee adulterated by the presence of union officials. For better or for worse, government was going to call the turn. It might call in outsiders for consultation and advice, but government itself was going to set the policies, make the decisions, and enforce them.

In other words, a barrier had been set up to prevent fundamental change in the economic system during the war program— at least to prevent fundamental change in one particular field. It happened that the barrier had been erected against the threat of change coming from the direction of finance capitalism, but it worked just as well when the threat came from militant labor. It was a barrier that the union men could not get over any more than the industrialists could get over it. For the duration of the war it killed off any consideration of the Murray-Reuther idea.

This left the OPM conference regarding conversion of the auto industry exactly where it started, with a burning issue to meet and no handy way of meeting it.

For the big idea of the conference had been to work out a comprehensive program for getting the auto industry quickly and completely into the production of war goods; and aside from the Reuther plan, which turned out to be illegal and hence inadmissible, as well as unthinkable, no plan was in existence.

Under the remorseless prodding of Leon Henderson, OPM announced that the manufacture of passenger cars would have to cease by January 31, 1942. The industrialists pleaded fruitlessly for a postponement of the cutoff date to February 28; OPM refused, but agreed that there was no good reason to stop production *before* January 31. The union men made a number of suggestions for the pooling of machines, dies, patents, and engineering brains in the various corporations of the industry, and OPM promised to set up a joint management-labor committee whose functions would be limited to giving advice. Then the armed services announced that they were prepared to place with the industry war contracts totaling some five billion dollars.

What happened next is best described in the words of an official OPM press release, issued on the evening of January 5.

"Representatives of the major automotive companies this afternoon were given the shopping list of the Army and Navy and asked to begin immediate plans for producing materials to the limit of their facilities," said the release. It added that Under-Secretary of War Patterson presented a memorandum entitled "Items of Munitions Appropriate for Production by the Automobile Industry," with a similar list coming up from the Navy Department. Then it went into its narrative:

"Mr. Knudsen opened the afternoon meeting by stating that many of the firms represented were already producing many of the items on the list. He was interested, he said, in the items not now under contract with the automobile firms.

" 'We want to know where some of these things will flow from,' he said. 'We want to know if you can make them or want to try and make them. If you can't, do you know anyone who can?'

"As he read off the list he acted somewhat in the role of an auctioneer.

" 'We want more machine guns,' he would say. 'Who wants to make machine guns?'

"As spokesmen for the companies indicated their desire to make a particular item, a note was made and it was expected that negotiations for more definite arrangements which may lead to contracts later will be opened soon. Many items will be studied by the industrialists after they have returned to their plants. . . .

"An interesting sidelight was the suggestion that the automobile makers who have long depended on the machine tool industry for tools may help out the latter group in supplying some simple parts for new tools. As one maker put it: 'Can't the machine tool industry send us some orders?'

"Some of the firms that had made war materials for the last war expressed their willingness to begin their manufacture again."

All of which had to be seen—or at least listened to—to be believed. Here we were, eighteen months after the beginning of the defense program and a full month after Pearl Harbor; and OPM, which had been set up to marshal the nation's industrial strength, was desperately asking, "Who can make what?" Conversion of the country's biggest mass production industry was being put on an auction basis, and it was piously hoped that "negotiations which may lead to contracts" might be the result. Some companies "expressed their willingness" to make the same goods they had made in the last war. And after long months in which the shortage of machine tools had been a desperate handicap, it was at last tentatively suggested—though not by anyone in government—that the industry which possessed upward of 50 per cent of the nation's total supply of industrial machine tools might, if no one could think of anything better for it to do, lend a helping hand to relieve the machine tool bottleneck.

Futility could go no further. Fortunately, it did not have to. OPM had had its last chance. On January 13 the White House announced that Nelson had been appointed chairman of a War Production Board, and left it entirely up to Nelson to say just what the War Production Board might be, what powers it might have, and what fields it might cover. OPM evaporated, without mourners.

Nelson appointed Ernest Kanzler, former Ford official, as the man in charge of converting the auto industry, and announced that there would be no joint committee of unionists and industrialists to help out with advice and counsel—"my experience in NRA," he remarked privately, "was that whenever you set up a joint committee of government, industry, and labor to handle something, the first thing you know industry and labor representatives get together to see how they can screw the public." He said that it was entirely up to Kanzler to use as much or as little advice as he chose, from separate industry and labor committees. The ban on new car production was riveted down, the War Department moved in with a host of contracts—and, more rapidly than anyone had expected, the auto factories began to produce war goods, the industry having at last discovered that all but a fraction of its tools could be used to make munitions, and government having finally discovered that the way to convert the auto industry was (a) to keep the industry from making autos, and (b) to hand out profitable contracts.

So the whole problem had been solved, at the purely nominal cost of OPM's official life? It seemed so, at the time; it *was* so, as a matter of fact, if the problem consisted exclusively of the question of getting tanks and cannon made instead of automobiles. But back of that problem there was a far greater one, and we did not in the course of the entire war even begin to solve it.

The real problem was nothing less than that of finding some way to fit tremendous industrial strength, with all of its unimaginable complexities and with its inexorable tendency to dominate men and institutions, into the framework of a free, democratic society; fitting it so that its full capacity is used, but also in such a way that the society which uses it remains free and democratic. Nothing less than that was what the war was all about. A stop-gap solution, which would meet the immediate need of the moment—the need for more munitions—might make military victory possible, but it would do nothing whatever toward meeting the real problem; and the real problem had to be met, if the military victory were to be worth its cost. The challenge of the war went far beyond a mere challenge to dig more iron and make more steel and fabricate the steel more cunningly than anyone else could do. The real challenge said: Your old way of controlling that intricate combination of money, machinery, markets, and human beings which you call modern industry is no longer favorable to the survival of human freedom—*find a new way.*

So it was not just the inadequacy of the well-intentioned men of OPM that is revealed in this dismal set-to over conversion of the auto industry. The real inadequacy that shows up is the inadequacy of any existing American philosophy, either liberal or conservative, to measure up to the situation.

The inadequacy of the conservative philosophy was obvious at the time. The leaders of the industry and the leaders of OPM— exponents of American conservatism, if any men ever were— simply had no answer at all. Put to the test, with the nation's survival at stake, they had not even been able to meet the immediate surface challenge: How to get more munitions made in Detroit? For the underlying problem they had nothing more than the assertion that industrial management's responsibility must not be divided or shared.

But the liberals had done no better. Faced with the need for a comprehensive and imaginative program, they had been able to suggest nothing but reliance on the antitrust laws. That, to be sure, was all to the good as far as it went; it ruled out unadorned corporate piracy, and it gained a breathing spell for free society. But it suggested nothing at all about what might be done with the breathing spell thus gained. Taken as a final answer it was just as frantic an attempt to cling to the status quo as the answer of the conservatives had been.

For if the conservatives had run out of new ideas at the beginning of William McKinley's second term, the liberals had done likewise at the beginning of Franklin Roosevelt's third, which was just the moment when new ideas were most urgently required. The old creeds were outworn and nobody was coming up with new ones; yet it was precisely the need for new creeds that was so dramatically high-lighted by the struggle to convert the auto industry. There was nothing in the books that would meet the situation. If the conservatives believed devoutly in the profit motive and in the rights of private property, the liberals were equally devout about labor's right to organize and the sacredness of free competition; but these articles of faith, excellent as they might be, were not in the slightest degree adequate at the beginning of 1942, simply because the dominant issues went so far beyond anything anyone had dreamed of when the creeds were put together.

All of the unsolved problems of the great age of industrialism, grown to enormous size and made explosive beyond all imagining, had come to a head in the war emergency; they had created the war itself and they had posed the challenge to all who hoped to survive the war; and nothing was going to be made available to meet this storm except the old familiar umbrella that had been used in the April showers of the past.

Into a situation which cried aloud for a transvaluation of values, the auto workers had dropped a plan. It was not just a proposal looking toward the faster production of war goods; for good or for ill, it offered a pattern, a core around which a new creed might be built, a vantage point for an approach by which new values might be found. At the very least it recognized that we were playing a new game, and suggested a new set of rules; suggested, in any case, the desirability of trying to create a new set of rules. Yet it was exactly that point which no one was prepared to face. The decision on the auto workers' proposal, despite the brief furore, was more or less automatic. The plan was dismissed, not because it had been carefully studied and found to be unworkable, but because it fell outside of the established points of reference. Reuther was in the position of the child in the fairy tale who tactlessly pointed out that the emperor was naked. That was the one thing nobody wanted to have to think about.

CHAPTER TEN

To Git Thar Fust

THE LUCK of the committee which was planning the Adam Gimbel Centennial Banquet was both good and bad. Good, because the committee had succeeded in signing up Donald Nelson to be the speaker of the evening; bad, because as events worked out Nelson wasn't able to be present. In the end, good luck and bad were neatly blended. Nelson wasn't there but his speech was—certified as official, and duly read to the assembled guests by a proxy—and a freak of chance decreed that this speech should be the first public statement of the views and policies of the new boss of American war production.

Plans for the banquet had, of course, been laid well in advance. It was to be held in Vincennes, Indiana, on January 14, 1942. It honored the centennial of a pioneer American merchant, and as one of America's leading merchandisers Nelson had been happy to accept the committee's invitation. He had worked on his speech with a good deal of care, trying to spell out for his audience just what the war was going to mean to the nation's economy, fully aware that in the present chaotic state of affairs in Washington a strong pronouncement by someone was badly needed. And then, twenty-four hours before the speech was to be delivered, Nelson was called to the White House and told that he was to be chairman of a brand new War Production Board, which would be in charge of everything Nelson thought necessary and would be armed with all of the authority he might see fit to ask for.

Among the many matters that Nelson had to think about, therefore, on the morning of January 14, this speaking engagement in far-off Indiana was one of the least important but most pressing. The one thing he could not do, on that particular evening, was go to Indiana. He could not even spare the time and energy to deliver his speech from Washington via leased wire or electrical transcription. Someone else would have to read it for him, if it were to be given at all; that was clear, and it was so arranged.

Then there was the speech itself. When he wrote it, Nelson

had been just one of a number of impatient officials who were watching the galvanic twitchings of the dying OPM and hoping that something could be done to bring real direction to the job of war production. In writing the speech he had tried to express his own idea of what the situation called for; not the organizational changes that were needed, but the fact that industrial America needed to take a deep breath and prepare to transcend all of its own limitations. He had designed his speech as a plea for the discarding of all preconceived notions, all prejudices or concepts or habits of mind that might in any degree stand in the way of victory. But now he was not just the critic; he was the boss. This speech would go out as an official pronouncement—the *first* official pronouncement—by the man who had just been put in charge of the whole works. He himself was the man who would have to live up to the fine sentiments which he had put on paper. Could he, as boss of the job, still say the things he had written when he had not been boss?

He could and he did. He called for the completed manuscript of his speech the first thing that morning—his first morning as chairman of the War Production Board—and read it carefully. Finally he said, "Well, it all stands up. I think it needs to be said. Let's say it." So his proxy made the speech as it was originally written.

It was an important speech. It not only showed the mental attitude of the man who had been put in complete charge of the nonmilitary side of the war effort; it reflected, unconsciously but very accurately, what turned out to be the key decision of the administration in regard to the waging of the war.

"We are going to have to rely on our great mass production industries for the bulk of our increase under this war program," Nelson said. "Wherever we can we must convert them to war production, and convert them quickly. The only gauge we can apply to this process is: What method will most quickly give us the greatest volume of war production in this particular industry?

"The answer to that question may be hard to swallow, at times; it may call for a pooling of tools, for a redistribution of skilled workers, for a concentration of civilian production in one set of plants and 100 per cent war production in others; it may, in fact, and probably very often will, call for utterly revolutionary changes in the method of operating that industry and the whole network of relationships as between government, management, suppliers, and workers. But what of it? The one thing that counts is to get the stuff out and get it out quickly. We cannot waste three months—or three weeks, for that matter—in wrangling and discussion; we cannot compromise this demand for all-out production, or accept a formula which gives us anything less than the absolute maximum of production, just because someone's toes are going to be stepped on."

Prave words, Captain Fluellen. Exactly what did they mean?

Two things. First, that the day of holding back was definitely over. What Nelson was saying was that he was ready—and the country must be ready—to try absolutely anything if it would help to win the war. Nelson was prepared to be ruthless, and he was not going to worry about labels like "radical" or "reactionary"; he could swallow, for instance, the Reuther plan, or any other conceivable plan, if he could be shown that the quickest road to victory lay that way. This bland, comfortable, hail-fellow-well-met from the mail order business was not going to boggle at formulas.

So far so good. But the second point, which grows out of the first and which went more or less unnoticed at the time, is that this declaration was in effect a statute of limitations. We would do, the war production chief was saying, anything under the shining sun that might be necessary for victory; but, by the same token, everything we did do would have to justify itself by that yardstick. The only consideration was the defeat of the Axis—the Axis, defined as a tangible, three-dimensional power to be conquered by armies and air fleets and warships and sheer weight of metal. Winning the war was all that counted. If we were fighting *for* something as well as against something, and if we would have to show what it was we were fighting for by the way in which we fought—well, all of that could be left to the great god of battles. We were getting a vision of a strange new world, maybe, in which all men worked together toward a common goal, and self-interest was gone with the mists of the morning, but the baseless fabric of that vision would dissolve and leave not a rack behind the moment the enemy laid down his arms.

Nelson wasn't trying to say all of that, to be sure. He was just trying to express his conviction that we were in a no-holds-barred fight, and that the crippling fear of change was not going to be allowed to handicap us any longer. He was not trying to set high administration policy, except as it applied to the business of making munitions. The trouble was that it was precisely in that field, more than in any other, that our underlying policy in respect to the war had to be made manifest, and our underlying policy had never been defined. If the word was to become flesh it had to become so in the way in which the flesh was put to work, and the word had not been uttered. Facing a problem in the production of war goods, Nelson took a leaf from Nathan Bedford Forrest's book and announced that our aim was to git thar fust with the most stuff. That was an excellent decision as far as it went, but it was framed and adopted in a vacuum. It was all the decision there was, and it became the controlling decision of the war, the point of departure for everything that was to be done.

Lacking any other prophet, we had gone back to Bill Knudsen's after-dinner speech three nights before Pearl Harbor. The Axis was a monstrous neighborhood nuisance and we were going to suppress it. The war was as simple as that and as limited. If, in the end, it refused to *be* simple, and if it turned out that it had no limits—well, that was not going to affect the way we fought it.

At the moment, however, there were other matters to think about. Before he could get his teeth into his new job, Nelson had to decide how he was going to handle two pressing issues: his relationship with the War Department, and the use that should be made of that useful, baffling, contradictory institution, the dollar-a-year man.

War Department first. Should it continue to sign the contracts for war goods, or should that job be taken over by a civilian ministry of supply—by Nelson's new War Production Board, to be specific?

Backward as OPM had been in getting a broad and speedy production program established, it had been no more backward than the War Department itself. Indeed, one of the chief criticisms of OPM had been centered on its inability to find any way to direct and to speed up the military procurement processes. Speed and volume of production depend, when all is said and done, on the contracts that are issued; the agency that issues the contracts, consequently, is apt to be the agency that ultimately calls the pitch on the production program. The War Department had given no faintest sign, up to the beginning of 1942, that it comprehended the size of the job that was to be done. Could it safely be left in charge of military procurement? Was military procurement, for that matter, actually a job for the Army at all? When the President announced that Nelson was to write his own ticket for the new War Production Board, and that he would be given any authority he asked for, it was pretty generally taken for granted that the first thing Nelson would demand would be the removal of the contracting power from the War Department.

He didn't do it, and while his decision not to disappointed his most ardent supporters, Nelson himself never doubted that it was the only decision he could have made. He estimated that to set up a new procurement agency would take many months; during those months, the all-out production job would inevitably be delayed. And there were no months to spare: not when the Axis was visibly winning the war on every front, and the turning of the tide so obviously waited on American war production. As Nelson himself said, there were not three months to spare—or, for that matter, three weeks, either. Furthermore, Nelson had a sneaking suspicion that to take over military procurement—to make himself the man who signed the contracts and actually placed the initial orders with industry—would be to cut himself in on the making of purely military decisions, for which he had no stomach. The man who signs the contracts for military goods can be, in the long run, the man who determines that weapon A gets made ahead of weapon B, that weapon C does not get made at all, and that weapon D is more to be desired than weapon E. For better or for worse, Nelson voted to leave procurement in military hands and to exert control through co-ordination and policy-setting rather than through outright expropriation.

Probably it was the only decision he could have made, under the circumstances. After the war ended he remarked that if he had it all to do over again he would do it exactly the same way. But it was a decision that was to fly up and hit him in the face, just the same, and in the end it had a profound effect on the shape of events. It was the enacting clause to the generalized decision that military victory was the only thing to worry about. Military victory is our one goal; and it is the military, in the end, that will tell us what we must do to reach it.

Hand in hand with this went the decision on dollar-a-year men.

The dollar-a-year man was in bad odor when Nelson took charge of war production. If the Roosevelt administration wanted to discredit business leadership and rob it of power and influence, as its more spirited opponents liked to believe, it certainly stood right on the edge of final victory in January of 1942. Business leadership had had eighteen months to show what it could do with a defense program, and the result had been bad both for the defense program and for business leadership. Maybe the choice of men had been bad, maybe the setup under which the chosen men had gone to work had been impossible; whatever the reason, the old idea that the only possible operators for an industrialized war were the industrialists themselves had suffered a sharp decline, and some sort of change was expected. If it was taken for granted that the new boss of war production would have to clip the wings of the War Department in order to get his job done, it was also assumed that he would have to get rid of the dollar-a-year men.

By no one was this conviction more deeply felt than by the Truman Committee of the Senate, which enjoyed more prestige than all other congressional committees put together, and which had earned it by being eminently fair, intelligent, and aggressive. The Truman Committee had come to the conclusion that the institution of dollar-a-year men ought to be abolished, root and branch, and it suggested as much to Nelson shortly after he took over his new office.

To the committee's pained surprise, Nelson flatly disagreed. He did announce that there would be some changes in the selection and use of dollar-a-year men, the principal change being an order that "no person shall be employed in any position in which he will make decisions directly affecting the affairs of his own company"—which, being interpreted, meant in substance that the president of the XYZ Refrigerator Corporation would not be allowed to fill a job which might require him, and no one else, to determine whether the XYZ Corporation could continue to make refrigerators in a limited and highly profitable market But with minor modifications Nelson continued the dollar-a-year system in effect, and presently he went before the Truman Committee to defend this decision vigorously.

His reasoning was simple and direct, a logical extension of his pronouncement for the merchandisers at Vincennes. He told the committee that he had just one standard for passing on all such questions: What will contribute most toward winning the war in the shortest possible time? Following that standard, he could see no alternative to the continued use of industrialists, loaned to government by industry and kept on the payroll of their own corporations, and he told the committee exactly why he felt that way.

"On this job we must get the maximum results from American industry," he said. "To do that we must have down here men who understand and can deal with industry's intricate structure and operation. In other words, we must have men with expert business and technical knowledge. For the most part we have to get them from industry itself. But no matter where we get them or how we get them we simply must have them in the places where they are needed, when they are needed."

In which case, why not put them on the government payroll and be done with it? Why let them retain their corporate ties and financial interests? The Truman Committee was deeply curious on that point, and Nelson had the answer:

"All things being equal, these men ought to be brought in to serve on a regular government salary. I wish that were possible. It isn't. You can't get all the help you need, of the kind you need, on that basis. The reason is simple: most of these men, many of them specialists, have been getting salaries much higher than those which can be paid government employees. Since they have been getting such salaries, they naturally have incurred extensive financial obligations over the years—mortgages, life insurance, income taxes which they have to pay this year, and so on—so that it is extremely hard for them to adjust themselves abruptly to a much lower income. In many cases it is literally true that the man in question simply can't make the change to a government payroll without extreme hardship to his family.

"Furthermore, when we bring these men in for this war effort we are not offering permanent careers to them. In the very nature of things we are offering them temporary jobs. So if we did not have any provision for dollar-a-year men, we should in every case be forced to ask these men to sever their old connections entirely to take temporary jobs at salaries which might not enable them to meet their fixed obligations. In practice, then, we would usually get from industry only older men who were independently wealthy and who could therefore afford to make the break, or those who have already retired. I do not think the Congress could approve the principle of such an arrangement, and I do not think the Congress would like to limit the War Production Board to the ranks of the very wealthy in the selection of personnel."

It must be admitted that this reasoning did not impress the Truman Committee greatly. Senator Truman bluntly told Nelson as much.

"I don't think there should be any special class," Senator Truman said. "I just received a letter this morning from a young man who is getting $25,000 a year. He is a Reserve officer. He is going to get $140 a month, and he can't draw his $25,000 while he is gone. He is satisfied to do that because he wants to win the war, just as you do and just as I do, by every means possible, no matter what it costs him, because if he doesn't win it his $25,000 a year won't be worth a cent.

"I am laboring, and have been, under the delusion, maybe, that if the government has the power to take these young men away from their jobs and their outlook on life for the purpose of this emergency, the dollar-a-year men could face the same situation and face it adequately, and would be glad to do it. However, if that is not the case, and their morale won't stand it—and you say it won't—we want to win the war. Therefore we are not going to hamper you in that effort and in your way of handling it."

A few days later Senator Truman spelled it out in detail in a letter to Nelson, making it clear that the committee—which for months had been demanding unified, coherent direction for the war production program—was going to support Nelson, now that he had been given the job, and was willing to go along with him even on his dollar-a-year policy, but that it still thought that he was wrong.

"The committee believed," Senator Truman wrote, "that the problem of substituting the right men for the wrong men was so great that the practice of retaining dollar-a-year men should be abandoned, so that those who were more interested in their remuneration than in their public service would automatically be eliminated, and those public-spirited individuals, like yourself, would be retained. You have informed the committee that you desire to retain some dollar-a-year men who, by reason of the standard of living to which they have accustomed themselves, cannot afford even temporarily to work for the government for $10,000 a year, or less. The committee does not like to have procurement matters entrusted to men who have given such hostages to fortune. Those who cannot forego large incomes temporarily cannot reasonably be expected to take a chance of foregoing them permanently by taking positions on behalf of the government with which the controlling officials of their corporations are not in sympathy. In the committee's opinion, this was one of the principal reasons for the now generally admitted failures of the Office of Production Management.

"However, the committee believes that the best interests of the procurement program require that it be administered by a single head who will be able to do things in his own way and who will be judged by his accomplishments as a whole and not by his position on individual matters. The committee will, therefore, support you even on matters in which it disagrees with you, and believes that all other agencies of the government should afford you a similar unquestioning support until you have had a full opportunity to achieve the success which we all hope that you will achieve."

With this highly qualified and reluctant clearance, then, Nelson's decision on the dollar-a-year men remained in effect for the duration of the war. Like his decision on the place of the War Department in respect to procurement, this decision may well have been the only one Nelson could have made under the circumstances; for the circumstances included, first and foremost, the binding imperative of the original decision—winning the war is all that counts, and right now winning the war involves getting the biggest possible volume of production in the shortest possible time.

Experts from industry *were* necessary; if they served no other purpose—and they served many others—they constituted, at the very least, an indispensable two-way channel of communication between government, which framed and issued orders, and industry, which had to carry the orders out. These experts were needed at once—not next April, but now, in mid-January. Was there time to stop for a reshuffle? Nelson thought not, and the Truman Committee refused to quarrel with him even though it clearly felt that he was mistaken.

So we kept the institution of the dollar-a-year man, for good or for ill; for good *and* for ill, since it was like most human institutions, a blend of the excellent and the deplorable. The decision, as noted, grew logically out of the fundamental decision that while we were fighting an all-out war we were going to fight it for limited objectives—which is to say, for purely military objectives—and it was a decision of the most far-reaching importance. In effect, even if not by conscious intent, it was a decision to cling to the status quo.

For the decision to keep on using dollar-a-year men did nothing less than preserve the existing corporate control of American industry; not just because the dollar-a-year man did things on purpose to safeguard that control, but because the possible alternatives to the dollar-a-year-man system were all so far-reaching.

The great feature of the dollar-a-year-man system was that it insured a high degree of understanding and co-operation between industry and government. It meant that when the rulers of industry were told by government what they could or could not do, or were called in by government for exhortation and exposition, they received their orders and their exhortations from men whom they were willing to recognize as big shots. Philip Reed, for instance, was in charge of consumer goods divisions for WPB in the early months of the war. What he said to the industrialists affected by the orders of his divisions carried weight, not just because he had a high position in WPB, but because everybody knew that in private life he was chairman of the board of the great General Electric Corporation. In or out of government, he was a leader of industry.

Reed was one of hundreds of dollar-a-year men, and the same thing was true of all of them in a greater or a lesser degree. Some of them were very big big shots indeed, and some of them were minor big shots, but all of them came from the businessman's own team. They were officials from whom the industrialist was willing to take orders.

Now contrast that with the position of such a man as Leon

Henderson. He had nothing to stand on but the force of his own personality, the power of his own intelligence, and the authority vested in him by law and by executive order. Industry did not listen to him gladly; it listened because it had to. He did get more co-operation than might have been expected, but his official career in OPM and OPA was one long dog-fight.

The whole basis of the nation's war production program was—in spite of the innumerable orders and controls—willing co-operation by industry. When Nelson was made chairman of WPB he was commonly spoken of as the "czar" of war production. Actually, neither he nor his organization, nor anyone else in government, really did very much czaring as far as the actual production process was concerned. America's enormous volume of war production grew out of a very few basic actions. WPB put progressive restrictions on the goods industry might make and the materials it might use—it said "no more automobiles," for instance, and it kept aluminum out of the hands of producers who weren't in war work—and the armed services flooded industry with enormous orders for munitions. WPB, in turn, then set up the machinery to distribute materials and component parts, and did various things to make sure that there would be enough of them to meet essential needs. All the rest was up to industry. And while it is true, of course, that government's part in all of this was almost incomprehensibly intricate, difficult, and important, the fact remains that the production job itself remained in industry's hands. Even at the height of the war, government did not—except, perhaps, by the standards of a few Neanderthal diehards—go in for "telling the businessman how to run his business." The most striking thing about the whole war production program was not that there were so many controls but that all of them fell within the established patterns of industry.

It all worked, and the quantity of munitions obtained startled everybody. But suppose, now, that the countless WPB officials who put this process in motion and kept it running had been Leon Hendersons instead of Philip Reeds; bureaucrats (by the industrialists' definition) instead of captains of industry; New Deal careerists, instead of dollar-a-year men. Beyond any question there would have been much less co-operation by industry, much less willing understanding, much less feeling that government talked the industrialist's lingo and relied on his brains and ingenuity. That would almost certainly have meant more compulsion. A New Deal government simply could not have let itself get into the position of being about to lose the war because it had refused to "use the best brains of industry."

So what? So the alternative to the dollar-a-year men was an entirely different kind of war effort. Almost inevitably, it would have turned out to be deeply and permanently revolutionary. Something along the lines of the Murray plan, for instance—some use of the industry council idea all up and down the line, with authority and responsibility directly vested in workers, technicians, and managers—would have been almost inescapable. There would not only have been more controls; they would have been controls of a different kind, controls which more explicitly asserted the right and duty of the central government to disregard the last vestige of property rights in time of crisis. To decide against using dollar-a-year men would have meant working out an entirely new kind of setup; and such a setup, created in the incandescent heat of war, would not have passed away quickly with the war's end.

The decision Nelson made was, fundamentally, a decision to bank on the existing order—and, banking on it, to preserve it. It was not without reason that Kiplinger's *Washington Letter*, on January 24, 1942, quoted "business-minded men within government" as saying that the WPB program constituted "the last stand of private enterprise." Kiplinger had it dead to rights. And as things turned out, this last stand was to be a honey.

CHAPTER ELEVEN

It Is Bloody Urgent

THIS wasn't the war. This was an exercise in top-level organization, a test run for the American economy, a trial marriage between the bureaucracies of government and business which made strange bedfellows out of the career men of Washington, New York, Detroit, and way stations; it was the War Production Board, crowned with dignity and power and fixed a little lower than the angels, properly busy in the air-cooled halls and offices of the modernistic Social Security Building, engaged daily in conferences, in arguments-by-telephone, in the fabrication and distribution of innumerable pieces of paper. The war that was fought here was a cold, bloodless war—a conflict of theories, of ideas, of programs, of orders—and while a good many feelings were hurt, first and last, nobody was actually getting killed.

But the trouble was that the other war, the real war, wouldn't stay put. The real war was tragedy and pain and death, and it was being fought by human beings, and the bits of paper that were being shuffled endlessly in the Social Security Building were due to turn up some day as the justification for somebody's bloodshed and agony; and the terrible question, "What are we really fighting *for?*" kept coming up for answer, demanding attention from men who would greatly have preferred to take their patriotism straight and let others worry about the abstractions. Yet the abstractions were at the heart of it, somebody had to work them out, the answers had to be found right here in WPB, and no sooner were items like the role of the dollar-a-year man and the handling of army procurement disposed of than the same problem would bob up again in some other guise. As, for example, in the matter of patent rights, technological advances, and industrial processes.

These are often fairly dull, unless you happen to be a technician, an economist, or an industrialist, but in the spring and summer of 1942 they offered the busy men in WPB one more chance to look the idea of an all-out war in the face and decide whether or not they could go for it. As usual, they found that they could not. For all-out war deals in absolutes; it means the last curtain and the final bugle call for Things as They Were; it means that this carefully formalized exercise in the Social Security Building might suddenly go haywire and become a swiftly-humming machine for building a new heaven and a new earth, so that the intangibles which men are dying for will transcend in value the sacred rights of custom, of property, and of Our Two Million Stockholders. And all of these matters were bound up in this question of patent rights, technological advances, and industrial processes.

It began innocently enough, as so many wicked things do, when a couple of Catholic scientists from Cincinnati visited Washington one day in March, 1942, to call on Maury Maverick, former congressman, former Mayor of San Antonio, and at that time the chief of WPB's Bureau of Government Requirements.

The two visitors were Monsignor Cletus A. Miller and Dr. George S. Sperti, both from the Institutum Divi Thomae, a Catholic institution for scientific research. They were interested, at the moment, simply in finding a means to protect public health during the war; Maverick's bureau, which was responsible for screening the requests made by state and city governments for materials and equipment, was their port of call because it was up to Maverick to determine whether a city water works, for instance, could have chemicals for water purification purposes. Thus the two men sat down to talk with Maverick, and presently they discovered that they had ideas in common about the necessity for an all-out war and ways and means of achieving it. As a successful inventor, Dr. Sperti had discovered a thing or two about the difference between perfecting an industrial device or process and actually getting it used; and before long the three had stopped talking about public health measures and were discussing the way in which scientific skills and techniques are sometimes monopolized in industry, the way in which such monopolies can interfere with an all-out war effort, and the importance, for war and for peace, of finding some way to take the shackles off the nation's productive power.

(And why should three men who sat down to talk about filtration plants and chemicals find themselves discussing big industry, monopoly, and the American dream? This was none of their business, as men's business was gauged in the spring of 1942; the war was being fought by and with big business, and nobody had asked these three to worry about the prospect that it might turn out to be fought *for* big business as well. The Social Security Building's war was Detroit and Pittsburgh and Chicago and Los Angeles, not to mention Wall Street, and the time to worry about monopoly was far behind anyway. . . . Except that this other war, the war in which the ordinary human being was proving once again his eternal and incomprehensible readiness to die for something bigger than himself, was going on too, and these three men somehow felt that they had to do a little thinking about what the ordinary human being was going to be given in exchange for his life. If all he stood to get was what would trickle down, ultimately, from the high centers of power, then he was being sold down the river and it was time to do something. And what better place to start doing it than right here in Maverick's office?)

It was wholly characteristic of Maverick that the discussion should have taken this turn. In the early days in Texas, Maverick's family name had been turned into a common noun meaning an unbranded critter that is out on the plains on its own hook, answerable to no one, and the noun fitted the man himself. He was short, stocky, swarthy, intensely irascible, and inordinately loyal—both to people and to ideas—and he was a scrapper who lost all his inhibitions in the clinches. The dollar-a-year men, for the most part, would have liked to look on him as a comic figure (he looked on most dollar-a-year men as figures out of the bad place, so that made it even) except that they felt he was too dangerous to be funny. He was an unconverted New Dealer, in whose eyes Roosevelt's one mistake was his reliance on captains of industry to help win the war—a mistake which, Maverick felt, was all too likely to be fine for monopolists and bad for ordinary folk who had to do the fighting.

So when the conversation got onto the problem of the monopolist, Maverick decided to take steps. After spending a good deal of time comparing notes and working out ideas with Monsignor Miller and Dr. Sperti, he prepared a memorandum on the matter. The whole business was outside of his field, but the war was still young and it hadn't been won yet, and Nelson was showing a refreshing willingness to consider any idea, no matter where it came from, that promised to bring victory more quickly; and, anyway, Maverick was a maverick and the range hadn't been fenced in yet. So Maverick sent his memo off to Herbert Emmerich, then executive secretary of WPB, outlining "a plan for the organization of the scientific research laboratories of the United States in a co-operative research program to meet the problems of shortages of materials and to assist industry and government in war production." The memo proposed that WPB set up a bureau to organize commercial and industrial research operations, and warned that it would be important to distinguish between "those problems which benefit private industry only and those problems which benefit the nation in the total war effort."

This memo was passed on to Nelson, who liked the idea. There existed, then and throughout the war, a most effective organization of scientists to help the Army and Navy develop new weapons—the Office of Scientific Research and Development, under Dr. Vannevar Bush—but there was nothing like it on the non-combatant side. If the military men needed a new explosive, a new range finder, a new fuse, or anything similar, Dr. Bush's organization could quickly bring the best scientific and laboratory skill of the country to bear on the problem. But there was no way to bring about a similar mobilization of talent for purely industrial problems, and there was no way to make sure that devices or processes which might be developed during the war would be made readily available to all manufacturers who might need them. Clearly, industrial production could be speeded and victory could be brought nearer if there were, on the industrial side, a good counterpart to Dr. Bush's organization. Accordingly, in mid-April, Nelson appointed a committee to look into the matter and recommend a course of action.

Nelson made Maverick chairman of this committee. Other members were Dr. Charles I. Gragg, a consultant to the chairman of WPB, on leave as member of the faculty of Harvard's Graduate School of Business Administration; Harold Stein, an officer in WPB's Division of Civilian Supply—the old Leon Henderson organization that made so much trouble for the auto industry eight months earlier; Lessing Rosenwald (*the* Rosenwald), chief of WPB's Bureau of Industrial Conservation, and

Dr. C. K. Leith, technical consultant to WPB's Materials Division, in private life a geologist on the faculty of the University of Wisconsin. These men were instructed to find out what kind of office or bureau WPB should set up in order "to make use of the scientific resources of the country," to keep abreast of industrial research, and to take action on inventions, new developments, and so on.

Late in April, 1942, then, these five men sat down together to examine what was currently being done along these lines and to see whether more should be added to it.

It was easy enough for them to conclude that WPB needed a much more vigorous direction and co-ordination of industrial research and development. What was already being done was good as far as it went, but it was clear that it did not go far enough. Dr. Leith pointed out that he himself was at the head of "an inadequate center, where there are only twenty of us" for the clearance of research problems. Ever since July, 1940, he recalled, the Defense Commission and its successors had been using the National Academy of Sciences for technological assistance, sending requests for aid to the Academy and getting the answers from scientific committees which the Academy would thereupon call into being. In addition, he said, WPB had from time to time used the services of such government agencies as the Bureau of Mines, the Geological Survey and the National Bureau of Standards; further, the several WPB branches and divisions were constantly asking for research of various kinds in industrial and university laboratories—the laboratories, for instance, of General Electric, Westinghouse, General Motors, Chrysler, the Mellon Institute, California Tech, and so on. There ought to be a much better integration and direction of the whole process, he said, with some such sum as $5,000,000 for a war chest; this board should take charge of all general requests for scientific research work, should be headed by an outstanding professional in the field, and should avoid setting up new committees or administrative units that might duplicate the work already being done by the WPB industry branches and divisions.

So far, so good; this was a war of technologies, and all five men on the committee agreed that America's technologies had better be good. But at that point the agreement ceased. For it was one thing to agree that all scientific and technological resources must be used; it was quite another to determine exactly where those resources existed, how they were to be discovered, and in what way they could best be harnessed. All of these resources "must be used"; and precisely what do we mean by "used"? Used how, by whom, for whose benefit? The answers to these questions determine, ultimately, who really runs the country. The committee split in two, with Maverick, Gragg, and Stein in one group and Rosenwald and Leith in another, and the split was permanent.

What the Maverick group was shooting at was a completely new approach to the whole problem. It believed in the removal of all the invisible impediments that stand between the age of scientific achievements and the fullest possible use of those achievements. What it was actually demanding was production-for-use translated to the entire field of industrial research and technological advance. Stein brought the point of view out clearly at one of the early committee meetings.

Industrial scientists and technicians, he said, were guided by the profit motive—that is, they looked for products or devices which would make money for their own corporations. Okay, they had to play it that way; the corporations are in business to make money, that's how we operate. But there was a war on now, and the war emergency needed something which the profit motive couldn't supply—"ideas of a revolutionary sort," as Stein put it, the determining factor regarding which being "not whether they are desirable for making money," but whether, all factors considered, they are desirable for the country as a whole, which might be quite a different matter. And he added:

"We have reached the curious point in our course where we have to think about things which in normal times would appear ridiculous."

True as four-ply gospel, but was there ever found on land or sea a human organization less prepared than this War Production Board to "think about things which in normal times would appear ridiculous"? How far do you gentlemen think you are going to get with this idea, anyhow?

Much farther than anyone would suppose; so far, in fact, that they almost got away with it. But first there was the committee itself to deal with. The committee was fully agreed that WPB should have an office to take responsibility for industrial research and development. But how should the men who would run that office be selected? Should they be technicians or laymen? Technicians, argued Dr. Leith, "because this is not a business matter" and because the office would be dealing with purely technical problems; laymen, argued Maverick, because the office would really be dealing with social problems and its responsibilities would be social rather than scientific.

Maverick undertook to illustrate with a case from his own experience as Mayor of San Antonio. They had had a civic orchestra, he said, which had fallen on evil days. Its governing body was composed of cultured and talented folk who knew a great deal about music but who did not seem to know very much about keeping an orchestra solvent.

"We finally got the most ignorant man in town and put him in at the head," said Maverick. "He had never been anywhere, and these cultured people had been to New York and many other places. But he made a howling success of it. Then he died, and the cultured people got control of it—and it went broke again. So you have to have—"

"What," interrupted Rosenwald, "is the moral of that story?"

"The moral of that story," said Maverick, "is that you have got to have a few people who are not specially trained along a certain line, and if you get all those men on a committee you look at it purely from a technical and research point of view, and not according to the economic, business, and social problems."

Dr. Leith protested that even so Maverick had not made his most ignorant man the conductor of the orchestra; but Stein got the argument back from Texas by remarking that what they were really up against was "the necessity for making decisions which the technicians are afraid to make." Synthetic rubber, for instance; the basic questions about that highly crucial program should be decided, not by the men who knew exactly how synthetic rubber is made, but by men who felt the terrible urgency of the situation and were resolved that the best technical processes should be used no matter whose vested interests or postwar expectations might be hurt.

Tied in with this there was a subsidiary question which revolved about the same central issue: Assuming that we must greatly intensify industrial research, do we continue to rely on the research agencies that are now doing the job, merely giving

129

the program better direction and a broader scope, or do we reach out to enlist the researchers who are not now being used at all—the men in the laboratories and experiment stations at small colleges and universities, the lesser research laboratories in private industry, the unattached scientists and inventors who have not yet been put to work in the war effort? Dr. Leith felt strongly that the established channels of industrial research were competent to do the job and ought not to be disturbed; Maverick argued heatedly for bringing in all of the little fellows.

Now this, dressed up in a different costume, was essentially the same breath-taking specter that had arisen to terrify the godly at the time the Reuther plan was up for consideration. This, again, was the proposal that the nation, beset by great dangers, increase the total of its strength by finding and using to the full all of its previously unused sources of strength. Beyond any ism or manifesto, this idea is revolutionary; for it presupposes a readiness to play the game in an entirely new way, an imaginative confidence that the nation will transcend itself by committing its future, without reservation, to the belief that it has at all levels the stuff that makes for greatness. Ultimately, it is this affirmation: What we are now is less than the shadow on the wall of what we can be if we trust ourselves.

All in all, a large idea for a modest committee of five overworked men; too large to be resolved, obviously. What the committee did, at last, was send to Nelson a dead-pan report which recommended the establishment in WPB of an Office of Technical Development empowered to co-ordinate active research projects, to use all available research facilities, to sponsor tested projects, to disseminate scientific information, and to give full consideration to all new proposals. This would fit either the Maverick or the Leith point of view, depending on the way in which the recommendation was put into effect. The report contained little hint of the deep disagreement which had split the committee.

The covering memo which Maverick sent to Nelson was not dead-pan, however. With a lofty disregard of normal government formality (after all, Maverick was the man who invented the word "gobbledegook" to describe regular governmental language), he headed the memo: "Report of Scientific Committee; Recommendations for Office of Technical Development; It is

Bloody Urgent." Then he went on to insist that WPB "must openly, freely, and honestly go into the matter of patents and new processes" and that it must approach the whole problem with the determination not to allow "certain special interests or individuals to get a superior interest over the public and the single will to victory." And just to give Nelson a fill-in on the current rumor that the five committeemen had been having quite a time with one another, Maverick added this paragraph:

"I can report to you now and authoritatively that the general relations of various elements who have been 'talking about each other' are much better now than when we started the committee hearings. However, I detect certain undertones of underground conflict wherein certain persons refer to each other by such names as 'politicians,' 'phuddy-duddies,' 'monopolists,' and the like. In MY opinion, certain persons referring to 'politicians' are THEMSELVES *politicians*, while there is much to be gained from some of the phuddy-duddies. In other words, all together, with the spirit of the Three Musketeers, we can win the war; and yet I must warn that there is much more to these hearings than would appear on the surface."

Having said which, Maverick closed his memo with the reiteration: "But the matter is bloody urgent, and I choose my words with care."

Dr. Leith was quite aware that Maverick was trying to put some backspin on the committee's innocent report. In a letter to his own superior, Alec Henderson, who was then in charge of WPB's assorted materials branches, Dr. Leith noted that "Mr. Maverick has transferred his effort to Don Nelson to get immediate action along the line of his philosophy," and added:

"A plan is being drawn up by one of the members of the Planning Board who is in touch with Maverick to establish a corporation with large funds to take over and promote new technological inventions and ideas and keep them out of the hands of business."

Quite correct. The Maverick committee might have turned in a compromise report, but Maverick's underlying idea had been picked up by a man who at that moment drew a great deal of water around WPB—Robert Nathan, author of the Victory Program and head of Nelson's official brain trust. Not long after becoming chairman of WPB, Nelson had made Nathan head of a three-man Planning Committee with broad authority to formulate and propose for the chairman such policies and programs as Nathan thought necessary; and the Planning Committee was now taking Maverick's plan and giving it some top-drawer elaboration.

Specifically, the Planning Committee presently recommended to Nelson that the Office of Technical Development be established as Maverick's group had proposed; but it further urged that there be set up under this office a War Research Development Corporation, with a capitalization of $100,000,000 and with complete authority to carry on scientific research in a wide variety of fields, to test new industrial processes, to build pilot plants, and to construct factories for the exploitation of processes or techniques which needed to be brought into full-scale operation. The Office of Technical Development would be the skipper of the operation, sifting technical ideas and suggestions and determining just what the country's important unfilled needs might be; aggressive development along the lines thus indicated would then be undertaken by the Corporation, and there would be a broad-gauge program not merely to provide industry with new processes and products but to make sure that the new processes and products were extensively used once they were provided.

This really added up to the most far-reaching, fundamental change that had yet been proposed by anyone in connection with the war program. If the Reuther plan had reached into the office of industrial management, this one reached straight into the board rooms and the counting houses. For what this proposal actually said was substantially this: If there is, or by any exertion of our best intelligence can be, any technical means whatever for increasing the productivity of our industry, then our government is going to see to it that it is used to the absolute maximum no matter what this does to competitive relationships, profit-and-loss statements, or who-owns-what. Period.

And Donald Nelson, the solid and conservative man of business from Chicago, promptly accepted the proposal and prepared to put it into effect. In his Vincennes speech he had said that fear of change was not going to hold him back. Perhaps he really meant it.

Perhaps other men did too, for that matter. Have a brief look at the Planning Committee which formulated and recommended the proposal.

The Planning Committee had three members. Its chairman, Nathan, was a kiver-to-kiver New Dealer, having come to the defense organizations from a spot as career economist and bright-young-man in the Department of Commerce. The second member, Thomas Blaisdell, was another New Dealer, drafted by the defense agencies from the National Resources Planning Board, the very seal and symbol of all that was abhorrent in government planning. But the third member was a crusty gentleman of the Republican persuasion named Fred Searls, Jr., and he was a solid and substantial mining engineer from private industry, about as much of a New Deal theorist as Senator Taft. Searls indorsed the new program along with the theorists, and in a letter to Nathan, written June 7, 1942, he explained why.

Previously, Searls said, he had opposed the Maverick plan, partly because of his own close friendship with Dr. Leith. Now, however, he was all for it; he had been forced to change his mind by facts recently uncovered "establishing the buck-passing procedure which has for the past several months successfully prevented utilization of the Schmidt process for the continuous nitration of glycerin by the Western Cartridge Co., which has a most urgent need for the use of this process."

Western Cartridge, Searls pointed out, was making a special explosive, on government contract, for rockets and other new weapons. To make this it desperately needed to use the Schmidt process, but in spite of the fact that there was a war on there seemed to be a great many reasons why the process could not be made available by its owners. Searls himself had done a good deal of work on the case and he was frankly fed up; he was convinced, he said, "that this whole situation is based on the fact that Western Cartridge does not belong to the 'club'" of high-powered corporations which held the Schmidt process. Acidly, Searls declared that "to further hamper the efforts to get production from them (i.e., from Western Cartridge) which cannot be had elsewhere, through the fear of giving them information that they might utilize commercially in competition with others after the war, should no longer be tolerated." And he concluded that "you can put me down as backing Mr. Maverick in his belief in the necessity for revision of the present setup."

It was exactly the point Searls touched on—the possible post-war effect of a genuinely all-out effort—that was upsetting people just then. It was easy to agree that WPB must have a center to direct scientific and technical research on production; the real question was whether such a center should have limited or un-limited objectives, because if the objectives were unlimited the changes in production processes which would occur were practi-cally certain to bring changes in the very basis of the production mechanism. But the striving for unlimited objectives is, by defi-nition, an essential part of an all-out war; and America's all-out war effort was in the hands of the War Production Board, most of whose big-wigs could face practically anything except the prospect of postwar change.

Nevertheless, Nelson had accepted the proposal just as Maver-ick and Nathan had outlined it. It remained to find a man who could run the new show.

This quest was a tough one. The fate of the whole venture would depend on the selection of a man who would be in charge. He had to be someone who was unassailable; a man with a good technical background but one who, as Stein had said, would be capable of making decisions the technicians were afraid to make; neither a New Dealer nor an industrialist with corporate ties; a man of unquestioned competence, acceptable both to the sponsors and to the opponents of unlimited production measures. If such a man could be found and installed, the long fight would be over; the very qualities that insured his approval would mean that he would take the Maverick-Nathan thesis and develop it to the hilt.

Nelson's choice finally fell on Colonel Royal B. Lord, of the Army Engineers. Lord seemed to fill all of the specifications. A regular army man with a brilliant record, he had been detailed to the Board of Economic Warfare, where he was then serving as assistant director, to the great satisfaction of the exacting Milo Perkins. The choice suited Nathan and Maverick to a T; they had seen a good bit of Lord when he served on a committee to study the possibilities of large cargo aircraft, and they liked the way he handled problems, his receptiveness to new ideas, and his obvious ability as an organizer and an executive. Lord's own concept of the job ahead is revealed in a letter he wrote to one of Nelson's assistants that summer, discussing the Office of Technical Development: "I am convinced that the Director of the Office should not have strong affiliations with large industry in view of the many criticisms that may be directed at this individual if patents or processes are commandeered by the government from industry." At the same time, Lord's record and his prestige were good enough to insure that the opposition would not quarrel with his nomination. Nelson wrote to Milo Perkins, who agreed to surrender Colonel Lord to WPB; then Nelson wrote to the Chief of Staff, General George C. Marshall, and asked that Colonel Lord be officially detailed to WPB as Director of the Office of Technical Development.

At which point a monkey wrench fell into the machinery. The War Department, thus reminded of Colonel Lord's existence, discovered that he could on no account be spared. On August 10 General Marshall wrote Nelson that "the shortage of experienced regular army officers will not permit the detail of Colonel Lord at this time." The War Department, said the General, had been concerned for a long time over the number of army officers who were on duty with civilian agencies, filling jobs which might just as well be filled by civilians, and steps were being taken to recall those officers for duty with the troops. It did not appear, the General continued, that the job Nelson had in mind for Colonel Lord really required an officer of Engineers. Therefore—sorry, no dice.

This did not simply mean that Nelson was out one director for his new office; as things worked out, it meant that the whole argument over the scope and functions of the proposed office was to be reopened. What had been a closed issue suddenly became wide open again.

Colonel Lord had been the one sure-fire choice. His removal from the scene meant, in effect, that Nelson had to shop around for a man, and in the process of shopping around all of the pressures for putting in a safe and sane man to do a safe and sane job would automatically be renewed. Lacking a director, the new office could not be formally set up; as long as it was not set up, the decision to set it up along the Maverick-Nathan line was not final; and if that decision was not final the various contestants were right back where they started, with the difference that the opposition was now thoroughly aroused while the proponents of the plan were obliged to fight with one hand because they had other pressing matters to attend to.

Nelson could not give more than a fragment of his attention to the Office of Technical Development in that August of 1942. The famous "rubber crisis"—which, by the way, was just the sort of thing an Office of Technical Development would have headed off—was just coming to a boil, with the Baruch Committee preparing its report. More urgent than this, even, was Nelson's bitter argument with the War Department over the feasibility of the war production program—an argument which not only consumed most of Nelson's attention but took practically all of Nathan's and the Planning Committee's. After having resisted for so many months all attempts to get the sights raised, the War Department had finally plunged ahead in patriotic fervor and raised them clear up to the moon. Instead of calling on the economy for much less than it could do the Department was now calling on it for much more than it could do, and it was translating this call into firm contracts specifying fixed delivery dates and quantities of material. Nelson and Nathan were fighting desperately to persuade the military men to grasp the simple industrial fact that to put a genuine overload on the nation's productive system would be disastrous. They had to show the Army men that industrial capacity was limited, while at the same time they sought to make an unlimited effort to increase that capacity.

And this was more of a handicap than the new project could carry. There never was a chance to get the War Production Board to sponsor such a far-reaching venture unless Nelson himself could make a continuous, overriding drive for it; and after the Army pulled the plug by removing Colonel Lord it simply was not possible for Nelson to make that kind of drive. The Office of Technical Development remained a paper creation, and the original report of the Maverick Committee came to look more and more like a preliminary study which ought to be supplemented by a report from recognized scientists and technicians; and at last, by mid-September, the battle had been lost and Maverick was sadly writing to Monsignor Miller, "insofar as this particular operation is concerned I have done all I can."

For by this time Nelson had pulled in his horns. Sometime in September, one of Nathan's assistants on the Planning Committee staff took a draft of the proposed order setting up the new office over to the War Department, to discuss it with an opposite number in the Army Air Force, and it came to the attention of Under-Secretary of War Patterson, who reacted promptly and sternly. Patterson wrote a sharp note to Nelson, protesting the whole scheme on the ground that it would duplicate work already being done and would make it harder to maintain secrecy about new scientific developments in the military field. Nelson's reply, on October 1, disclosed that the WPB chairman had dropped the fight. The projected order, he told Patterson, "never had my approval and was merely a suggestion proposed by Colonel Lord as a basis for fuller consideration." WPB, he added, did need some kind of central scientific group to pass on new production processes; and, he concluded, "to review the whole matter and provide recommendations upon which I may make a decision, I am having this whole question studied by a small but highly competent committee of scientific people from whom I expect a report shortly."

That did it. The most ignorant man in town was not going to run the orchestra, after all. The small but highly competent committee was the kind of group Dr. Leith had been urging from the beginning. Its chairman was Dr. Webster N. Jones, Director of Engineering at Carnegie Tech, and its members were scientists and technicians from outside of WPB; and on October 12 it submitted a report stating that WPB should have an Office of Technical Development, under a competent director, to "coordinate technical efforts," pass on new ideas and processes, make use of existing research personnel and facilities, and so on. As a final kicker, the report stipulated that the office should "start with a modest appropriation and should be allowed to grow as its effectiveness is demonstrated."

In the end it was so ordered. Early in November the new office, now named the Office of Production Research and Development, was formally opened under the directorship of Dr. Harvey N. Davis, president of Stevens Institute of Technology. There was a last minute effort to save some vestige of the original idea, by inserting in the administrative order a proviso that "the director shall secure from the Alien Property Custodian information on foreign patents and shall make full utilization of patents important to war production." But this was stricken out, as was another paragraph that would have required the director to

137

"make a comprehensive survey of national research facilities, including laboratories, scientists, engineers, and technicians, so that these resources may be utilized most effectively in the war production program." The program went ahead, did a considerable amount of useful work before the war ended, and disturbed nobody; and the War Production Board was not, after all, compelled to "think about things which in normal times would appear ridiculous."

In the end Maverick had the last word, after all, although by that time matters had reached the stage where words did not make any particular difference. He became chairman of the Smaller War Plants Corporation, and in 1946 he transmitted to the Senate Small Business Committee a report of the Corporation entitled "Economic Concentration and World War II."

This report showed that during the war the government spent nearly one billion dollars for scientific research in industrial laboratories (exclusive of money spent on atomic research). This money went to some two thousand industrial organizations; the ten largest got two-fifths of it—say $400,000,000—and the 68 largest got two-thirds of the total. After pointing out that this centralization of research would almost inevitably increase the existing concentration of economic power—since the peacetime uses and applications of the technical knowledge gained at government expense would be enormous—the report of Maverick's corporation continued:

"Obviously, the companies in whose laboratories this research work has been carried on will be its chief beneficiaries, not only because of their direct acquaintanceship and knowledge of the research but also because of patents. The investigations of the Subcommittee on War Mobilization of the Senate Military Affairs Committee show that over 90 per cent of the contracts made between government agencies and private industrial laboratories for scientific research and development placed the ownership of patents with the contractor, the government receiving a royalty-free license for its own use. . . . This means, in effect, that the large corporations which carried on the great bulk of the federally financed wartime industrial research will have control, through patents, of the commercial applications of that research."

Maybe it really was bloody urgent, at that.

CHAPTER TWELVE

Something Beyond Victory

LIKE a genial and slightly owlish bonze in steel-rimmed spectacles, Donald Nelson settled himself comfortably in the chair at one end of the table and looked dutifully at the big easel at the end of the room. This was a fairly busy day—he had been chairman of WPB for no more than a month, and his time was pretty well occupied—but the advertising agency people had come all the way from Detroit and the least he could do was look at the agency's presentation.

An agency presentation is one of those landmarks on mankind's long journey upward from the primitive stage of communication by grunts and sign language. You have an idea and you want to tell people about it, so you get them together in a room. But instead of just telling them, you have your idea written out in a series of punchy, one-sentence paragraphs, and you print each paragraph in large colored letters on a yard-long cardboard placard, and you hang all of the placards on an easel. Then you stand beside the easel with a long pointer in your hand while a stooge flips the pages; and as each sentence comes up you point to it, and—in case anyone present happens to be inattentive, or nearsighted, or slightly illiterate—you read it aloud as you point. After half an hour you run out of placards, the presentation is over, and your audience departs, a bit numb, perhaps, but deeply impressed.

So it was on this February morning in the Social Security Building. The Detroit agency was unfolding for the WPB chairman an idea for stimulating war production. The idea was aimed squarely at the honest working man—who, it was felt, ought to be made to realize that there was a war on, so that he would work harder, and in patriotic fervor would abstain from yelling for higher wages—and it was filled with straight-from-the-shoulder exhortations and admonitions, devised and phrased by experts in the art of breaking down sales resistance. The general theme (for each presentation has to have a theme, and there is no nonsense about being afraid to say the same thing six or eight times, either) which permeated all of the placards was the slogan: "You *Too* Can Be a Hero!"

The presentation finally ended, Nelson thanked the agency people politely and went back to his office, and there were no untoward remarks—except for a muttered "Well, for Christ's sake!" which Information Director Horton felt either unable or unwilling to suppress. The agency people returned to Detroit, leaving their idea to germinate if by chance it had dropped upon fallow soil. . . . Here it is, Mr. Nelson, and if the War Production Board would like to use this in all of the war plants in America we would be glad to be helpful; we are currently using it in the Zilch factories in the Detroit area, and it seems to be most effective. We would of course contribute the services of our agency gratis; and those services, bought in the open market, come high—the expense of the brain-power that went into the preparation of this presentation would be enough to keep all of the Social Security Building stenographers in stockings for a year. Which might not be a bad way to spend the money, at that. . . .

This was the winter of 1942, and in a world where many things were obscure one point was crystal clear, to Nelson and to many others: it was going to be necessary to make munitions in enormous volume and at tremendous speed, and these munitions were going to have to be made by people, most of whom had got themselves organized into labor unions of one kind or another. It seemed (so went the prevailing thesis) to be up to somebody to make sure that these people put forth their best efforts at all times.

But—up to just whom? To the industrialists who employed the workers? That might be fine, except for the fact that the channels of communication between worker and employer did not appear to be completely free from sinuosities and obstructions. Furthermore, the industrialists had a way of doing their talking through advertising agencies and public relations experts, and the presentation which Nelson and Horton sat through was a fair sample of what came out of that kind of spigot. Patriotism —the great intangible, which could pull the unpurchasable out of men's hearts—was looked upon by these gentlemen as something which had to be sold just as a new depilatory is sold. It was to be sold in the same way, using the same techniques, by the same expert salesmen, infused by the same cynical contempt for human intelligence and human motives; and the salesmen could hardly be expected to notice if, in the process, the product being sold happened to be debased to the depilatory level. (It was just about at this time that some ardent soul in the WPB Information Division, wearying of the advertising approach toward the problems of democracy's greatest war, doodled himself a fancy poster. I don't remember exactly how it went, except that it began, in heavy red letters: "The War That Refreshes—Try Those Four Delicious Freedoms!" Horton threw it away, lest some dollar-a-year man see it, take it seriously, and order it put up on billboards all across the land.)

Clearly, the whole proposition called for some careful thinking. Nelson definitely was not going for the You *Too* Can Be a Hero stuff, but the underlying problem was still there: there had to be some way to communicate with the man at the machine. Since Horton was prepared to bleed and die to prevent adoption of the theory that the ordinary citizen needed to be advertised into supporting the war, it was up to Horton to find the way.

It wasn't too hard to figure out, once you stopped thinking of the man at the machine as The Worker, who was in a class apart and had to be sold something, and began thinking of him simply as another American citizen who wanted to know what the score was. What this man needed, Horton believed, was information—no more and no less. He needed to know about the size and urgency of the job his own shop was doing, its relation to the war as a whole, the tie-in between his own daily stint and the progress of the effort to lick the Axis. Take, for example, the man at work in a factory that produced valves—just valves, useful but extremely uninspiring. It might be very hard for this man to see any direct connection between his daily job and the winning of the war, since as far as he could tell the factory was making exactly the same kind of valves it had been making for the past dozen years, and since he had no idea what they were going to be used for anyway. Unless someone spelled it out for him he could hardly be expected to know that unless America produced three times as many valves as it had ever produced before it would have neither the navy nor the merchant ships which it had to have in order to wage war successfully. This worker didn't need to be scolded and cajoled into working harder; he simply needed to be given the facts that would reveal to him the crucial importance of his own prosaic job. Once he got that information—well, he was an American, this was his war, and he could be trusted to do the rest. If he couldn't be so trusted, the theory and practice of democracy were both so defective that it didn't matter greatly whether Hitler got licked or not.

Horton therefore got together a staff of technically qualified people and began preparing to produce posters, banners, and the like for use in war plants—material designed to inform rather than to entreat.

But that was only the first step. Producing the stuff was fairly easy, given the proper approach; the next step was to move the material into the factories and to make sure that the workers for whom it was designed would actually pay a little attention to it after it got there. The government, of course, could simply send a bale of the material off to each factory manager with the injunction, "Put this on display where your workers can see it"; but the big idea was not just to have the material put on display but to have it create a visible effect in the form of fast, sustained production, and there was plenty of reason to suspect that the worker was not going to pay very much attention to anything that was handed down from above. In addition, a great deal of the material would have to be specially designed for individual factories. The men in the John Smith Plant No. 1 wanted to know just what the gadgets they were making meant to the war effort, what they were used for, what the finished product actually looked like, and how it helped beat Hitler; they wanted to know how many they were supposed to make, how much of a rush there was, whether they were behind schedule, and if so how much of a push they needed to make to catch up. And no group of experts could sit down in Washington and work all of that out for them on a mass production basis.

It began to look as if the worker himself ought to have a hand in the whole operation.

This checked with the advice Horton was getting from Sidney Hillman's Labor Division. Hillman's people had learned a thing or two about labor co-operation since the defense effort began. Labor appeared to be co-operative enough whenever it was allowed to share in directing the operation in which it was supposed to co-operate. A deep and abiding cynicism in regard to the aims, statements, and good faith of management was certainly evident, and this in turn created a latent cynicism toward almost any kind of appeal or pep talk from the outside. But this was just the obverse side of the coin; if labor did not care to be talked down to, and if it was inclined to suspect that hurry-hurry-hurry slogans from the front office were just another effort by the bosses to get something for nothing, it was definitely responsive whenever it was treated as a full partner in the undertaking.

As Horton talked his posters and streamers over with Hillman's men, the application to his own immediate problem was clear. If he had a job lot of information aimed at the men in the factories, and if much of this needed to be specially tailored for the individual plants, and if some direct and acceptable system of distribution was called for, why not turn the job over to the labor people themselves? Make labor itself, in other words, responsible for appealing to labor for the extra effort that was required to keep production up; was that the answer?

Not quite. The factories in which all of this was to take place were, after all, owned by stockholders, not by labor unions; and if labor had a good part of the responsibility for increasing production, the rest of the responsibility indubitably rested on management. Furthermore, management was just as cynical regarding labor's aims and motives as labor was about those of management. To set the whole business up as a straight labor union operation looked like a deal that couldn't be rammed down the throat of industrial management with anything less than a pile driver.

The logic of the situation thus pointed toward some sort of joint effort by labor and management. This was what Hillman's men recommended; also, it was what the British had been doing for some little time, with excellent results. (Horton got a study of the British experience from David Wills, press man in Washington for the British Supply Council. Wills cabled London for a detailed report, and Horton shaped his own plans in the light of the British operation. Wills subsequently was reprimanded by his own bosses for being so helpful, possibly on the ground that labor-management co-operation wasn't a fit topic for discussion on His Majesty's cables, but this happened too late to do any harm.)

Once the joint-operation idea took hold, the whole subject began to broaden. Herbert Harris, one of Hillman's aides, suggested that it needn't be confined just to the collection and distribution of information about the need for greater output; why not let it include some means by which the workers themselves could contribute any ideas they might have about ways to increase production? If the man in the shop had found a short cut to some production operation, why shouldn't this short cut be passed on to other workers? If the men in one plant found a good way to arouse a healthy competitive spirit which raised production rates, shouldn't there be a way to make their scheme available to men in other factories? In short, why not go all out with the project and have a joint labor-management operation responsible for doing practically everything that might be needed to make the production effort fully effective?

There was in all of this a groping toward something incalculable. . . . Labor is more than brawn and skill, hired by the week and paid by the hour, and there is in these men at the bench and the machine a resource we have never begun to use. The economics of war are cockeyed and are not to be found in any textbook, war is production-for-use carried to the highest power; and if industry's sole function now is to produce, then half the responsibility is labor's and nothing is needed as much as a recognition of that fact and a means of making the responsibility bear its fruit. Our whole struggle for survival in this war is a struggle to find how much we can do by extending the pattern of our democracy, and here is a good place to begin. . . . This was implicit in the new plan for labor-management co-operation, and Horton took the completed program to Nelson with high hopes.

Nelson went for the idea with enthusiasm. It tied in with one of his favorite wartime theories—that the American people would do anything that was asked of them, provided that they fully understood what it was all about and believed they were being treated fairly. This looked to Nelson like the ideal means for showing the men in the factories what the big push was all about, and the joint labor-management operation seemed likely to convince all hands that they were getting fair treatment. Furthermore, buried away where he could not easily bring it out and talk about it, there was in Nelson's make-up a deep, instinctive feeling for democracy, and this project struck him as a seed from which a genuine industrial democracy might grow. It drew from him an emotional reaction such as few other WPB programs ever got; to the end of the war he took about as much pride in having sponsored and pushed through the labor-management committee system as in anything he had done.

With Nelson's blessing, Horton got tentative approval from the War and Navy Departments and from the Maritime Commission. Then came the task of obtaining a formal directive from the White House. That worked out like this:

First Nelson talked to the President about the general idea and discovered that the President liked it just as much as he did. Then Nelson's aides drafted a letter for the President's signature, addressed to Nelson and instructing him to "take every possible step to raise production" and "to bring home to labor and management alike the supreme importance of war production this crucial spring." This letter was sent over to the White House, put on White House stationery, signed by the President, and formally transmitted to Nelson. Nelson, in turn, wrote a reply stating that in obedience to the President's instructions he was going ahead with a big campaign in all war plants which would involve, among other things, the establishment of joint committees "to consider suggestions from all quarters for increasing production." And finally these letters were made public, and it was announced that Nelson would go on the air to explain the proposition to the nation.

So far everything had been plain sailing. What had begun as an attempt to find a way to get patriotic posters into war plants had evolved into a device for enabling the worker to contribute his own ideas about ways to increase production. But it seemed that there were misgivings about it. This project did vest in the worker a measure of responsibility for successful operation of the plant, and to a man of nervous temperament and solid conservative leanings this might look like the camel's nose coming under the edge of the tent. Horton ran into these misgivings a day or so after the campaign was publicly announced, when he went to an interagency meeting and heard a civilian from the Navy Department denounce the plan as a scheme "to sovietize American industry." Shortly afterward he discovered that Nelson had begun to hear the same complaint.

Nelson made his broadcast over a national hookup, announcing the plan and calling for the formation of joint committees in war plants all across the country. A couple of days later he called Horton into his office. Horton found the WPB chairman looking glum and harassed.

"Bob," said Nelson, "this just can't go on."

"What can't?" asked Horton.

"This labor-management program. It's just raising hell among the businessmen. People are calling me up from all over. They don't like it, they're afraid of it, they're saying it won't work, they're calling it another of Roosevelt's revolutionary ideas. Honestly, Bob, it's got me down to the point where I think I'll go back to Chicago."

Horton meditated briefly. He knew Nelson well enough by now to know that Nelson did not intend his "I think I'll go back to Chicago"—uttered privately, within four walls—to be understood as an actual statement of intention to resign; it was simply Nelson's way of saying that he was baffled and bruised. For Nelson, called to serve in a spot which guaranteed his participation in at least one major fight a week, was a lover of peace. The slings and arrows he encountered along the way never deflected him from his purpose, but they certainly did make him suffer en route. He was suffering now, visibly.

"Who has been calling you up?" asked Horton.

"Lots of people. Charlie Wilson called me."

"Which Charlie Wilson?"

(It was an oddity of the industrial war effort that among the captains of industry on whom the government most relied for munitions production there were two corporation chieftains named Charles E. Wilson: the president of General Motors and the president of General Electric. General Motors Wilson had been a frequent visitor to Washington during OPM days, when ill fate cast him in the role of target for the implacable Leon Henderson; General Electric Wilson had been down less often, was known as an all-outer.)

"Both Charlie Wilsons," said Nelson.

"What did they say?"

Nelson brightened a bit.

"Well, General Motors Wilson is against the whole idea. He doesn't want to have a thing to do with it. But the other Wilson is all for it. He asked me: 'When can we get going on this? Do we have to wait for a government man to come up here and set it up, or can we go ahead on our own hook?' "

Horton grinned.

"Did anybody tell you that this is a scheme to sovietize American industry?"

"Oh, Lord, yes. I meant to tell you. A lot of people said that. I tell you, Bob, a good many businessmen are awfully scared of this program."

The point that worried Horton was not Nelson's mood of discouragement. That would pass; it was just part of the price Nelson paid every so often for being the man he was. The troublesome part was this recurring remark about sovietizing American industry. That phrase was appearing altogether too frequently; so frequently that it couldn't be entirely accidental. It began to smell as if the same kind of brains that knew all about selling depilatories had cooked up a slogan and injected it into the industrialists' blood stream, and while there wasn't much danger that Nelson himself would be infected, the situation could easily reach the point where he would be seriously handicapped in putting over the labor-management plan.

But at this moment Adolf Hitler himself came to the rescue.

A few days after Nelson had blown off steam, Horton brought to his desk a State Department intercept of a German radio broadcast. In this broadcast Hitler had taken note of Nelson's plan to set up joint labor-management committees in war plants. Reminding his countrymen that Germany was the one unfailing bulwark against Bolshevism, Hitler had exultantly branded the Nelson scheme as "a plan to sovietize American industry." Nelson quoted the intercept in full in a second radio talk, and the slogan dropped out of circulation without a trace. Maybe the boys had done their work too well.

Panic in the upper income brackets having subsided, Nelson turned his attention to the letters and telegrams that came in following his first two broadcasts. There were many thousands of them—so many that after the first two or three days his office staff gave up all pretense of trying to acknowledge them all—and they were almost uniformly favorable. (One that struck Nelson particularly was a penciled note from a member of a longshoremen's union on the west coast. This writer condemned the bosses up, down, and across as connivers and enemies of the working man; but co-operation was worth trying, the war had to be won and everybody had to work together—and as for the bosses, "we'll fix their wagons after the war.") The writers of these letters were not in the least worried about sovietizing American industry; something in this labor-management plan had touched their imaginations and aroused their hopes. It was almost as if this limited and imperfect program, devised so hastily and introduced with so little preparation, appeared to the people to be a sign and a portent regarding the path that America must travel. They were looking for something beyond victory, they wanted bread instead of a stone, they wanted to see democracy working somewhere besides the polling booth, and maybe this was it.

Maybe. At any rate, wobbling on its pins but tolerably healthy for all that, the labor-management system was brought into being. Careful rules were laid down to keep the venture from getting out of hand. The joint committees were to do anything and everything that would increase production, but they definitely were not collective-bargaining groups or grievance committees. Over and over again, Nelson tirelessly reiterated that this was neither a means for enabling labor to take over the factories nor a dodge whereby management could take over control of the unions; it was just co-operation, and its one aim was to help win the war. The rules were codified and distributed, machinery was set up in Washington to run the whole operation, and eventually joint committees were established in some five thousand factories.

In the long run the committees were useful. The WPB files list many hundreds of devices for speeding and increasing production that were brought forth, and contain innumerable letters from individual plants testifying to the value of the joint-committee system. In the aggregate, the program unquestionably added substantially to the volume of munitions production. Some of the best work done by the committees probably was in connection with that complex of problems which, lumped together, came to be known as "absenteeism." Not only did the committees find ways to remove this evil; they showed that it was not just a display of cussedness by unpatriotic workers but was the result of perfectly tangible causes which could be found and removed, if anyone took the trouble, so that there was no point in merely trying to scold the evil out of existence via newspaper editorials, speeches in Congress, or pronouncements by angry cabinet members—of which manifestations, from one end of the war to the other, the country had rather more than enough. All in all, the joint-committee system was well worth what it cost.

But in the first bright flush of dawn it had looked as if it might be worth a great deal more than that—as if it might be a bold and daring attempt to work out a new pattern for industrial democracy, desperately needed then, desperately needed today. That hope was never realized. It remained unrealized because too many men were afraid of what might happen if the attempt were made. This venture in co-operation by labor and management was limited by fear, and the fear was born of the deep suspicion, jealousy, and enmity which existed between labor and management—the very elements which made the venture necessary in the first place. That fear was never overridden; instead, it was specifically recognized and accepted, and nothing was ever done to remove its causes. In the middle of 1943, for instance— more than a year after the plan had been launched—WPB felt it necessary to issue a statement over the signatures of the four recognized leaders of labor and industry: William Green and Philip Murray, for labor, Frederick Crawford, of the National Association of Manufacturers, and Eric Johnson, of the U. S. Chamber of Commerce, for management. This statement said:

"The labor-management committee program now being promoted by the War Production Drive Division of WPB, under the direction of Mr. T. K. Quinn, endorsed by us, is not designed to increase the power or position of any union. It does not interfere with any bargaining machinery or undertake its functions. It is not designed to conform to any scheme that contemplates a measure of control of management by labor or labor by management. It does not put management in labor or labor in management. It is not a labor plan or a management plan. It is the War Production Drive Plan to increase production by increasing efficiency through greater management and labor co-operation."

Taking one thing with another, this is probably the most completely negative bit of sales talk in the history of salesmanship —a move to sell something, not by explaining what it was but by emphasizing what it was not. Is the highway to a better democracy paved with that kind of talk? Why was it necessary to get the top men in labor and industry to issue this baffling and extended catalog of it-is-not's? What was Banquo's ghost doing at this feast, anyhow?

After the war, Nelson remarked of the labor-management plan: "The whole thing strikes me as just one more proof of the most valuable lesson that we got out of the war—our American democracy *works*, and it works better than any other economic and political system on earth."

Which is, certainly, one way of looking at it, a way that can be argued for and justified. But if American democracy on the industrial sector worked during the war, the record indicates that it worked under conditions much like an armed truce. The bitter, deeply rooted hostility and suspicion which made the it-is-not statement necessary and caused its strange, negative phraseology—this remained, untouched by anything industrial democracy was able to do in the course of winning the war, and in the years following VJ-Day we had an excellent glimpse of its fruits.

We brought this condition of hostility and suspicion out of the war because we had it when we went in, and we faithfully bound ourselves—having taken counsel of our fears—not to fight the war in such a way as to make any basic changes in the conditions that prevailed before the war began. The joint committees were useful, and they grew out of honorable motives, and high hopes attended their birth; but any hope higher than the hope that the Axis might be defeated was not destined to be realized.

The whole chain of it-is-not explanations amounted to a signboard for a people at war: Whatever it was you were looking for, this isn't it.

CHAPTER THIRTEEN

Creation of a Mess

SPEAKING in rather general terms, the government of the United States managed to maintain its reputation as an honest woman until the early summer of 1942. About that time virtue (which is its own reward) became more of a luxury than anyone was prepared to pay for, and the administration began to look for the easiest way out. About all that can be said by the defense is that the fatal first step downward looked like a good idea at the time.

Official Washington was feeling frustrated and harassed, as the spring of 1942 wore away, and there were plenty of reasons. The nation had been at war for several months and victory was not yet in sight. The Philippines and the East Indies had been lost, toppling the historic white man's burden and all that went with it into the dark backward and abysm of time. In Russia the Nazis were getting ready for a new offensive, and no one had any idea whether such an offensive, once started, could ever be stopped. In North Africa German columns were preparing for a dash at the Nile, and people were openly wondering whether Nazi and Jap might not presently be meeting somewhere in the neighborhood of Calcutta. On the east coast of the United States the beaches were smeared with a greasy film of oil and littered with broken lifeboats, debris from wrecked steamers and corpses of merchant seamen, in testimony to the appallingly effective work of the German submarines.

And at home nobody could buy a new automobile tire, which seemed to be what bothered Washington most of all and was the proximate cause of the government's stately descent from virtue.

The most sensitive single nerve in American life had been touched with an iron finger, violently, and the administration reacted with unco-ordinated vigor. It was bad enough, in all conscience, to reflect that the war might be lost for lack of rubber; it was even worse to consider how the average American might feel if, through official bungling or the contrariness of fate, he was prevented from making free use of his own auto.

Facing this prospect, the government simply lost its nerve. It was prepared to do whatever needed to be done to provide the necessary rubber, but it emphatically was not prepared to look the people in the eye and say that pleasure driving had to stop—which, in the end, was exactly what it was obliged to do. It went to great lengths to avoid doing this, and it thereby created an unholy mess—the famous "rubber mess," which was such a burning issue in the summer of 1942. This mess, like the rubber itself, was synthetic, created by man and not a natural growth. It came into being because President and Congress assumed that the American people were neither bright enough nor brave enough to face hard facts without flinching; it was a phony, and in the end it had to be removed by resort to a phony solution. And it was at this point that the government fell into sin.

It was of course perfectly true that the rubber problem had been sadly mishandled from the start of the defense program. Bill Batt, who called things just as he saw them, made this clear in testimony before the Truman Committee on March 24, 1942. Batt was in no mood to pull his punches; he flatly told the Senators that "you and I are not going to get an automobile tire for the length of this emergency." Then he went on to explain why.

He made an impressive witness. Physically solid, graying, with pleasantly bushy eyebrows, Batt in his lighter moments had a way of making you feel that he would make an ideal uncle, if an uncle was what you needed—and not just because he was so eminently solvent, either; but today he was grim, and so was his message, and the Truman Committee listened attentively.

As far back as the summer of 1940, Batt recalled, he had been made chairman of a committee set up by the Defense Commission to survey the rubber situation. Early in September of that year his committee submitted a report asserting that America's capacity to make synthetic rubber—then about 5,000 tons a year— should be expanded as quickly as possible to at least 100,000 tons. This, the committee felt, would cover the needs for strictly war purposes, and in case of an emergency would tide the country over until more synthetic rubber plants could be built.

The Defense Commission tried to get this program translated into actual factory capacity, Batt continued, but was balked by the indomitable banker's caution of Mr. Jesse Jones, the boss of the Reconstruction Finance Corporation, which would have to provide the money to finance construction of the projected factories.

"Mr. Jones," said Batt quietly, "thought we were much too pessimistic and were making a rather wasteful approach."

The upshot, he added, was that the plants were not built.

By now, he said, a program had been established, contracts had been signed—the turn of events, apparently, having convinced Jones that this was no longer to be considered wasteful—and construction of the new plants was under way. But it was going to be a tight squeeze. Leaving entirely out of consideration any question of rubber to make tires for civilians, and taking into account only the rubber that had to be produced in order to win the war, this brand new synthetic rubber industry would have to turn out at least 300,000 tons of the stuff in 1943. That, said Batt, would just meet the most urgent needs; also, it was very close to the most that could possibly be done no matter what magic might be exercised. The deduction was inescapable: no new tires for civilians, now or at any time in the visible future.

This was clear enough as far as it went. The problem had been botched before Pearl Harbor, and if apportioning the blame was important, it was obvious that Jesse Jones didn't deserve all of it; OPM was entitled to some, too, for it had failed to push through either an adequate synthetic program or a proper stock-piling program. But that was water over the dam, by the spring of 1942. What mattered then was the question: Are we doing all that must be done in order to meet our essential needs for rubber?

Interestingly enough, by the time Batt went before the Truman Committee the rubber program was beginning to make pretty good sense.

Shortly after he organized the War Production Board, Nelson had made Arthur Newhall head of the Rubber Branch, expanding his authority a bit later to make him Rubber Co-ordinator; the papers referred to Newhall as the "rubber czar," and in a sense the designation was fair enough, since Newhall was in charge of the whole program, although he was a czar with rather limited powers. It was Newhall's misfortune that he was a pleasant, quiet, soft-spoken sort of chap; Washington suffers from a deep unwillingness to believe that a government official is on top of his job unless whatever drive and energy he may possess appear right on the surface, and Newhall was neither the cold, curt, incisive type—like Forrestal of the Navy—nor a hell-for-leather, shouting, desk-thumping character like his own ultimate successor, Bill Jeffers. But he did plan, organize, and get rolling the rubber program that finally carried us through the war, and the "rubber mess" that at last bogged him down was not of his making. Newhall had been a rubber manufacturer for many years, and he had come to WPB from the presidency of a company that made zippers. (He used to keep on his desk a little zipper demonstrator, if that's what you would call it—a four- or five-inch zipper with all the essential parts made out of transparent plastic, so that you could open and close it and see with your own eyes exactly how it operated. It was fascinating, and I used to study it every time I entered Newhall's office, but it didn't do me any good; I still don't understand how zippers work.)

Anyway, Newhall's first step as boss of the rubber program was to find out what the existing situation was. This, it developed, wasn't too promising; if everything that was on paper came out right the country would obtain some 25,000 tons of synthetic in 1942, about 125,000 in 1943, and maybe 400,000 in 1944. When this program was matched against the visible needs for rubber, its inadequacy was quickly apparent. By the latter part of March, Newhall had raised the 1944 program from the original 400,000 tons to 600,000 tons, and during the following month he raised it again to provide for the production of 350,000 tons in 1943 and 800,000 tons in 1944, with plans for supplemental capacity of 200,000 more tons ready for use if it appeared necessary. This program was formally okayed by WPB and, in essence, was the rubber program on which we got through the war.

Actually, therefore, before the great to-do over the rubber problem even started the crisis had been passed; and it was passed without any public outcry whatever, even though it was perfectly clear that no new tires could be made for civilians. By the time Batt went before the Truman Committee there was unanimous agreement that the tires which at that moment were on the wheels of the nation's automobiles were all the tires those automobiles were going to have until the war had been won. This fact had been repeatedly made public, and had been accepted without protest.

Furthermore, by the spring of 1942 an adequate synthetic rubber program was well under way. The processes by which

154

synthetic rubber could be made were understood, the plants in which the rubber would be made were under construction, the importance of providing top priority for their construction had been agreed to by WPB. We were going to have the rubber we needed to win the war, although the margin of safety was going to be narrow.

Where, then, did the "rubber mess" come from?

Primarily, it came from a refusal by the administration to face the facts; or, more accurately, a refusal to admit that the American public could face the facts without recoiling angrily, losing the war, and making life unpleasant for elected officials. (The fact that there was to be a congressional election that fall was one of the imponderables, never mentioned but never forgotten.) The President and Congress simply got scared.

Along with this, by sheer coincidence, was the activity along the Atlantic shore line of the German submarines.

Observe, now, how the various elements which created the mess began to work together.

It really began with the submarines, although they had nothing on earth to do with the supply of rubber.

They had started to swing in close to the coast shortly after Pearl Harbor, and by the middle of the winter they were having a field day. The Navy couldn't stop them; it had pressing commitments in all of the seven seas, it was rushing the biggest naval building program in history, it was converting yachts into patrol vessels and it was using sailing craft for scouting purposes, but it couldn't stop the ravages on coastwise shipping; not right away it couldn't, not until many months had passed, not with the best direction and the most untiring energy in the world. For the moment the cards were stacked in the submarines' favor, and the Nazi skippers made the most of it. They sank American ships faster than new ships were being built; and especially they sank the coastal tankers. This sinking of tankers, furthermore, came just at the moment when military necessity was forcing the Navy to requisition as many tankers as it could lay its hands on for service overseas.

The result was a desperate oil shortage on the eastern seaboard. Before the war, 95 per cent of all the gasoline and fuel oil used by the east coast states came in by tanker. By the spring of 1942 this had been cut to the barest trickle. The railroads were doing

155

their best, but although they raised average weekly tank car shipments from 3,000 to 27,000, the supply still fell far short of needs. Secretary Ickes, who was doubling in brass as Petroleum Co-ordinator, had applied early in the war for steel to build a pipe line. He had been turned down, on the ground that the steel, the pumps, and the valves were more urgently needed elsewhere, and at the time the decision was made it was a perfectly good one; but now the situation had changed beyond all anticipation, WPB had to reverse itself and let the pipe line be built—but it would be a year or more before that could provide any relief. By April the whole east coast was critically short of liquid fuel, and on April 22 Henderson announced that gasoline rationing would be instituted in the seventeen states on or near the eastern seaboard on May 15. The ordinary motorist, he said, would get a basic allowance of something between two and one-half and five gallons a week.

This touched off a furious argument, in which almost everybody joined. Secretary Ickes protested that the cut was too severe. Spokesmen for the oil industry agreed, and asserted that Henderson's plan was "half-baked, ill advised, hit or miss" and "indicative of the lack of intelligent understanding which that government agency has shown in dealing with a problem so vital to the people." There was a confusion of tongues and a blowing of great winds, and it seemed at times as if the proposed rationing rested on no firmer basis than Henderson's malicious desire to make people unhappy. Unperturbed, Henderson went ahead with his plans, the basic ration for motorists was finally set at three gallons a week, and the rationing program got under way on May 15 as advertised.

It was admittedly a stop-gap system, with motorists placed pretty much on their honor to turn in accurate estimates of the amount of gasoline they needed for strictly essential driving; OPA explained that a regular card-rationing system could hardly be perfected and put into operation before July, but the shortage was too pressing to wait that long before cutting down on consumption. (By way of an aside: during the last week before rationing began, both the press and a number of government officials had freely predicted that the final, ration-free week end would see an unprecedented amount of gasoline-buying and pleasure driving, with motorists rushing to beat the gun by taking a final fling, and the selfish thoughtlessness of the American people had been widely deplored in advance. The papers of Monday, May 11, however, revealed that the rush had not taken place; on the contrary, auto traffic in and around eastern cities had been markedly below the normal week-end level, indicating that the people had displayed more good sense than Washington had been willing to expect.) Anyhow, the rationing system went into operation, and eastern consumption of gasoline was reduced to proper levels; but in the process the luckless members of Congress got a sharp jab right where it hurt most.

Under the stop-gap rationing system, OPA had prepared a set of "X" cards, whose holders were entitled to unlimited quantities of gasoline, the theory being that these cards would go to persons whose essential public services made it necessary for them to use their autos without any restriction whatever. Picture, then, the welkin and how it rang, when it was revealed that more than two hundred members of Congress had asked for, and had been given, the greatly desired X cards.

Congress at this time was more than commonly sensitive to public criticism. With singular lack of a good sense of timing, the Congress had chosen the month immediately after Pearl Harbor to pass a law providing pensions for retiring Congressmen. This had aroused a great chorus of criticism, culminating in the derisive "Bundles for Congress" campaign in Washington and Oregon. Congress had hastily canceled the law and the tumult had died down, but the memory lingered; Congress was in a mood to avoid like grim death anything which might look like an attempt to get special favors for Congressmen in wartime. And this business of the X cards reopened the old wound, and Congress came in for a new buffeting. The result, naturally enough, was that the mere idea of gasoline rationing became intensely irritating to the average Congressman; he was conditioned to believe that it was unnecessary, to suspect that Henderson (whom he disliked anyway) was an antisocial monster for putting it into effect, and to feel that the executive branch of the government needed very careful watching.

All of this, to be sure, had nothing whatever to do with the rubber situation. There was a shortage of gasoline and fuel oil on the east coast, and on the east coast alone, due solely to a lack of transportation, which in turn was due solely to the German submarines, and that was all there was to it. But this stop-gap rationing system for the east coast speedily got most thoroughly involved in the very center of the rubber situation and contributed materially to the formation of the "rubber mess."

Because automobile tires wear out.

Fact Number One, admitted by everybody, was this: the tires on your car are all the tires you are going to have until the war ends. From this it followed that something had to be done to preserve those tires. It was not enough to assume that when John Citizen had worn out his tires he could walk, or ride the street cars, or go to and from his job by bus. The country was no longer set up that way. The Japs had waited until America had made the complete transition to the automobile age before cutting off America's supply of crude rubber. People might give up pleasure driving, they might ride buses and street cars, they might walk until they were both blue in the face and sore in the feet; the fact remained that the nation was organized in such a way that the use of the privately owned auto was essential to its ability to go on functioning. Any given individual, chosen at random, might indeed be able to get along after a fashion without his car; no city, no mass-production factory, no essential industry could possibly do so. The vast bulk of America's autos simply had to be kept in operation or the country would come apart at the seams.

(A striking illustration, right there, of the way in which the very existence of a highly organized community modifies traditional ideas about private property rights. A man's auto is indubitably his own personal possession, and he has a right to use it in any way he sees fit; and yet the community can, and in time of crisis must, compel him to use it for the common good rather than for his own.)

This was perfectly evident to the War Production Board, to the War and Navy Departments, to every Washington official who shared responsibility for keeping the nation's war economy in operation. From the first of the year, therefore, a good part of their attention had been directed toward the problem of keeping the rubber tires that were then in use from collapsing before the end of the war.

To do that, clearly, some sort of mileage control had to be devised. The number of miles the citizen's car could be driven had to be rationed. There was no conceivable alternative. But rationed . . . precisely how?

The late Joseph Eastman, head of the Office of Defense Transportation, worked out a system which was theoretically sound enough, involving the use of car stickers, speedometer readings, weekly inspections, and so on, all directed to the end that the motorist should drive no more than necessity compelled. It was a good theory, but it was so obviously unworkable that Eastman never made any converts; indeed, while he argued for his plan he apparently was not too thoroughly converted himself.

Which left exactly one other way to do the job: gasoline rationing.

By early spring Nelson, Henderson, and Newhall were convinced that this was the only course to adopt. They talked to the President about it, and apparently they convinced him; on May 19, at a press conference, the President indicated that he was in favor of nation-wide gasoline rationing in order to save rubber, and said that a rationing plan was being drafted. A few days later Nelson revealed, at his own press conference, that rationing would go into effect just as soon as plans could be worked out; he and Newhall explained that every bit of synthetic rubber that could be made, as well as all existing stocks of crude rubber and reclaimed rubber, would be needed for direct or indirect military use.

And at this point the storm broke. Congress got the proposed nation-wide rationing system hopelessly mixed up with the already-existing east coast rationing and never succeeded in getting the two untangled. It greeted the news with a mixture of confusion and fury—born of such diverse elements as the approaching elections, dislike of Leon Henderson, and the sting left by the X card episode—and it began erupting all over the place, a fair sample being this outburst by Congressman Leland M. Ford:

"Here we have the spectacle of our government telling seventeen states they cannot have gasoline, giving as a specific reason the lack of transportation facilities in the way of tankers, pipe lines, and tank cars not now available. They say there is a tremendous shortage of gasoline. Now then, when resistance and objection is made by the seventeen states to this program, these officials say it is going to be made national.

"In those districts where they have more gasoline than they

159

know what to do with, and have no facilities to store it, cannot get priorities to build such facilities and will therefore have to resort to burning it, these people are told that their gasoline consumption will have to be curtailed. The reason given to these people out there is, 'It is not a gasoline shortage but a rubber shortage.'

"What is the whole program? Why are not our people told the plain, honest-to-God truth?"

This was unadulterated nonsense, of course, for the plain truth had been laid on the line repeatedly, and if there was something just a bit left-handed about rationing gasoline, which was abundant, in order to save rubber, which was scarce, the project after all was simple enough to be grasped by anyone who really wanted to grasp it. The time had arrived for somebody to proceed boldly on the theory that the people were intelligent enough to understand what was being done, since what was being done (up to this point) made perfectly good sense. The people had a right to expect something in the way of leadership.

But they did not get it; not in connection with the rubber problem, they didn't. There never was a president who adjusted more rapidly to an expression of public sentiment than did the revered FDR. What was coming out of Congress at the end of May sounded like such an expression, and the President adjusted at his next press conference. He deplored "overexcitement" about the dark outlook for motorists, and said that if various experiments which were currently being made on rubber substitutes turned out well he thought people could get to town all right.

This was true enough as far as it went; experiments were being made with wooden tires, plastic tires, tires made of heaven-knows-what-all. The catch was that no one who was familiar with them saw any prospect that any or all of them would actually turn out to be even a partial answer to the nation's need. The net effect of the President's airy remark was unquestionably to minimize the rubber shortage and to discount the need for a tight control on driving; instead of quieting the wild cries that were being raised in Congress, it justified them. As soon as this appeared on the news tickers the reporters who covered WPB came boiling up to the fifth floor of the Social Security Building, demanding audience with Nelson, with Newhall, with anybody at all who knew anything about the rubber program, to see if what the President said made sense. Nelson, Newhall, and Henderson were flabbergasted; the President had cut the ground out from under their feet. They went into a hurried huddle, and shortly afterward Nelson held a press conference. As tactfully as he could, he said that he assumed Mr. Roosevelt was merely voicing the hope which he, Nelson, held—that substitute materials might be found to prevent a crisis in transportation. He added that while this was indeed his hope he saw very little chance that anything would actually come of it, and he reiterated that no rubber for civilian tires was in sight for at least two or three years.

This was about as much as could be done to salvage the situation. After all, a government official can't flatly and publicly contradict the President who appointed him . . . not and go on being a public official. But more than this had to be done. Nelson considered the idea of going ahead with nation-wide rationing without further ado, and went so far as to tell reporters that an announcement on the subject might be issued within a week. But no conceivable rationing system would work if the President—who was given to expressing his doubts in public, when he had them—remained doubtful about the need for it. Furthermore, there was Congress. News had just come down from the hill that one-hundred-odd members of the House had caucused and had adopted a resolution opposing gasoline rationing "until such time as Congress was convinced" that it was really necessary. This, to be sure, was unofficial and did not bind anyone, but as a straw in the wind it was about the size of a haystack.

At last Henderson, as a veteran New Dealer, suggested that what was called for was a heart-to-heart talk with the President. If the President understood all of the facts, Henderson believed, he would go along with the gasoline-rationing program without further delay; therefore, why not descend on him, indoctrinate him in the facts as they were known to the men in charge of the rubber program, and see what happened?

Agreed. A meeting at the White House was arranged for June 5; present were Nelson, Henderson, Newhall, Ickes, Eastman, and Archibald MacLeish, head of the Office of Facts and Figures.

This meeting promptly backfired. Instead of convincing the

President that gasoline rationing should begin at once, it brought from him a new attempt to avoid gasoline rationing altogether. After Roosevelt had opened the meeting by remarking, "Personally, I'm not worried about the rubber situation," Henderson stated the case for rationing and got nowhere; then Secretary Ickes suggested that the rubber shortage might be greatly alleviated if the government would just collect all of the available scrap rubber and reclaim it. He had been assured, Ickes said, that the right kind of collection campaign would bring in a million tons of rubber scrap.

Newhall protested that this estimate was fantastically high; all of the tires on all of the pleasure cars in America, he said, would hardly come to a million tons; but the President liked the idea and it quickly became apparent that his mind was made up—and his mind, when made up, was of a remarkable fixity and hardness. He told Ickes to launch a rubber scrap collection campaign right away, and the meeting ended. Three days later the President made public announcement of the collection campaign, saying that its outcome might determine the answer to the question of gasoline rationing. Since the experts couldn't agree, Mr. Roosevelt explained, on the amount of scrap rubber that might be available, the only way to find out was to collect all the old rubber and weigh it. It was of course true, he added, that there was no way to provide new tires for ordinary motoring, so it behooved the civilian to drive carefully and make his tires last as long as possible; and the President hoped that it would not be necessary to go any farther in solving the rubber crisis than to convince motorists of the need for saving their tires.

Thus the President simultaneously warned people to take care of their tires and encouraged them to hope that relief would quickly be provided; and the rubber salvage campaign, blessed by a presidential radio chat, got under way. The public responded nobly . . . but it was quickly apparent that someone had greatly overestimated the amount of scrap rubber that was available. At the end of two weeks the total collected was just over 100,000 tons; William Boyd, chairman of the Petroleum Industry War Council, said that this figure was "encouraging," but Secretary Ickes sharply disagreed and said that unless collections increased considerably, requisitioning of tires might become necessary. . . . The gasoline shortage in the eastern states grew worse than ever, Henderson remarked that "car owners will do a lot of walking from now on," and on June 30—the day the campaign was scheduled to end—Roosevelt extended it for another ten days, announcing that collections to date came to 219,000 tons and were sadly disappointing.

On no one was this rougher than on Secretary Ickes. He had sincerely believed that a million tons of scrap rubber were waiting to be collected and that the collection would go a long way toward solving the rubber problem, and he was in a belligerent mood when it became necessary to extend the campaign. He told reporters that "we suspect that there are people hoarding rubber, and there may even be people in official life who are doing a little hoarding," and he tried to contribute to the campaign the rubber floor mats from the Interior Department buildings. These mats were owned, however, by the Public Buildings Administration, over which Ickes had no control, and the Public Buildings Administration stopped him, saying that the mats were needed to keep people from slipping on the polished marble floors. Visiting the White House one day, Ickes seized a rubber mat at the doorway to the executive offices, rolled it up, handed it to his chauffeur, and told him to take it to the nearest scrap rubber collection center. White House Secretary Early told reporters this was perfectly okay; nobody at the White House would try to get the mat back. As a means of dramatizing the need for extensive scrap collection this stunt was all to the good; Newhall fumed about it privately, however, pointing out that rubber door mats were made of reclaimed rubber and that if they were collected about all they were good for was to make more rubber door mats.

So the campaign finally dragged on to its end, with 335,000 tons collected. The emotional temperature in Washington by the end of June was beyond measurement by any thermometer known to man. Rommel had passed through Tobruk and was just eighty miles from the Nile delta ("East, or west?" asked some grim wag, when the news came on the ticker); the Russians had evacuated Sevastopol, and the way to the oil fields of the Caucasus appeared to be open; the Japs were digging in on the Aleutians, and the FBI had just nabbed eight Nazi saboteurs who had been landed on an east coast beach by a submarine. Clearly, this was no time to be playing duck-on-a-rock with the rubber problem, and Roosevelt reflected awareness of that fact at his next press conference.

It might be necessary, he said, for the government to requisition every tire in the United States if the war got any worse. A reporter asked if rationing of gasoline wasn't really the most effective way to save tires. Roosevelt replied that he really didn't know, that he couldn't tell what the answer to the problem might be. He knew, he said, more about the gasoline-rubber situation than most people, but he doubted if he himself could write an intelligent story about it; personally, if he lived next door to an oil well, had an auto, and owned four good tires, he could see no reason why he should not use his car freely, if he needed to, in his own business.

This really did it. Any citizen who had not yet been confused by the situation had ample warrant for confusion now. All in the space of one minute the President had hinted darkly that the outlook was so desperate that government might have to commandeer everybody's tires, had said he didn't know whether gasoline rationing was really needed, had indicated that he could see no harm in driving as usual where there was plenty of gasoline, and admitted that he was completely confused. After these remarks had appeared on the front pages, the one certainty was that it would take something like a convulsion of nature to put gasoline rationing across now. The rubber problem had become the rubber mess, complete with white tie and tails.

Which meant that one of the genuinely essential parts of the war program—a measure needed to keep the economy from collapsing—could not be put into operation.

A point to bear in mind is that this mess had no relation whatever to the WPB program for making synthetic rubber. The original argument was confined strictly to the question of saving the motorist's tires, and all of the confusion grew out of the fact that the one effective way to keep the nation's cars rolling for the duration—mileage control through the rationing of gasoline—was a step which neither the President nor Congress could contemplate unemotionally in an election year.

But behold, now, how swiftly the argument broadened. Men began by discussing the desirability (or otherwise) of rationing; before long they were heatedly questioning the rubber program as a whole, and were going on from that to question the competence and the good faith of the industrialists who were running it.

Arthur Newhall, who was fast becoming the unhappiest man in Washington, was made fully aware of this as the spring wore away. All of the freak inventors in the land were bringing him processes for making synthetic rubber, and Newhall was referring one and all to the Bureau of Standards, where the processes were tested and without exception were found wanting; but the net result was to bring a storm of criticism on Newhall's head and to reveal that a great many people were ready to credit almost any accusation against a dollar-a-year man. Most of the disappointed inventors had access to the public ear, through Congressmen or newspaper columnists or radio commentators, and the burden of each one's complaint was: "WPB doesn't *want* to solve the rubber crisis." It was of course perfectly natural for the inventors to complain in this way; what was ominous was that their complaints were so promptly publicized and were listened to so attentively. Each self-deluded or felonious-minded "inventor" who yelled to heaven that WPB (guided by The Interests) had turned down his simple, inexpensive means for providing rubber for everybody's tires, found a susceptible audience. Anything could be believed, or at least half-believed; the very worst was likely to be true. (It even got so, at one stage, that men wagged their heads at Secretary Ickes, who was so flagrantly incorruptible it was almost offensive, and muttered darkly that he had somehow or other come under the thumb of the Oil Crowd.)

The same attitude was evident in Congress, where it was much more serious. Senator Guy Gillette of Iowa flatly charged that WPB was not following the best and simplest approach to synthetic rubber. Newhall's program was based largely on the use of petroleum as the raw material; Gillette pointed out that he could just as well be using alcohol, made from corn, which the nation had in abundance—which was, in fact, raised in quantity in the senator's native state. Yet it was all but impossible, Gillette complained, to get any consideration whatever from WPB for this suggestion, because WPB was slanted in favor of the oil industry.

Senator O'Mahoney of Wyoming, the Senate's principal authority on monopoly in America, carried Gillette's complaint a

step further, declaring that the men in WPB were "more interested in preserving the opportunity for large aggregations of
capital to exploit the people than they are in winning the war."
He added:

"More than a year ago the experts of OPM said that we had
enough aluminum with which to fight the war. They were
wrong. They told us we could get enough rubber for the war.
They were wrong. They told us we had enough steel to provide
the needs of the nation in the midst of war. They were wrong."

And Senator Truman, who knew more about the record of
OPM and WPB than any other man in Congress, and who was
not given to loose talk, asserted:

"We are now beginning to suffer the results of the inefficiency
of OPM and its refusal to admit the prospect of shortages in
strategic materials and to force soon enough plans for increased
production thereof irrespective of the effect on the financial and
competitive positions of industry."

Something drastic had happened to America's traditional faith
in the leadership of businessmen. That leadership, as exemplified
by the dollar-a-year system, had ceased to command confidence;
yet that leadership was the one element which might have ended
the rubber mess if the old faith had still existed. It might, in
happier days, have retrieved the situation; there was a time when
it could have put expert, disinterested, businessman's advice into
the scales to balance political hesitancy, thereby rallying public
support and stiffening the spines of the timid. But it was on the
defensive now, its old prestige was gone, and the very fact that
dollar-a-year men were for a program was a handicap rather
than an asset. Instead of being able to retrieve the situation,
business leadership in WPB was hard pressed to justify its own
decisions.

So the confusion about rubber covered everything from the
factory worker's right to drive his car to the technical processes
for making butadiene. The situation by the end of June was
completely out of hand. What had to be done could not be done
because confidence was lacking. Something dramatic had to be
done to restore confidence—which meant that the object of the
game was no longer to find and execute the best possible program
but to make people think that the best possible program was being

found and executed. A great change had come over the face of the waters. Government had begun by hunting the best formula for artificial rubber, had gone on to seek the best formula for saving tires, and had now brought itself down to a search for the best formula for affecting public opinion.

CHAPTER FOURTEEN

Down to the Sea

C ONSIDER briefly, at this point, the difference between the statesman and the cynic. The difference is rather substantial, and it can be very important when a democracy is fighting for its life.

The statesman in a democracy has little enough to go on; nothing, as a matter of fact, but faith, which may be no larger than a grain of mustard seed. But this faith is a faith in the people, and out of it can come courage, and the strength which moves mountains, and the people are ennobled thereby. For this faith assumes that the people, in the long run, are just as good as they are required to be; that they are brave enough to know the worst and intelligent enough to do what has to be done, and that their one great need is a leadership which trusts them. It is an assumption that has been justified in the history of America at various times and places—whenever leaders have been inspired enough to act on it.

But the cynic knows better than to make any such assumption. His faith is a faith in salesmanship and in the devices of the public relations counsel. The people must not be forced to look at unpleasant facts, and if such facts exist they must be dispelled or hidden; matters won't be quite so bad if you can just make people believe they aren't so bad; people's minds lie entirely on the surface, where you can manipulate them to your heart's content if you are just clever enough, and public emotion is something you can create rather than something which arises from what the people are actually doing. . . . It is all a business of techniques and mental attitudes, and what a pity we weren't around to help Lincoln when the bad news came in from Fredericksburg and Chancellorsville. . . .

It must be granted that in most matters the government of the United States lacked neither faith nor courage, in the summer of 1942. It put through a hundred-billion-dollar budget, it took the offensive in the Pacific with a crippled fleet and a few brigades of marines, and it planned an invasion of North Africa with a ᴸolly untested army, and for these projects great courage and passing faith were needed. But the simple, basic faith in democracy itself, which was required when the strong winds began to blow around the issue of rubber and gasoline, simply wasn't there at all; so the administration turned the rubber problem into a public relations problem and then resorted to an elegant variety of hocus-pocus to solve it.

Do a little post-mortem on this rubber business. It was profoundly significant.

By mid-June of 1942 the rubber situation was exactly what everyone said it was—a mess. But it was not a mess because the operating people—Henderson, Newhall, Nelson, *et al.*—had botched the job of analyzing and meeting the rubber problem, for they had not botched it; on the contrary, they saw what had to be done and they had blocked out a tolerably effective program for doing it, and as far as synthetic rubber was concerned the program was being put into operation fairly rapidly. They had not done their job perfectly, to be sure. The program they had started needed to be broadened and tightened, and more drive was required for its proper execution. But the fact that the rubber program in the spring of 1942 needed broadening and tightening and a greater impetus was not what created the mess; and the improvements that were finally brought about in these respects were not what settled the mess.

The mess had come into being because elected officials—specifically, Congress and the President—had spent their time worrying about what people were going to think, rather than about the action the facts in the situation demanded. Because of that mental attitude at the top, the rubber problem became the rubber mess; because of this desperate, overpowering fear that the people might think the rubber situation was in a mess, the people finally did think so—with, by that time, abundant justification. Because they did think so it was at all costs necessary to get them to think something else—because one of the key steps in the program, nation-wide rationing of gasoline, could not be put into operation when public confidence in the program as a whole was lacking. And so the rubber mess was finally settled in exactly that way, by a public relations device pure and simple. The device worked because it relieved Congress and the President of the necessity of trying to make the harsh facts about rubber look other than they actually were.

Take Congress first.

Admittedly, Congress was in a tough spot. The move to ration gasoline on the eastern seaboard got off to a bad start. The brief public argument between Henderson and Ickes, over the exact amount of gasoline that would be available for the individual motorist, had spread more heat than light. The matter of drawing the boundary line for the rationed area had been most vexing, too. How far west of the coast should the line be drawn? At Harrisburg? At Pittsburgh? Wherever it was drawn, there was going to be a border region where the whole operation looked absurd, with rationed scarcity in one town and unchecked plenty three miles down the road; and with the best will in the world, bewilderment and resentment over that absurdity were bound to be reflected in Congress. The fantastic episode of the X cards, with its echoes of Bundles for Congress, was ideally designed to throw the Congressional temper off balance. And then, in addition to everything else, the final proposal to save rubber by restricting driving by rationing gasoline was hard to digest, especially when it dovetailed with a regional rationing system which was due solely to a bottleneck in the transportation system.

But it could have been digested, and there was some sort of responsibility resting on elected persons to make the effort to digest it. Instead there was an irrational explosion.

We're short of rubber, so we're going to conserve it by restricting driving, and the only way we can do that is by rationing everybody's gasoline.

Hell, you can't do that; that's crazy; why, there's plenty of gasoline!

Something just a little bit better than that might reasonably have been expected, in time of war; but something better than that was not forthcoming, because senators and representatives kept insisting that the people just wouldn't understand being deprived of gasoline when they knew that there was abundant gasoline everywhere except on the east coast. The preoccupation in Congress, in other words, was not on what had to be done to meet a crisis; it was on what the people might think about what was done, and there was no effort whatever to broadcast the available facts so that the people would have a decent chance to draw intelligent conclusions. Instead there was a frantic concentration on the effort to evade the facts, to show that the whole rubber program had been so badly mishandled that this demand for gasoline rationing couldn't be necessary, to find a scapegoat somewhere (at which point the personal unpopularity of Leon Henderson and the miserable past record of the dollar-a-year men came in very handy), to spare the people a hardship which the people might resent.

To which the President added more than enough. He began by publicly supporting Nelson's contention that it was going to be necessary to ration gasoline. Then he qualified his support and expressed the hope that rubber substitutes would be developed so as to make rationing unnecessary. Then, hearkening to the uproar in Congress, he qualified it still further, saying that if enough scrap rubber were collected the dreadful cup might be averted. Then he agreed that he couldn't blame any man who lived where gasoline was plentiful for driving his car as he pleased. Finally, he confessed that he was completely confused—so much so that he himself could not write a story on rubber that would make sense.

What confused him? Not the men to whom he had entrusted the handling of the rubber program, the conduct of the civilian economy, or the supplying and equipping of the armed forces. Their advice to him had been clear and consistent from the very start. Nelson, Patterson, Henderson, Forrestal, Newhall—without exception, they had told him, right from the beginning, exactly what the situation was and exactly what needed to be done, and their stories never varied. The only possible conclusion is that the President shared the feeling of Congress—that this was too tough a dose to inflict on the public palate, that the people just wouldn't understand, that the people had to be nursed along . . . and that there must, somehow, be a Way Out.

And as the final curdling element, of course, there was the widespread distrust of the industrialists who were running the war economy. The people had grown cynical about them and about the entire system they represented, and in this depth of their cynicism they were suddenly called on to fight a war in defense of abstract ideals—the supreme war of their national existence, in defense of the highest ideals that had been evolved by all their generations of living. The people were entitled to something better than a matching cynicism at the top, a cynicism which finally found expression in a public relations approach to the job of leadership.

But from first to last they did not get it. They got eloquent words, from time to time, but they did not get the summons to find within themselves, by their own heroic actions, the supreme values they were seeking. While the war lasted the people were going to live by bread alone. . . .

So the simple question of rationing gasoline became the rubber mess, and government was unable to do what it knew it must do, and assorted publicists complained that the people—the heedless, thoughtless, selfish people!—believed in fighting a soft war. Something had to be done but it couldn't be done until the crisis was brought to a head. It was brought there, presently, by act of Congress.

Senator Gillette provided the impetus. He introduced a bill to establish a brand new agency, completely independent of the War Production Board, to handle rubber. This agency would have all of the priority powers it needed to allot materials and component parts both for the building of rubber factories and for the making of rubber; and because Congress strongly suspected that WPB was biased in favor of petroleum, the bill provided that a substantial part of the synthetic rubber program must be based on the use of grain alcohol as the raw material. This bill would indeed foil the dollar-a-year men, and—other things being equal—it might ultimately produce large quantities of rubber. Unfortunately, it would also disrupt WPB beyond hope of repair, and with WPB thus disrupted there would either be complete chaos in the whole war production program or a forced and probably unwelcome reorganization of the entire system for running the war economy.

Nelson hastened to the hill to testify on these points before Senator Gillette's committee. He admitted freely that alcohol was an excellent raw material to use in the production of synthetic rubber, and said frankly that WPB had erred in failing to recognize the fact earlier. But the fact had been fully digested by now, he added, and WPB was currently planning to make at least 200,000 tons of rubber out of alcohol—about one-fourth of the entire program. An even higher percentage probably would be theoretically desirable, he agreed, but it was too late now; to

172

change the factory-construction program for that purpose would take too many essential materials away from the most urgent munitions programs; 200,000 tons was about the limit. But the effect of the Gillette bill, he continued, would be nothing less than disastrous. It would take priority control out of the President's hands; worse yet, it would divide it, and priority control was indivisible—it was the very heart of the mechanism for operating the war economy. The disorganization would be complete; it would not only reduce the production of munitions, but it would almost certainly mean the production of less rubber rather than more. For all of these reasons he pleaded with the senators not to give the bill their approval.

He had no luck whatever. The senators liked Nelson, and from first to last they trusted him about as much as they trusted anyone in the war agencies, but they were not impressed by his testimony on the Gillette bill. Senator Gillette did say that he was delighted to learn that 200,000 tons of rubber would be made from alcohol, although he added a caustic crack about "this death-bed repentance." Nelson's dire warning about the evils of dividing priority control and wrecking WPB the senators simply disregarded. After brief debate and deliberation, the Gillette bill was passed by both houses of Congress and was sent to the White House for signature.

To this pass, then, had the administration been brought by its reluctance to face the disagreeable and politically dangerous issue of gasoline rationing. Congress had given the President a law which had to be vetoed if the war were to be won: Nelson had not been exaggerating in the least when he warned that this would wreck the painfully-erected mechanism on which the nation relied for war production. But a mere veto was by no means enough. In addition, the President had to get the rubber mess straightened out so that everyone would agree that it *was* straightened out—a task which by now was many light-years beyond the reach of any mere cabinet member or agency head. The eternal verities still applied, or had to be made to apply; the rubber needed to win the war had to be produced, the tires on people's cars had to be saved, the country had to be able to go on working. It was time to pull a rabbit out of a hat—preferably, a rabbit about the size of a Shetland pony.

Fertile in expedients, the President found one that worked. He vetoed the Gillette bill; simultaneously, he called to his aid, once more, a Great Reputation—this time, that of Bernard M. Baruch. Announcing his veto, he announced also that he was appointing a small committee of impartial and unimpeachable experts, with Baruch at its head, to explore the entire rubber situation from Alpha to Omega and to turn in a report which the entire country could, would, and must accept as the final, authoritative word on the whole business. The committee would determine whether there was in fact a rubber shortage to begin with. It would find out, once and for all, whether the existing program for making synthetic rubber was adequate. It would answer the supreme riddle: Do we need to ration gasoline? All in all, it would set everybody's mind at rest and the country could then get on with the war, which at that point needed getting on with quite badly.

Baruch was an excellent choice for this job, because he had many virtues. He had been the production man in the other war; he was a master of high finance and he was familiar with heavy industry and with the men who ran heavy industry, and if there was any justice in such matters it was clear that he knew all of the answers to production riddles. Much more important, however, was the fact that he had reached the kind of apotheosis which all public men desire but which only a very few ever attain. He had become a great name, a sage, an elder statesman, a Sacred Cow (using the expression with all reverence) for publishers and for editorial writers, an oracle whose word it was sheer impiety to doubt. He was girt about with a kind of Wall Street homespun; when he visited Washington it was widely reported that despite his years he shunned such luxuries as ordinary office suites and did all of his work on a wooden bench in Lafayette Park, impervious to the suns of summer, the chill winds of winter, or the impudent squirrels on the prowl for peanuts. All in all, he was a reputation that reached from here to there, and he was exactly what the administration needed.

Baruch and his committee got busy promptly. They spent the rest of the summer examining witnesses, studying statistics, surveying and analyzing reports and taking counsel with themselves. Finally, in the fall, they produced their report.

The rubber shortage, the report found, was not a myth. Drastic restrictions on civilian driving were needed, since the most that could be done with reclaimed rubber was to provide recaps for essential driving. The government's present program for making synthetic rubber—tardy as it might have been in its inception, and handicapped by the qualms and hesitations of bygone OPM— was technically sound and had the required breadth and range. It needed to be expanded a bit to provide for contingencies; there should be new mechanisms for supervising the operation of the rubber plants, and there should be a new office of the Rubber Director, technically answerable to the chairman of WPB but effectively independent, to jam the whole program through; if all of this were done, the rubber program would meet the necessities of the situation.

And, as a final kicker: nation-wide gasoline rationing was absolutely unavoidable and must be instituted as quickly as possible, no matter how much gasoline might exist away from the eastern seaboard.

So ordered. By presidential edict there was established a new Office of the Rubber Director, to rank with-but-after WPB, as military men would say. William N. Jeffers, burly president of the Union Pacific Railroad, was brought in to take charge of it, and was instructed to amplify the rubber program along the lines recommended by the Baruch committee and to drive the program through regardless—this latter being an order he was temperamentally fitted to comply with if any man in Washington ever was. Luckless Arthur Newhall, of course, had to go. He had coped with and solved the real rubber problem, but this was something else again; there had to be a new broom and the new broom had to make a clean sweep, and Newhall was dropped into obscurity (and continued usefulness, fortunately) in the offices of the Combined Boards. The Baruch report was the Bible and Jeffers was its expositor, and the rubber mess had at last been settled—a thing for gods and men to marvel at.

There was one final flare-up on rubber, and it came nearly nine months after the Baruch committee's report. Jeffers, a hard-driving Irishman who seemed to be nearly half as wide as he was high, and solid muscle all the way, had been given what amounted to a presidential order to get rubber made no matter who stood in the way. Jeffers was not the man to let an order like that go to seed, and all of the war production and supply agencies quickly became aware that any official or administrator who got in the path of the Rubber Director was going to suffer bruises and abrasions. There was a good deal of chance for conflict, too, since the plants in which synthetic rubber is made need all sorts of complicated machinery and equipment which are also needed by the plants which make high octane gasoline and, in addition, are essential in the construction of warships and merchant vessels. Jeffers, therefore, was in the position of competing for these articles with the Petroleum Co-ordinator, with the Navy Department, and with the Maritime Commission—while the War Department, whose entire aviation program depended on the production of high octane gasoline, stood by as an intensely interested spectator.

Nelson, as chairman of the War Production Board, was the umpire who had to settle all of these conflicting claims and determine which programs, or parts of programs, had top priority. Nelson's WPB not being at the moment set up to do a first-rate job of doling out the scanty components, and umpires never being popular anyhow, all of this brought woe and grief on Nelson's head until he brought in Charles E. Wilson of General Electric, late in 1942, and turned over to him the job of scheduling the production and delivery of the critical components.

In any case, by the spring of 1943 the various programs were rocking along fairly well—fairly well, that is, for the heat and pressure of wartime, when nothing is ever in genuinely satisfactory shape. But the Army, which by now was neck-deep in air warfare, began to worry about a possible shortage of high octane gasoline, the program for which, the War Department felt, was being crippled by the favored position given the synthetic rubber program. Dissatisfied with Nelson's assertion that industry could provide adequate quantities of both rubber and aviation gasoline, the War Department took its complaint to the public prints. In the latter part of April, Under-Secretary Patterson submitted to an interview in which he expressed dark forebodings about the probable necessity for grounding fighter planes because of a lack of high octane gasoline, and intimated that the rubber program was being allowed to hog the necessary materials and was, therefore, threatening to prolong the war.

So far this was just standard operating procedure. Patterson's blast was aimed at Nelson, who was the War Department's favorite target at all times; but when the story appeared in print everyone assumed that the Under-Secretary was really shooting at Jeffers, who wasn't the same sort of target at all. Nelson made a pretty good target, most of the time, because he was a regular sitting duck—he never moved out of the way, and he could rarely bring himself to shoot back. An intimate WPB associate once deplored this trait, saying: "One of these War Department generals will stick a knife into Nelson and all Nelson does is pull the knife out and hand it back and say, 'General, I believe you dropped something.' And the general will say, 'Why, Don, thanks, I believe I did'—and right away he sticks it back in again."

But Jeffers was a different breed of cat. As soon as the Patterson interview was printed the rubber director began to make noises like a man who proposes to hit back with everything he can lay his hands on, up to and including the tenpins from the nearest bowling alley. The Truman Committee sighed wearily—*another* public row over rubber, after everything had been fixed up!—and hastily called hearings to inquire into the matter. For a moment it looked as if 1942 were back in full flower.

But only for a moment. The hearings passed off rather quietly. Everyone concerned voiced discontent with Nelson's decisions on the competing programs, but everyone agreed that someone had to make such decisions, that they had to be stuck to, once made, unless excellent reason to the contrary should arise, and that rushing to the newspapers with complaints was not the proper way to get them overruled. And while it became very apparent—as everyone in Washington already knew—that relations between Patterson and Nelson were seriously strained, the hearings quickly showed that if Jeffers had got hit by any flying fragments it was all a regrettable error.

Patterson was explicit on this point. He began his testimony by declaring: "I have no personal quarrel with Mr. Jeffers. I hold him personally in high esteem and I respect his character and his patriotism. I deeply regret that my recent remarks should have been interpreted as reflecting on him. I had no such intention." Warming up, as the hearing progressed, and getting onto an old-pal basis, he testified further that "we have no quarrel on that—Jeff and I," and disclosed that since publication of his interview a mutual friend had arranged a meeting between himself and Jeffers, at which they had agreed to make a joint inspection trip to the field to see just how the synthetic rubber plants were coming along.

"Jeff and I have exactly the same aim, to win this war," he asserted, quite as if this made them unique in Washington.

Senator Brewster, a member of the committee, commented dryly that "this accord in which it seems to be a case of Pat and Jeff" struck him as distinct progress, and the whole sensation died down, with everyone but Nelson having confessed membership in a little band of brothers. And that was the last of the great public disputes about rubber.

For the rubber mess—to repeat—had been settled, disposed of once and for all; and the means of settlement—the appointment of the Baruch committee and the publication of the Baruch report —had been essentially an essay in public relations. The government had been jittery, and because it had been jittery the public mind was disturbed and confused—or so Washington assumed, at any rate; and the great object of the means of settlement had been to quiet this disturbance and end this confusion.

And this helped to set a pattern. The process it started was self-perpetuating and carried the most far-reaching consequences. In the end it conditioned not merely the way the war was fought but the way the country came out of the war and the things that happened after the shooting had stopped.

See how it works. Once you begin to sugar-coat the facts you create a gap between the real world and the world you want people to believe in. Then the things you need to do can't be done because the gap is there. So you have to take elaborate measures to get across the gap; as a result, you have to undertake another manipulation of the public mind and heart; and because you have to do all of this—which usually takes you all the way around Robin Hood's barn—you come to the conclusion that the people themselves must be to blame for it all. The people are overoptimistic, they are complacent, they don't realize how bad the situation actually is, they think the war can be won without sternness and sacrifice. You have to move mountains to induce yourself to impose gasoline rationing, for instance; before long you begin to assume that the heedless, careless people think more of driving their cars than they do of winning the war. This is a state you naturally deplore, because complacent and self-indulgent people don't win wars. So you have to make a still greater effort to force public opinion into the shape which you think it ought to have.

The residue of distrust which all of this deposits grows by accretion, like some calcareous growth that stiffens the joints. At last it affects government policies themselves, so that government's most important actions arise from the desire to affect public opinion. Manipulation leads to still more manipulation, and there is no end to it. No immediately visible end, that it. Unless you can look over the edge of the steep place that leads down to the sea.

CHAPTER FIFTEEN

The Gentleman Need Not Wait

ALTHOUGH they never quite realized it, the we-hate-Roosevelt people were successful beyond their dreams during the war, and 1942 was the year of their first big triumph. Their strategy was simple, and it was all the better for being purely instinctive rather than rational. It began with the excellent assumption that any action which the administration might take (other than those actions directly concerned with military matters) was sure to be unsound and ill-advised and was more than likely to be revolutionary; thus they always had something to criticize, and the criticism never had to be documented since it was based on an axiom rather than on facts and reasoning. Better yet, this created a game in which both ends could be played against the middle; for the very fact that this criticism was being made could then be used as a basis for further criticism, the idea being that there must be something terribly wrong or the administration wouldn't be under so much attack. The war could not be won unless there was national unity, and there couldn't be national unity unless the administration bought off its critics by desisting from the actions of which the critics complained. It made a lovely game, and the tragedy was that the administration wasn't able to stand up against it.

The newspaper files for the spring and summer of 1942 give plenty of illustrations. A minor sample can be found in a front-page outburst which appeared in the morning papers of March 22, 1942—a solemn warning issued by Thomas J. Wallner, president of the Southern States Industrial Council:

"This war cannot possibly be won—ever—and may be irrevocably lost—this year—unless there is an immediate and extremely far-reaching reversal of policy and direction by our government.

"America is losing the war for one fundamental reason and only one; our government—meaning primarily the President of the United States—still stubbornly persists in the attempt simultaneously to fight a foreign war and wage an internal economic revolution—and wars are not, never were and never can be won that way."

This of course was off the beam for a number of reasons, one being that the administration had very definitely committed itself not to fight the kind of war Mr. Wallner was talking about and another being that wars often *are* won in that way, a notable example being the war that accompanied the French Revolution. But nobody took the time to make any reply, partly because a frank reply would have been embarrassing (after all, the administration was vulnerable: it had won three landslide elections on the theory that something resembling an internal economic revolution was necessary) and partly because there were more important beefs to attend to.

For at just this time the Baltimore *Sun* weighed in with the "disclosure" that nearly 10,000 machines and metal-working production tools were scattered about in 124 training centers of the National Youth Administration.

This complaint was one to rock the rafters, or at least to disturb all of Mr. Roosevelt's political opponents. The NYA had been set up to train young men for jobs in industry; it had been set up by Roosevelt, at a time when there were millions of unemployed, and—without any ifs, ands, or buts— it was obviously impractical and wasteful, a stupendous boon-doggle tinged with radicalism. Now there was a war on, and a shortage of machine tools was one of the great handicaps of the munitions program; the mere fact that NYA was still in existence was enough of a scandal to the righteous, but the added fact that it had been given custody of some thousands of machine tools was clear proof that the New Deal wasn't paying proper attention to the war emergency. There was no need to argue the point; the mere fact that NYA had the tools was all that need be known. Amid general applause, Senator MacKellar introduced a bill to abolish both NYA and, for good measure, the Civilian Conservation Corps.

Sidney Hillman rushed into the breach first. He was working as hard as he could to meet industry's fantastically increased need for skilled workers, and he explained that these NYA training centers had been set up at the express request of the defense authorities, and that most of the NYA tools were ancient, reconditioned, and largely unsuited for use in war factories. This didn't help much, because Hillman was a union leader, he was one of the prime symbols of the administration's radicalism, and anyway he talked with a terrible Russian accent, and what he said didn't count. In the end Nelson had to take time off from his other duties and go before a congressional committee to bring the matter into perspective. Nelson emphasized that the NYA training centers were of direct service to the war effort—so much so that if they did not exist it would be necessary to invent them. Industry's need for tools, he continued, had to be balanced against the need for tools to develop and train new workers. The tools in question were far more useful in the NYA training centers than they would be anywhere else, and in any case as an added safeguard WPB for some time had been making a careful running survey of the tools, to be sure that none were being kept in the training centers if they would be of more value in the factories.

That ended that; and the issue was dropped, amid mutterings. It was immediately succeeded by an energetic campaign to force repeal of the forty-hour-week law, a campaign promoted with vigor and emotion by influential sections of the press and Congress.

This was as completely phony a campaign as the country ever saw, since it rested on a flat and willful misinterpretation of the law and its effects. The forty-hour-week law did not prevent an employer from working his men any number of hours he chose; all it said was that the workers should get time and one-half for all hours in excess of forty worked in any one week. In addition, at the time the campaign was going strong the law was almost completely inapplicable to war work, since the overwhelming bulk of munitions production took place in factories where there were union agreements governing overtime pay, and since most war plants had not yet been geared to go much beyond forty-hour operation in any case. All of this was a matter of record; the Army, the Navy, and the War Production Board had reviewed the situation and had reported to the President that the law had no appreciable effect on war production and should remain unchanged.

But these facts made no difference. The campaign to repeal the law went ahead regardless, definitely based on the assertion that this law made it impossible for industrialists and patriotic workers to go beyond the forty-hour limit. It lent itself to fine phrases, such as "The Boys of Bataan don't limit themselves to forty hours a week," and "There's no forty-hour week in the fox-holes"; the Washington *Post* solemnly remarked that men in the Army resented "life as usual, and better than usual" for the workers; and Mark Sullivan, in his column published March 25, asserted:

"The atmosphere of Washington this week is not that of foreign war. It is of domestic battle, the battle of the New Deal to keep and increase its power, of New Dealers to hold onto their offices."

In the end, the great campaign evaporated without leaving any measurable traces—except for such additional misunderstanding, suspicion and bitterness as may have been created along the way—but its evaporation didn't change matters much because it was promptly followed by a brand new scandal. This one centered about an innocent-looking jerry-built frame building, erected on a vacant triangle in the heart of downtown Washington, which quickly became known as "Mellett's Madhouse."

The Madhouse, officially opened for business at the end of April, was a government information center, the idea being that it would provide an accessible point where visitors to crowded and confusing wartime Washington could get quick, authoritative information on all government activities. Particularly, it was de-signed to handle inquiries from businessmen, who were coming to Washington in battalions without in most cases any but the foggiest notion what agency or department had jurisdiction over their problems or where the said agencies and departments might be situated. The whole inquiry branch of the Department of Commerce was quartered in the building; staff specialists from WPB, OPA, Treasury Procurement, and the Civil Service Commission were on hand to answer questions; all government documents were on sale there, and the Coast Guard and Marine Corps had recruiting headquarters in the building. The District of Columbia Council for Defense maintained there its informa-tion booth for service men, and the building also housed the offices of the Defense Homes Registry. All in all, the project would appear to have been an honest attempt to meet a pressing public need—a whole series of pressing public needs, as a matter of fact.

But it was a scandal, just the same, before it ever opened its doors; for the venture was under the jurisdiction of the Office of Government Reports, and the Office of Government Reports was in charge of Lowell Mellett, and for many years Mellett had been accused of being the President's private Goebbels. Furthermore the place was an *information* center, and "information," in Washington, means press agentry pure and simple. Consequently, there was hell to pay, and construction of the building was treated as prima facie evidence of a vast plot to glorify FDR. Senator Harry F. Byrd, a wealthy Virginian who had made a career out of denouncing New Deal press agents, took the Senate floor to denounce the entire project as an unadorned publicity racket. The local press took up the cry, and it re-echoed back and forth in newspaper columns and in the halls of Congress. The East Indies had fallen, Bataan was gone and Corregidor was going, but for a time it seemed as if the crucial issue of the whole war was the projected opening of Mellett's Madhouse. Not since a reformed fan dancer had been detected on the payroll of the Office of Civilian Defense had the republic stood in such danger.

Like all the other burning issues, this scandal fizzled out at last—and fizzled rather abruptly. One day it was a front-page scandal and a cause for alarms, and the next day everybody was talking about something else. The Madhouse opened for business on May 4, and the republic did not fall. In fact, the Madhouse did a land-office business; on its first day it had 2,500 callers, with 1,500 more making their inquiries by telephone; it was obviously serving a useful purpose, and anyway the boys had had their fun.

Now there are two points to all of this—to the uproar over the Madhouse, the forty-hour law, and all the rest. The first is the highly ironical one that the pallid remnant of what had originally been elected and operated as the New Deal was being kept alive, in those days, almost solely by the bitter attacks on it that were being made by people who supposed that it was still healthy. At the very moment when the administration was definitely and finally turning its back on the kind of war effort that would be adequate to meet a world revolution, it was being hotly accused of straining every nerve to make that kind of effort and no other. It had swung far over to the other side of the street, but the swing went undetected because the opposition was busy bombarding the spot where the New Deal had been the last time the opposition had bothered to take a good look.

The other point is that through all of this welter of complaints, accusations, and dire forebodings, the administration had been getting a very bad press. Its public relations, so to speak, were not good, and the mere fact that it was innocent of most of the charges that were laid against it did not help. The attacks on the NYA training centers, on the forty-hour law, and on the Mellett Madhouse were indeed unworthy of reasonable men; nevertheless, the mere fact that these attacks were made became an additional cause for complaint. The New Deal was fighting a soft war: obviously it was—for wasn't it spending much time and energy defending its pet domestic reforms against criticism, instead of getting on with the business of licking Hitler? At the very least, there was "confusion in Washington." When would the government get down to cases, cease disturbing and alarming the public, and start thinking about nothing but victory?

The administration, unfortunately, was not in shape to stand up under this sort of thing very well—precisely because of its own increasing desire to manipulate public opinion. On questions of strategy, logistics, and supply it was as hard-boiled and ruthless as anyone could have asked, but as far as publicity was concerned it was fighting a soft war. Not only was it wrapping up unpleasant items like the gasoline-rationing problem in swaddling cloths of breezy optimism; it was doing much the same with its announcements about the actual fighting. Ship losses, for instance, were not announced until it was certain that the enemy knew about them anyhow; a defensible practice, to be sure, but one which developed into a habit of withholding bad news until it could be balanced by good news, and which brought about a definite minimizing of the genuinely critical situation at sea. On May 21 as sober a commentator as Walter Lippmann declared in his syndicated column that "it is hard to see what good purpose is served by the cheery official publicity which was issued over the week end," referring to remarks from Army, Navy, and White House about the effect of the submarine war on American shipping. Lippmann added: "Surely, the effect of such publicity is to give the people a false sense of security and to promote complacency and inertia in the face of a danger which is becoming so acute that it may mean, if not defeat, then an unduly long and bloody and costly struggle." For the war was not going well; was, in fact, going very badly indeed, and everybody sensed it but could get little inkling of it in anything the government was saying. When General Joe Stilwell came out of Burma, about that time, with the blunt statement, "I claim we got a hell of a beating," his grim candor was welcomed all across the country.

The administration, then, had bad public relations—partly through no fault of its own, and partly because it was spending too much time worrying about its public relations. And finally it undertook to remedy this bad situation by doing the obvious, traditional thing: by hiring a new public relations man.

On June 12, 1942, Mr. Roosevelt announced the formation of a spanking new Office of War Information, with Elmer Davis as its chief.

This step, the President said, was designed to bring about "an informed and intelligent understanding . . . of the status and progress of the war effort and of the war policies, activities, and aims of this government." Davis would have authority to "issue directives to all departments and agencies of the government with respect to their informational services"; he was expected to eliminate any overlapping or duplication of effort that might exist in the informational field, and he had power to discontinue any such activity that was not helping the war effort.

Thus was born OWI, to the tune of muffled thunder on the left; an organization which had its faults, like all man-made things, but which from first to last was infinitely more sinned against than sinning.

It was the inheritor of many fragments. Into it were consolidated MacLeish's Office of Facts and Figures, Mellett's Office of Government Reports, and most of Horton's Division of Information; into it, also, went the Foreign Information Service of William J. Donovan's Office of the Co-ordinator of Information, which put OWI into business as the government's overseas propaganda arm. (The remainder of Donovan's outfit was transferred to the jurisdiction of the Joint Chiefs of Staff and became the Office of Strategic Services, a highly useful organization in spite of the Hollywood cloak-and-dagger atmosphere that gathered around it.) With these diverse organizations blended into one, as harmoniously as could be expected, OWI set out to tell the people about the war.

The choice of Elmer Davis as its chief was especially fortunate. As a veteran newspaperman and radio commentator, Davis was

186

admired and respected as a completely honest, forthright, and intelligent man, and it is worth noting that he was still so regarded when the war ended even though OWI by then was pretty well discredited. OWI's failures were not hung on Davis, for the simple reason that he went to work with two large strikes on him.

The first strike was a matter of basic principles and organization.

In setting up OWI the administration was following the same course it followed to settle the rubber mess: using a public relations technique for solving what was at bottom an operating problem. The administration was on the pan for many reasons, in mid-1942, but the biggest reason of all was that it was not unified. It was not unified as between the White House and Congress, or within the executive branch itself. Conflicting and opposing viewpoints and purposes were at work from one end of Washington to the other; everybody wanted to win the war, but agreement ended there. To remedy this situation, the administration decided—not to take the kind of action that would create unity, but to do something which would make it look as if unity had been created. It set up OWI to take charge of all government publicity connected with the war, and charged OWI with responsibility for seeing to it that the government told a clear, coherent, single-track story about what it was doing. That might have been fine if there had in fact been a single-track story to tell, but there wasn't. Columnist Ernest Lindley put his finger on the defect in this approach a few days after OWI had been created when he pointed out:

"On the whole, it is better that the public should be confused temporarily than that opposing viewpoints should be muffled or suppressed. Most of this confusion arises in the stage of policy-formation rather than after binding decisions have been made. It is the President's job, in most cases, to make these decisions."

This was 100 per cent correct, but handing the responsibility to OWI meant that the cart was being put before the horse. As far as the domestic side of the war was concerned—the "home front," as they used to say in Washington, until the absurdity of calling the unimperiled life of civilians a "front" began to dawn on everybody—the government was simply wading hip-deep through a swamp toward a quite undefined goal, and making pretty heavy weather of it, too. The real remedy was to define the goal, and to make it something that would command the allegiance and inspire the ideals of the people who had to fight the war and pay for it; but this remedy had already been put aside as impractical, and—since a floundering government in wartime is not an encouraging sight—it was put up to OWI to stop the floundering. Because that task was far beyond any conceivable powers that OWI or any similar agency might have, what this really meant was that OWI somehow was to make it look as if the floundering had stopped whether it had or not.

OWI did its manful best. Speeches, public announcements, and ordinary press releases of all war agencies were cross-checked, to make sure that no official or agency was saying something with which another official or agency, having responsibility in that field, felt obliged to disagree. This failed to help much, partly because the basic disharmonies had not been removed, and partly because any official who wanted to carry an unresolved argument to the public could always get around the OWI clearance mechanism simply by leaking his story to a chosen reporter or two. The immediate effect of this clearance procedure was chiefly to make it harder to get out legitimate news; in the end, the procedure was to become a handy mechanism for enforcing a party line.

In addition, OWI had two very different jobs. Overseas, it was a propaganda agency; at home, it was supposed to be concerned with straight news. Davis was perfectly aware that there had to be a complete divorce between propaganda and news handling, and yet the very nature of his assignment put OWI into the propaganda business at home. OWI was put in charge of all publicity and promotional operations that might be used in connection with any official government campaign. A drive to collect waste paper, to check inflation by persuading people to buy government bonds rather than spend their money on consumer goods, or to induce war workers to take jobs in foundries: any venture of that kind was bound to rely heavily on promotional and advertising techniques, which meant that OWI had to enter into a morganatic marriage with the advertising, radio, and motion picture fraternity so that it might determine precisely what appeals or exhortations would be launched upon the public. The campaigns themselves were necessary, and by and large they were extremely well-handled; but the result was a steady absorption, by OWI, of the sales-promotion ideas and techniques. When government wanted to explain to the people the need for doing this, that, or the other thing required by the exigencies of war, it ceased to address them direct; it simply turned the job over to the advertising profession, which knew very well how to get results but which was not privy to the idea that the government of a democracy undertakes to propagandize its own people only at its peril. OWI not only had to keep a clear separation between its overseas propaganda work and its domestic news job; in the domestic field it had to make a similar separation between the news job and the campaign job. This was a little too much to expect of any organization.

When OWI came into being the curtain was finally pulled down on that thorny, difficult, and spiritually incorruptible character, Robert Horton, with his tactless insistence that government information had no function beyond the simple one of handing out all the facts and letting the people make up their own minds. An effort was made to fit Horton into the OWI organization, and for a time he was in charge of the domestic news desk, but the experiment was an impossible one. Horton had made too many enemies, and a goodly number of them had become important officials in OWI. He did not like the influx into this informational agency of high-powered advertising and promotional experts, and he made his dislike very evident. Davis once remarked to him: "Bob, I've asked a lot of people about you and all of 'em either say that you're an S. O. B. or say you're a swell guy. There doesn't seem to be any middle ground." Eventually Horton departed, going over to OPA to serve as Henderson's press representative until Henderson himself was forced out, and then returning to the Maritime Commission to finish the war in charge of press work there. Currently he lives in the mountains of Vermont, operating a summer hotel and meditating on the errancies of government life.

With Horton there departed something essential from the administration's approach to the task of telling the people about their war—not because Horton was a more honest man or a greater believer in democracy than Davis, because he wasn't, but simply because the administration's own attitude had changed. Originally, all that had been required was a clear channel of information from the government to the people; what was wanted now was a mechanism that would put an end to the appearance of confusion in Washington. OWI had been given an impossible assignment.

The second strike that Davis took up to the plate with him had to do with the military, and it proved exceedingly significant.

In his comments on Davis's new assignment, Columnist Lindley had remarked:

"It is doubtful whether any war information service can win confidence in this country until it gets more authority over the information services of the Army and Navy." That expressed the view of the newspaper group in Washington perfectly. It was assumed that Davis had been given that authority; certainly his presidential directive looked clear enough. But getting authority over even the most remote fringe of the War or Navy Departments in wartime is not just a matter of official directives but of slugging it out and getting whole-hearted support from the White House, and everybody knew it; so the press corps kept its fingers crossed and waited for a test case.

It did not have to wait long for the first tip-off, which came from Secretary of War Henry L. Stimson himself, at a press conference he held a few days after Davis's appointment. It was generally known that Davis had gone to see Stimson, to talk about the possibility of having Army news announcements handled by OWI, and the reporters wanted to know about it. One of them, accordingly, asked Stimson if Davis would have the power to supervise Army and Navy communiqués.

Stimson looked dour and a little surprised, as if someone had mentioned the unmentionable in polite society, with ladies present.

"Is Mr. Davis," he asked, heavily, "an educated military officer?"

Mr. Davis obviously was no such thing, and as far as Stimson was concerned that was that. It might possibly have helped if someone had arisen to remark that however great Davis's ignorance of military matters might be it could not, through time and eternity, come within many miles of matching the deep, abysmal, appalling, and arrogant ignorance of civilian emotions, motives, morale, and ideals which sat entrenched under the brass hats on the skulls of Army officers at the Pentagon

Building, and that it was in the highest degree important, in a people's war, that someone with at least a faint understanding of such matters should have something to say about the way in which the people were told about the fighting. But you don't row with cabinet officers at press conferences, Stimson obviously did not want to hear any more about it, and there the matter rested.

The actual test case came a few days after that.

Davis was appointed on June 12. On June 27 the FBI announced the capture of eight Nazi saboteurs, fresh off the boat from Germany. That set the stage for the showdown.

The saboteurs were military prisoners and the Army naturally took over. On July 2 the President announced that the men would be tried behind closed doors by a military commission appointed by himself. The commission, he added, would be headed by Major General Frank R. McCoy, and it would have power to make such rules as it deemed necessary for a fair trial. The prisoners were lodged in the District of Columbia jail, which became an armed camp surrounded by military guards, and carpenters went to work preparing a trial room on the fifth floor of the Department of Justice Building. Nobody involved would say anything; Army secrecy covered every detail of the case; it was impossible to get anyone to admit even so much as the time or the place of the hearing. The men had been caught, they were going to be tried, and in due season the result of the trial would be announced, and that was all there was going to be to it.

This irritated the press, which does not admire star chamber proceedings, and the press went to Davis to see whether some ray of light might not be shed on the proceedings. No reporter in his senses, of course, supposed that the trial of these spies could be held in open court, like the trial of a damage suit against a street railway company; the need for keeping a good part of the testimony very much off the record was readily admitted. But the boys had seen Army security at work before, and they knew it for what it was—an unfathomably, irrationally stupid proposition whose one guiding principle is: Tell nothing to anybody. The people (who, to repeat, were after all fighting the war) had a perfect right to know as much as possible about the trial, and any intelligent man could easily see that a great deal might be told them without hurting military security in the least.

But where matters of simple intelligence in respect to news are concerned, the Army just naturally belongs to the Jukes family. Something had to be done, and OWI had been set up to do it.

Davis played it straight. He realized that it was useless to try to get reporters admitted to the trial; the necessities of the case could be met, however, by assigning a responsible official of OWI to sit in on the case and issue news releases periodically, the releases being carefully edited to avoid giving useful knowledge to the enemy. Accordingly he sent one of his principal officers, Henry Paynter (a veteran New York newspaperman, inherited by Davis from the Horton organization), over to the opening session of the trial.

Paynter's first effort was to try to see General McCoy and work out arrangements—arrangements, at the very least, to permit him to get inside the room where the trial was being held. He waited for an hour without getting anywhere. Finally McCoy sent him a note. It read:

"The General does not wish to see the gentleman. The gentleman need not wait."

That was that. OWI never did get in—not because handling news about the trial did not come within OWI's proper province, but simply because the Army did not propose to be bothered. The Army ultimately unbent so far as to issue a communiqué, of its own wording and editing, over McCoy's name, at the end of each day's session, and it permitted OWI to publish the communiqué through the OWI news room; but the communiqué said little beyond revealing the fact that the trial was in fact going on and that the eight saboteurs were actually in court. In his news story in the Washington *Post*, Reporter Dillard Stokes commented that this "spelled failure for the efforts of Elmer Davis, director of the Office of War Information, to inform the American public of the sensational hearing and to forestall anticipated Nazi propaganda charges that the eight spies are being put away in a star chamber proceeding." On the following day, Stokes wrote that Davis "had been getting one of the most brutal brush-offs ever witnessed in Washington."

Brutal indeed, and Davis did not propose to take it lying down. He and Stimson went to the White House for a showdown . . . the sole result of which was McCoy's agreement to issue his skimpy communiqués through OWI. The Army was upheld all along the line. Davis admitted as much at a press coference he held on July 11 to discuss the scope and functions of OWI.

The Army and the Navy, he explained, would still largely determine when and how much the public was to be told about battles and military operations generally. They had promised to keep him in touch with military developments and to let him make suggestions when he thought the news wasn't coming out fast enough, but the generals and admirals would still have the say-so on matters of military security—which, as everybody in Washington knew, meant anything the Army and Navy felt like making it mean. No one in OWI would be permitted to discuss military matters for publication; comment and background on military news, along with all battle communiqués, would continue to come from the armed forces.

Defeat, with far-reaching consequences. Witness the editorial comment in the Washington *Post* following the Davis press conference:

"This agency [OWI] was created in response to rapidly mounting indignation over the inadequate, confusing, and often contradictory items concerning the war supplied by the myriad government press agents and 'spokesmen.' The chief offenders have been the departments of the armed services. The OWI, it was expected, would bring order out of chaos, and the appointment of Mr. Davis to head it was widely hailed by press and public alike as an excellent one. Must the public now be left to understand that the setting up of this new agency was merely for the purpose of stopping this public clamor? Was it never contemplated that Mr. Davis is to be given powers to correct the appalling situation he inherited? It begins to look like it."

It certainly did look like it, and with good reason, for it was in fact the case. And the whole business was not just another case of an administration failing to make sense out of its press arrangements, or of the Army getting its own purblind way in the matter of military communiqués. It reflected an underlying condition that was frightening to contemplate at the time and became even more frightening a few years later when some of its consequences began to be more clearly recognizable.

For what Davis was really up against was exactly what Nelson was beginning to collide with over in WPB, and exactly what the people themselves, in the end, were to come up against: the fact that a crippling and inadequate pattern had been set for the whole war effort.

The basic decision had been made, by this time, and the kind of war we were going to fight had been determined. Militarily, the decision was good; everything for victory and for the quickest possible victory, and the devil may take any other considerations than those of strategy and tactics. That was all to the good—except for the fact that every other wartime decision stemmed from it. Military needs not only came first; they were the only needs that anyone felt obliged to worry about very deeply, the only needs the government was really prepared to meet. For only our military goals were clearly fixed, only our military policy was sharply defined. Everything else was left hazy. This was to be a purely military war, a straight exercise in strategy, tactics, and logistics, a strictly military war in place of the all-out *people's war* we thought we were fighting.

That meant military dominance, for the military men were the only men who knew exactly where they were going. Anyone who fought against that dominance, as Davis had already discovered and as Nelson was to learn during the next two years, was doomed to fight a series of rear-guard actions. The cards were stacked against him. What the critics would take for personal weakness, as he struggled with ill-success against military encroachment, was actually a weakness in his basic position, about which he could do nothing. Neither Davis, Nelson, nor anyone else could keep the War Department from throwing its weight around and making far-reaching decisions in purely nonmilitary fields, because that was inherent in the kind of war we were fighting. We were not following the theory that the work of the military was only part of the job; in practice that was just about all the job there was, or at least it was all that really had to be done, and the military was always in a position to put the screws on.

But military dominance didn't just mean that Army officers ran things, to the dismay of good civilians. It meant, of necessity, an inflexible commitment to preserve Things as They Were.

Hitler had challenged the fundamentals of the American dream. By force of arms he had asserted that his own frantic, nightmare society was the only kind of society which could survive amid the interlocked complications of modern finance, industrial cartels, and the unsolved problems of the age of machinery. He himself might be beaten by hot lead and cold steel, but it was going to take more than that to defeat the idea back of him; was going to take, indeed, an idea of even greater clarity and vitality. His armies and air fleets were, in the end, only the cutting edge of the menace. They were our military objectives—but military objectives were the only objectives that mattered.

To meet the challenge by posing an even greater challenge of our own, to find, by the very process of fighting for survival, new ways of making old values enduring, to transmute the tremendous hopes and vitality of democracy into something that men would know and passionately believe in and gladly die for because they had been a part of its birth and growth and had shared in its transfiguration—all of this, at the last, was beyond us. Something happened, every time we tried, and the final excuse was always the same: from a purely military viewpoint we didn't have to. We could win the war without doing anything drastic. The General does not wish to see the gentleman. The gentleman need not wait.

CHAPTER SIXTEEN

O King Agrippa

NAKED we came into the world, and naked we must go out of it. As it was in the beginning, so must it be in the end. Read Genesis and you get a fairly good line on Exodus. Which is to say that we came out of the war, at last, precisely as we went into it—unready; unready in spite of the most elaborate preparations, unready because the price of getting ready was a price which the men at the top simply were unable to pay. The story of 1944 and 1945 is the story of 1940 and 1941 all over again. In each case men saw a crisis over the horizon and undertook to prepare for it; in each case, when the showdown came, the right answer just wasn't there. Like that bright phrase, "all-out defense," reconversion was a concept which brought the men of destiny squarely up against the limitations imposed by the Old Order. The limitations were not removed.

The reconversion program, in other words, was a failure. There was no spectacular pillar of fire from Pearl Harbor to dramatize the failure, as had been the case with the earlier effort. Dramatic values were lacking, this time; the prophets of gloom themselves were wrong, for the end of the war was not followed by mass unemployment, total disorganization of industry, and an outraged people clamoring at the gates of the palace. But the reconversion problem was not just a question of getting through the twelve months following the end of the fighting. Rather, it was a matter of setting long-range directions, of retrieving earlier losses, of facing up to the issues which had been dodged, of making it possible for the nation to meet the test of peace. There was a complete failure to meet this problem.

There were many causes for this failure, and they can be spelled out in a great deal of detail, and when they are all added up they are not so terribly important after all. For the real failure was a failure of vision. And perhaps this is a good place to tell the story of Dick Scholz, which has nothing whatever to do with reconversion but has a good deal to do with this matter of vision. . . .

Dick Scholz was a young reporter who covered the defense agencies in the period leading up to Pearl Harbor. Dick was a handsome chap of twenty-three or twenty-four with wavy black hair and a friendly smile, and he was well on the way to becoming a top-notch newspaper man; he had recently gone from the Washington *News* to the staff of *Time* magazine; he was a hound at digging out the news and he knew how to write, and in addition to being as likable and admirable a young American as you could find anywhere, he was obviously a young man with a future. He took the defense program very seriously—so much so that it may have lessened his value as a reporter, for it destroyed his objectivity, although worse things than that can happen to a reporter, probably. Anyway, Dick thought that the leading officials of OPM were botching their job and doing the nation a disservice, and he was forever on the prowl for news stories that would prove his point. He was a daily caller at the offices of the Information Division, where we used to greet him with some such remark as "Well—here's Junior again!" for we were old-timers and we were worldly-wise, and we figured it was good for him to be reminded that he was young and innocent. Dick would grin and sit down with us, and together we would arrange to put him in possession of some fact or set of facts which would show that the defense program was not coming along nearly as well as the men in charge wanted people to think it was.

So finally Pearl Harbor day came, and almost immediately afterward Dick joined the Navy and went off to be trained as an aviator. He figured he ought not to wait to be drafted. "After all," he said, "I've been raising hell for months because the government hasn't been moving fast enough to win the war. Now it's time to show that I really mean it." So he wound up at Pensacola, and the next thing we knew he had his wings and an ensign's commission and was all ready to show whatever it was that he had to show.

About that time I got a letter from him. Dick was a bright lad, and he apparently had been graduated at the head of his class and had made something of an impression on the officers in charge of the flying school; at any rate, he had been informed that if he wished he could remain at Pensacola as an instructor instead of going to the fleet as a combat pilot. In a mild way they had even put the heat on him, explaining that he would actually serve his country more effectively by staying there in comparative safety, training other young men, than he would by going off to fight. This had given him something to wrestle with. The wrestling was all finished and he had made his decision, but he wanted to tell somebody about it so he wrote to me.

He knew perfectly well, Dick said, that he had a bright future as a newspaper man. It was a future he very much wanted to enjoy; in plain English, he wanted to live, he wanted to survive the war and come back and pick up the old threads and make the most of the fine life that was clearly ahead of him. This proposition to stay at Pensacola and be an instructor for the duration looked like manna from heaven. It was conscience-proof, too, or at least it ought to be; his superior officers were urging him to do it and were telling him that that was how he could make his biggest contribution to the defeat of Germany and Japan. All in all, what could be better?

But he had been doing a good deal of thinking, Dick continued. (Unless you are far too hard-boiled to weep, don't ever sit down to meditate on the *thinking* that was done in those days by millions of kids who were just a few years out of high school. They had so much of it to do, and so little time for it.) He would be perfectly justified in taking the instructor's job, to be sure; but at the same time, if he did he would know, all the rest of his life, that his real, inner reason for taking it was his selfish desire to go on living. And while it was natural and harmless enough for a young man to want to go on living, nevertheless it seemed to Dick that something big was at stake in this war—something that had made it impossible for him to watch OPM and its inadequate work without getting angry, something that had made it impossible for him to wait quietly to be drafted; and therefore, taking one thing with another, he had decided that he could not take this instructorship. Instead, he had put in for assignment as pilot of a torpedo-bomber (the most dangerous of all the Navy's flying jobs, he had been told at Pensacola), had been given the assignment, and would be going to sea shortly. He just wanted me to know about it.

That's about all there is to the story. Dick went to the Pacific on a carrier and was shot down on his first combat mission. He had made his choice and he had paid for it with his life, and—

—and. And what?

It doesn't do to grow emotional about the war. War calls for cool heads and clear thinking, and while an upsurge of deep feeling may help get young men into the armed services, where they are needed, the real business at issue has to be handled by men who can be objective, matter-of-fact, and practical. So they say, anyway, and so it is done. But our victory in this war was bought for us by a great many thousands of young men like Dick Scholz, who had a deep understanding that the real issue was something more than a mere challenge to their manhood, who somehow believed that they were buying something unspeakably precious by giving up their lives—which, one and all, they valued and wanted to hang onto precisely as Dick did. And there is no way to estimate the weight of the obligation which those lads who died put upon us who stayed safely at home, except perhaps to say that it was—and it still is—at all times incumbent upon us to recognize the vision they died for, and to live up to it.

The vision: something beyond price, purchased for us at a cost beyond human comprehension; it was in the keeping of assorted government officials in Washington, who had to be cool and clear-headed and realistic but who also had to be capable of understanding the values they were dealing with. For they were the men who, by their day-to-day actions, by the accumulation of their decisions on many routine matters, were going to determine how we would meet the responsibility and the opportunity of victory.

In the end, they failed. Instead of having a vision and following it, they had fear and distrust—fear and distrust of any future which might turn out to be different from the old, familiar past; fear and distrust of the people to whom the future might belong. So the boldness and imagination which might have turned the reconversion program into a means of achieving the goal the young men were dying for were lacking. Instead, reconversion became a matter of playing it safe, of guarding established interests, of settling feuds personal and political; and it was made so because the men who had the power in their hands were canny and practical in all things and were far too level-headed to be in the least visionary.

(But they had to be canny and practical, because so much was at stake? So should Dick Scholz have been canny and practical, because much was at stake for him, also. Four hundred thousand young Americans killed, and men of affairs should not try to see and follow a vision? What *was* the war all about, anyway?)

The different threads that go into this pattern of failure are badly tangled. There is no one place where you can put your finger on the text and say: Here is the point where the big mistake was made. Studying the whole process, from the moment when reconversion began to be talked about down to the death of the Office of Price Administration (to take a handy milestone) is a little bit like studying a game of chess. No single move appears to be decisive; each one seems to grow out of some previous move, and only a long-range view shows the general plan of campaign. Yet the pattern is there and it does emerge, inexorably, out of many factors.

One of these factors, oddly enough, was the progressive decline in the prestige and power of Donald Nelson; and this decline both grew out of and helped to determine the long and disastrous struggle between the military and civilian sides of the government. The struggle was dramatic only by fits and starts, and it was a queer sort of drama anyway since its heroes were not consistently heroic and its villains were not personally villainous; but it had the most far-reaching effects, involving mundane matters like the new house you were unable to buy after the war ended, the apartment you couldn't rent, the jump in the cost of your food and in the price you had to pay for shoes and children's underwear, the prospect of your having a job a few years from now and, indeed, the chance for a continued peace. For this struggle was more than just a set-to between soldiers and civilians. In the end it became a showdown between those who were afraid of the future and those who were not. Nelson became the key figure in this contest, and before it came to a climax he had been whittled down to the point where he couldn't carry the load.

In one sense, many of the troubles which descended upon the WPB Chairman were of his own making. It will be remembered that his first act, on becoming boss of war production, was to decide that his civilian agency would not take over the Army's procurement powers. During the next two years the chickens which were thereby hatched out came home to roost by flocks and droves and myriads. The War Department, retaining the power to buy the munitions it needed, promptly translated that power into an assertion, endlessly repeated, of the right to say how the munitions should be produced and how the civilian economy should be operated; and there was no final way to deny that assertion because any agency that spends sixty-odd billions of dollars a year in the American market is going to have a good deal to say about how that market operates, whether it theoretically ought to have such a right or not. The Army bought enormous quantities of heavy goods such as tanks, artillery, motor trucks, and the like, which required vast tonnages of steel; and because the Army was actually placing the orders for these items, and negotiating with the manufacturers who were to produce them, and not merely notifying a civilian agency that it had to have them, the Army was inevitably concerned with such matters as the ultimate supply of steel, the uses to which that steel was put, the way in which it was divided up, and the decisions that were made on other claims for a part of the steel. Since the Army, of necessity, was geared to think only about its own supplies and the deadlines that had to be met on them, it was forever in the position of complaining that too much steel (or rubber, or wool, or wood-pulp, or lead, or manpower) was being devoted to nonessential activities, even though those activities and the ways in which they were provided for were obviously none of the Army's business.

This meant that the activities of the War Production Board involved an endless series of head-on collisions between the civilians and the military. Was it necessary to allocate steel for machinery to keep the iron mines running? The Army could be counted on to oppose such a move vigorously, with acid words about "coddling the civilian economy." Newsprint was short; the Army, therefore, argued that newspapers should be kept from printing comic strips since that was a clear waste of critical material, and the mere fact that this would involve the government in a highly effective form of censorship of the press was brushed aside as utterly irrelevant. Enormous new factories for the manufacture of ordnance items had been built, turning cross-roads villages into humming little manufacturing cities; but although the need for new housing for the men who were to work in these plants was admitted, any use of material or labor to increase the output of building materials or to provide the community services needed by a vastly expanded labor force was bitterly opposed. In selecting targets for its strategic bombing force in Europe the Army assigned top priority to the German railway networks, on the ground that a highly industrialized community could not operate efficiently without good railway transportation; yet when the War Production Board undertook to provide more materials and equipment to keep American railroads in good working order the Army opposed the move as a waste which would detract from the war effort.

The chairman of the WPB had been set up as a combined planner and director of the broad, intricate production program, and as a species of umpire to decide between the conflicting claims of the different war agencies. The planning and the directing were doing fine, but the umpiring—as might have been anticipated—was not going too well, partly because umpires are never popular but chiefly because, under the terms of the game as it was being played, the Army as one of the contestants was always claiming a share in the umpire's power.

This led good men to call their shots wrong. The War Department voiced bitter objections to Nelson personally and to his manner of running WPB when what it was really shooting at was the fact that the Army had some control over the civilian economy but not final control. Nelson, in turn, had equally bitter objections to Under-Secretary Patterson and General Somervell, although his real cause for complaint was the fact that the War Department had some control instead of no control at all. Given the arrangement that existed in those days, unending conflict between civilians and military men was inevitable.

This hurt Nelson's prestige. When he was appointed, he had been greeted by press and Congress as the "czar" of war production. All well and good; yet the czar, it appeared, was forever having trouble with his subjects. Should not the chairman of the War Production Board be a man who could get along with the Army people? Or, alternatively, shouldn't he be able to impose his will on them once and for all, and so end the bickering? Such questions began to be asked more and more frequently, which irritated the President. He had put Nelson in as chief of WPB to end the disputes and provide unified control over war production. War production did seem to be coming along nicely, but the disputes continued and had a way of getting space on the front pages of the newspapers. The inevitable result was that Nelson presently ceased to be one of the true inner circle of White House favorites.

The unmistakable sign came from the White House in November, 1942, when former Senator James F. Byrnes resigned from the Supreme Court to accept a presidential appointment as Director of Economic Stabilization—a new office which ultimately was to become the Office of War Mobilization.

The creation of this new office was a typical bit of Washington overlayering. For one reason or another the WPB setup had not worked out quite as expected. The remedy, therefore, was—neither to serve notice on all and sundry that what the boss of WPB said went, nor to put a new man in as head of WPB with instructions to pull things together regardless of breakage, but to create a new agency overlapping everybody. Byrnes was designated as the super-umpire, a visibly embodied extension of the final power of the President. Did the different agencies row among themselves, did the decisions of the old umpire fail to sit well with the disputants? Then take it to the new umpire and let him decide; this time it's final, and let's hear no more about it.

The choice of Byrnes was generally accepted as a good one. He was suave, likable, an able politician, gifted with a knack for inducing rival claimants to compromise. A WPB official once remarked ruefully: "Suppose you and I have an argument in arithmetic; you claim that two and two make four, while I claim two and two make six. We take it to Jimmy Byrnes for a decision. He's apt to get us both to agree that two and two make five." Clearly, if anyone could make the war machine run smoothly, it ought to be Byrnes.

News of his appointment, nevertheless, landed on Nelson with the impact of half a ton of brick falling from a high building. He learned about it in the same way Knudsen had learned that OPM was being superseded—via the news ticker; and he at once assumed that he himself was being fired, just as Knudsen had been fired. After some twenty-four hours word came through from the White House: Nothing of the kind, you're doing a grand job, keep right on as you are, this is just an arrangement for taking work off the President's desk. . . . This was comforting, and Nelson stuck to his post. But WPB had slipped down a notch in the official scale of values. The wind had veered a trifle. There was now an agency to which WPB's decisions could be appealed, conceivably an agency that would presently be deciding the issues WPB used to decide, possibly even an agency that would take over the direction and operation of WPB itself.

This would not have mattered so much if it were not that Washington, the front counter and the show window of democracy, is exactly like an oriental court. In the executive branch of the government, most especially in wartime, practically all power comes from the President; appointed officials operate largely on authority given them by the President, who may at any time take it away from them and give it to somebody else. Consequently, all over town there is an amazing alertness to detect and analyze the frowns, smiles, snubs, and who-talks-to-whom of the throne room; a great preoccupation with the changes in atmosphere which indicate that so-and-so no longer enjoys the personal confidence and last-ditch backing of the source of power, and that who's-it is now the rising man. And by the end of 1942 it was clear for all to see that in Nelson's case the sultan had administered an unmistakable snub. Nelson was no longer unassailable; he was a man who could be had, if you went at it right, and people promptly went to work to have him. The scheming and conniving that followed would have been harmless enough—except that we were at war, and the values war was buying for us would, in the end, have to be worked out as part of the bitter struggle for place and authority.

First step in this struggle was a bitter scrap between the War Department and WPB over the extent of WPB's powers.

WPB controlled the distribution of raw materials through the exercise of its priorities authority. This control, originally, was incomplete; a good part of the priorities power had been vested in the Army and Navy Munitions Board, and there was a good deal of conflict. Nelson solved that, in the middle of 1942, by bringing the bulk of the Munitions Board operations over into WPB; and to operate this expanded chain of control over the distribution of raw materials he brought into WPB the man who had been running the Munitions Board, Ferdinand Eberstadt.

Eberstadt was out of Wall Street. He was quiet, cold, immensely able, with a spring-steel brain to which the intricate task of allotting the nation's basic raw materials seemed clear and simple. He perfected and put into operation the mechanism which was to make that task effective—the famous Controlled Materials Plan, an immeasurably useful device. Under his direction the materials-distribution part of WPB's job was well taken care of.

But now the War Department began to argue that WPB's job should end there. Let WPB handle the distribution of materials and nothing more; the procurement agencies would do everything else, WPB could pass out materials at their direction, and there would be no more conflicts or regrettable clashes of personalities. (You and I will get along fine, said the General in the old Army story, but you will do most of the getting.) Since this was not at all the idea back of the formation of WPB—since it clearly and immediately meant full military control over the whole war economy—Nelson balked. Balking, he persuaded the President to call in Charles E. Wilson—General Electric Wilson, the fabulous production expert and driving force. When Wilson arrived, Nelson announced that he would be expected to devise and operate a means of scheduling the production of all of the items that were being made out of the materials whose distribution Eberstadt was supervising.

The question then was: Who is to be the Number Two man in WPB—Eberstadt or Wilson? If Eberstadt, then WPB becomes in effect what the Army wants it to be, a materials-control agency pure and simple; if Wilson, then WPB is what Nelson wants it to be, an agency that exercises the basic controls over the economy of a nation at war. Naturally enough, the Army backed Eberstadt with everything it had. Fully aware of this, Nelson countered—early in 1943—by dramatically enlarging Wilson's job and diminishing Eberstadt's, thereby serving notice that Wilson was going to be the Number Two man and that Eberstadt was going to be just another subordinate official.

The War Department countered by trying to get Nelson fired.

Nelson learned about it just in the nick of time. Coming to his office one morning in the middle of February, 1943, Nelson was informed by his grapevine that his head was to be laid on the chopping block that very afternoon. The Secretaries of War and Navy, Stimson and Knox, accompanied by their Under-

Secretaries, Patterson and Forrestal, had a date to see the President at two o'clock; they were going to take with them a draft of a letter which had been prepared for the President's signature, removing Nelson as chairman of WPB, putting Bernard Baruch in his place, and naming Eberstadt as Baruch's principal deputy. Justice Byrnes had given his approval; apparently the President was ready to sign. Nelson hastily did a little checking, by telephone, and found that this grapevine report was correct.

Nelson tried to get in touch with the President. No luck: the President was tied up, and so forth. Then Nelson got a member of the White House secretariat on the telephone and complained that he was about to be executed without being given a hearing.

"The President expects you to take things in your own hands," replied the man at the White House. "This whole row seems to be centering around Eberstadt—yet you've been keeping Eberstadt in your own organization all this time. Do something about *that*, and then see if the Boss doesn't invite you in for a chat."

Nelson meditated. There was no time to lose. It was then about ten o'clock in the morning; in four hours the White House conference would take place, and Nelson would become the man who used to be. Nelson couldn't reach the President. After all, though, he could reach Eberstadt.

So he did the one thing that could save his job. He dictated and speedily issued a press release announcing that he had asked for, had received and had accepted Eberstadt's resignation. (In other words, he fired him—or, as a little stenographer in the Information Division remarked, "Mr. Nelson has resigned Mr. Eberstadt.") He did this so fast that the announcement was ready for distribution in the OWI press room before Nelson got around to telling Eberstadt about it. By noon it was on the news tickers and in the papers.

This move was either very smart or very lucky; for it was the only thing Nelson could have done to prevent his own dismissal. Obviously, if the President fired Nelson immediately after Nelson fired Eberstadt, nobody would ever believe that he hadn't fired Nelson *because* Nelson fired Eberstadt. To fire Nelson now was to reinstate Eberstadt. But the President, as it happened, was not fond of Eberstadt. Early in the war, Eberstadt had flatly refused to carry out some specific request which the President had made.

He may have been right in that refusal or he may have been wrong; the point is that FDR had an elephant's memory and was singularly unforgiving. He had been ready to go along with the elevation of Eberstadt, as part of the general reshuffle, but with Eberstadt out he would not bring him back in.

So the whole project fell through, the White House conference was not held, and Nelson retained his job. A little later that afternoon Nelson telephoned the White House advisor to whom he had talked earlier in the day. "I just thought I'd tell you," he said, "that I have an appointment to see the President at five this afternoon."

But if this was a victory, it left the victor in rather bad shape. Nelson had escaped destruction by the skin of his teeth. At one moment the President had been perfectly ready to drop him, and everybody knew it. If that had happened once it could happen again, and the one certainty in an uncertain world was that the opportunity for it to happen again would be provided. The breach between Nelson and the War Department was permanent now. Before the war ended, one or the other was going to be licked.

And this was not just one more chapter in the dreary history of bureaucratic rivalries in Washington. Underneath the personal animosities, what was really involved was the theory that the Army confines itself to military matters and that civilians govern the country, which is basic to American democracy if anything is. With all his weaknesses and all his faults, Nelson stood for civilian control; the man and the idea were tied together so firmly that civilian control, in the end, would stand or fall with Nelson.

Nor was that the end of it. Having re-established himself—on however shaky a footing—as boss of war production, Nelson began to take thought about the end of the war. Late in August, 1943, he sat down and wrote to the President about it. He told the President that while "we obviously must continue to arm for a prolonged, hard war," it would be wise to begin making real plans for meeting the domestic economic problems which would arise once the Nazis finally surrendered; the domestic economic problems, which would be so momentous that the way in which they were met would determine what the country did with the peace after it had been won.

After sending this letter, Nelson began work in earnest on the preparation of a reconversion plan. This was all to the good, of course; but the upshot was that in addition to representing civilian control, Nelson also came to represent postwar planning. It was certain that he was going to be fought, and because he was slowly sinking in the official scale of values the odds were that he would eventually be defeated. Yet these two issues were tied to him. They would fare as he fared. The men who, for reasons of their own, opposed civilian control, would presently find allies in the men who (also for reasons of their own) opposed a positive reconversion program. Nelson was becoming a symbol of something much bigger than himself.

Nineteen forty-three was the year of the false dawn. It no longer seemed absurd to start thinking about victory. Despite all of the warnings about overoptimism (which were sounded, at regular intervals, by every Washington official who possessed a press agent) the mood of officialdom at that time was definitely hopeful. The dark days of early 1942, when the very worst anyone could imagine might easily turn out to be true, had been left behind. The war was looking better in the Pacific, Italy had given up, Russia obviously was in the war to stay, and the Army Air Force was plastering Germany with bombs—and was press-agenting its achievements so lustily that it was not uncommon to find writers and speakers seriously discussing whether Germany might not presently be knocked clear out of the war by bombing alone, without invasion.

Most encouraging of all was the change in the war production picture. The arsenal of democracy was living up to its name so well that it was going to be able to ease up on its operations; the Army was beginning to reduce its programs, and its contracts. Production for November, 1943, was the record high for the entire war. From then on, with all its ups and downs, production was on the downhill slope, and by the end of the year the goal which had seemed almost unimaginable two years earlier had clearly been reached; the country at last was able to make more stuff than was needed to win the war.

But it was not optimism which led Nelson to urge a quick start on reconversion planning; in the beginning, at least, it was a concern over war production itself. Postwar planning would help win the war. Industry knew perfectly well that such planning had not been started, its absence made the future look uncertain, and the uncertainty was beginning to hamper the production of war goods—not seriously, but still noticeably. Some companies, as Nelson told the President, were holding their inventories of parts and materials down below efficient operating levels because they suspected early contract cancellations; others, whose contracts had run out, were hesitant about taking on more war work because they wanted to be in shape to resume peacetime production promptly whenever the wartime restrictions were canceled. Therefore, as Nelson put it, "there is a real need at this time to create confidence that the government is taking vigorous measures to assure an orderly and equitable reconversion of the economy to a peacetime footing, as and when military developments permit."

This letter to the President accomplished nothing in particular, from a practical standpoint, except that it did put Nelson out in front on the subject of reconversion planning. He had by no means drafted a reconversion program, as yet, but he had served notice that such a program must be drafted well in advance of the war's end. Going into the war, it had been necessary to realize that the wartime task was so enormous that simply doing the job would have far-reaching and incalculable effects on the nation. Exactly the same was true of reconversion; it was altogether too big to be left to chance and aimless drifting. Furthermore, Nelson had made a point of cardinal importance: that the war economy itself would run more smoothly and efficiently if the government openly and vigorously made arrangements for a smooth transition to peace.

During the next few months Nelson laboriously hammered his ideas into shape. Early in the autumn, he wrote: "Whether German resistance collapses soon or in the more distant future, as the war progresses toward a successful conclusion and as it becomes possible to shift at an increasing tempo to civilian production, an uncontrolled inflationary production boom might well develop, with subsequent deflation and crisis, unless the progress of reconversion is systematically regulated." * A little later he

* Note that in the end the progress of reconversion was *not* systematically regulated, and that it was precisely this anticipation of an inflationary boom followed by deflation and crisis which became a cardinal point in Soviet Russia's postwar attitude toward the United States.

209

explained to a caller that the absence of industrial controls in a period of demobilization might have disastrous effects, with the industrial giants using their war-increased weight and muscle to slug their way through to control over parts and materials; the reconversion program, therefore, ought to be planned on broad lines, with special reference to meeting the country's needs in such fields as housing, transportation, and consumers' durable goods.

These, to be sure, were only statements of general principles. It was still going to be necessary to work from them to a concrete program. Nelson was groping toward one, but he hadn't found it yet. What he had found, however, was basic: recognition of the overriding fact that the country had enormously increased its own strength during the war. Industrially, it was half again as powerful as it had been in 1940. For better or for worse—for prosperity or for depression—its potentialities were greater than ever before. It could rise higher and it could also fall farther. It was going to have the future in its hands—*if* it had the vision to see it.

Vision, once more. In a world of hard, common-sense practicalities, the most imperative practicality of all was this need for men who could see and follow a vision: a vision of what the war had meant, of what all the young men had died for, of what America had gained by its ability to bring forth some hundreds of thousands of boys like Dick Scholz, who wanted to live because life was going to be good but who wanted something else just a little more. This vision would have to be found in the course of working out a prosaic, matter-of-fact program for reconversion; that program, in turn, would have to be built around the vision, if the vision were not to be dishonored and lost. . . . Wherefore, O King Agrippa [said the Apostle Paul], I have not been disobedient unto the heavenly vision. . . .

But if America needed a few visionaries in high places, what America actually had was a dog-fight between WPB and the War Department, a complex and unedifying tangle of clashing personalities and discordant motives, out of which would have to come whatever the nation was going to get in the way of a plan to meet the future.

CHAPTER SEVENTEEN

What Price Facts?

THE YEAR 1944 was the great year of decision, the year of omens and portents, the year that swung like a gate to the future. America was the Valley of Dry Bones, waiting for the word that would bring life and hope and the vision without which men perish; and what America was given, as the great year opened, was a public scolding.

On New Year's Day the papers front-paged a long, impassioned, and somewhat startling interview with an impressively unidentified "personage high in the councils of the United States and the United Nations," who felt that the populace had got into a disgraceful frame of mind and who did not hesitate to say so.

His particular targets were two recent events: one, a railroad labor dispute, which had resulted in a presidential order directing the Army to take over the railroads; two, a Christmas Eve walkout in a number of steel mills, which had affected some 170,000 workers in nine states. These events, said the high personage, may well have prolonged the war by six months, thereby causing hundreds of thousands of needless casualties. The railroad labor dispute, he declared, was "the damnedest crime ever committed against America"—which, apparently, gave it top billing over the treason of Benedict Arnold, Aaron Burr's conspiracy, the sinking of the *Maine*, and the attack on Pearl Harbor.

"Well-posted strategists," the interview went on to explain, had hoped that unremitting Allied pressure, plus stepped-up aerial warfare, might cause German collapse by spring—perhaps even as early as February. Now, however, said the highly placed one, German propagandists had just the weapon they needed to bolster their nation's failing morale. The threat to American production caused by these labor difficulties, he added, was not the important thing; what really mattered was the setback given to anti-Hitler forces behind the German lines.

This outburst was more than a little surprising. The railroad labor case had been disturbing enough, but it had not caused any trains to stop running. The administration had taken the dispute out of the hands of the National Mediation Board (where it had gone, under the regular provisions of the Railway Labor Act) and had undertaken to bring about agreement by direct intervention. This attempt had been bungled, strike notices had been served, and the Army had been directed to take control. Freight and passengers continued to be hauled in the regular way, and the row obviously was going to be settled without the slightest effect on the nation's transportation service.

The steel strike had been even less harmful. Sporadic walkouts following the expiration of contracts had involved a comparatively small portion of the industry, and had ended after four days when the War Labor Board issued a directive guaranteeing that whatever wage scales were provided by the new contracts would be made retroactive to the expiration of the old ones. One factor in the steel situation, incidentally, was a recent decline in the Army munitions program which had resulted in cutbacks on steel orders and had brought about the closing of a number of blast furnaces. All in all, the two strikes together had hardly seemed serious enough to disturb even a Republican Congressman.

But now there was this denunciation by a highly placed personage. It was obvious, from the prominence which the papers gave the story, as well as from the awed, slightly breathless way in which the story was written, that the man who had given the interview was very highly placed indeed. William Green, president of the American Federation of Labor, asserted that the personage was none other than the Army Chief of Staff, General George C. Marshall, and this assertion went undenied. Reporters at the White House inquired whether this appraisal of the steel and railway strikes was shared by the President; Presidential Secretary Early replied that the President "seemed to be thinking along the same lines."

That made it official. This was not just a nervous explosion by an overburdened Army chief who was under great strain; it was a calculated thrust, aimed at producing an effect. It was speedily followed by others. The people, it seemed, had to be reminded that there was a war on; they were getting complacent, they were letting down, they needed to have the stern realities of wartime brought home to them.

(At that moment there were some ten million Americans under arms. Someone might have asked: Where did those boys come from, if not from the people? The people, who gave these boys, need to be told there is a war on? Anguish of separation, heart-sick anticipation of tragic loss, aren't enough to tell them: it needs *our* voices yet?)

Thus: shortly ahead of the crime-against-America statement, another equally anonymous but highly authoritative government spokesman revealed that there would be 400,000 casualties in the American armed forces by mid-April (which turned out to be a whopping overestimate, but by mid-April everyone had forgotten the forecast). A bit later the Army and Navy jointly revealed the sickening facts about the terrible "death march" on Bataan. On January 5 the Office of War Information got out a full dress release warning against optimism. The War Department, OWI said, had found no evidence that the German home front was cracking; on the contrary, "German war production is still high, despite allied bombings," and "the German army is still powerful and resourceful, and its morale is high." The release added that "our military leaders, while they would welcome a crumbling of the home front, aren't counting on it." (Somebody seemed to be kidding someone, in all of this; the OWI statement was a flat contradiction of the highly placed personage's assertion that a German collapse might have occurred inside of two months if it hadn't been for the steel and railway strikes. But no matter, the public memory is short, and stern indoctrination is needed.)

And on January 11 President Roosevelt went before Congress and called for "total mobilization" under a national service act. He declared:

"Disunity at home—bickering, self-seeking partisanship, stoppage of work, inflation, business as usual, politics as usual, luxury as usual—these are the influences which can undermine the morale of the brave men ready to die at the front for us here."

The President did not specify the precise form of national service act that was needed, and no official White House draft of such legislation was offered by any Democratic party leaders on the hill. Indeed, the President left a wide-open escape clause in his appeal, since he asserted that he favored national service legislation only if Congress adopted the rest of his projected war program simultaneously—ferociously stiffer taxes, tighter war-profits control, food-cost legislation, and effective stabilization of the wage-price relationship. There was no chance whatever that Congress would go along with him on this; within a fortnight the Senate, for instance, passed a tax bill providing about one-fifth of the revenue he had called for in such a measure. It was the national service law that got all the attention.

As well it might. A national service law, dressed up by no matter what fine phrases, was a labor draft pure and simple. Two years earlier such a law could have been argued for very cogently, and could probably have been passed without too much trouble. Now, however, it simply was not needed, and everybody knew it. War Production was coming down. Employment in the munitions industries had been declining for some time—not because the factories were unable to hold their workers, but because a lower level of employment was adequate. Three days after the President's speech, the War Manpower Commission announced that it was not counting on further increases in the munitions industries' manpower, and cut 600,000 from its estimate of the total labor force that would be needed by July 1. It was admitted that Paul V. McNutt, head of the War Manpower Commission, had been opposed to the proposed legislation. Nelson, head of WPB, similarly saw no need for it. The President himself, in calling for it, had admitted that the war could be won without it, but had added that it might be helpful.

But the War Department did want it.

Immediately after the President had spoken, a draft of a national service act was introduced in Congress, jointly authored —not by the President's own party leaders, but by two Republicans, Senator Austin of Vermont and Congressman Wadsworth of New York. This bill provided that all males between eighteen and sixty-five, and all females between eighteen and fifty, would be liable for service, in selected jobs for which they were qualified, under a conscription system closely patterned after the Selective Service Act. The Senate Military Affairs Committee opened hearings on the bill, and Secretary of War Stimson appeared as the first witness.

Stimson pulled out all of the stops. A manpower draft, he told the Senators, was needed very badly. He spoke of deepening resentment among soldiers over "industrial unrest" and "irresponsibility" on the home front, and he asserted: "If it continues, it will surely affect the morale of the Army. It is likely to prolong the war and endanger our ultimate success." Such a draft, he continued, would not only mobilize needed manpower, but would assure the soldiers that all Americans were willing "to accept the same liability which a soldier must accept for service to country." His voice rose in anger, the newspaper stories related, when he referred to the home front as "on the point of going sour."

"I say we have a situation of anarchy," declared the Secretary of War, "and this is a step to cure that situation of anarchy and to restore law and order."

These were high-powered words, and no mistake about it, and they highlight one of the strangest episodes in American history.

Bear in mind that the American industrial economy—which is to say the American people—had just accomplished the impossible. Munitions production had just gone to its all-time high; the country was at that moment making more war goods than were needed, and the requirements were coming down; this had been done in spite of labor disputes, in spite of all of the hesitations and reluctances of management, in spite of the shortcomings of dollar-a-year men, in spite of the bickerings and rivalries within government. The people had just shown, by the most fantastic production of goods in all human history, that they could and would do anything that was asked of them—and now they were being told, on the highest authority, in a shrill voice that cracked with emotion, that they were in a state of anarchy, that their selfish irresponsibility was prolonging the war and endangering victory itself, and that the sternest of measures was needed to restore law and order.

From the day its independence had been won the republic had passed through grave perils and had had strange experiences, but it had never seen anything quite like this.

What was going on, anyhow? Here was this big push for a manpower draft, accompanied by a furious flagellation of the public. By open admission, this law was needed—not to make people work as they should, but to make them think and react emotionally as they should. This was psychological warfare, naked and undisguised, and it was psychological warfare directed at the American people themselves.

Once more the chickens were coming home to roost. An administration that had pulled its punches—as in the handling of the defense effort before Pearl Harbor, as in the handling of the rubber problem, as in the handling of military news—on the theory that the people could not assimilate the harsh facts without paternal assistance, had finally got to the point where it had to blame the people for that assumed defect. It had acted as if the people were complacent; now, driven by ineluctable logic, it had to cure that complacency. Its desire to create an emotional effect was finally beginning to determine what it did; for the final propaganda is the propaganda of acts, not of words.

But in undertaking to whip national psychology into the desired state, no matter what it might cost, the government was compelled to work at cross purposes. It was beginning to suffer from a marked case of schizophrenia, which affected everything it did from this point on.

The nation had been at war a little more than two years, and the government was demanding, not without a trace of hysteria, the sternest of all war measures; a measure that could be justified only by the argument that the people were not doing their job and that the war would be lost if they *didn't* do it. But just at the moment when it was making this demand, the government was finding that its gravest and most immediate problem was arising from the circumstance that the people had done their job faster and better than anyone had anticipated. To a steadily increasing extent, the government was finding itself compelled to worry about the use that might be made of workers, factories, and raw materials which were no longer needed for war work. The invasion of Europe was still months in the future, but the industrial picture was so encouraging that the administration, in spite of itself, had gone feverishly to work on reconversion plans; had done so, not because anyone supposed the war was nearly over, but because the growing surplus of industrial energy could not be ignored any longer.

Consequently the government was now embarked on two mutually contradictory campaigns. On the one hand it was demanding a manpower draft, on grounds of stark and desperate necessity (situation of anarchy: damnable crimes committed against America); on the other hand it was trying to find a way to ease the nation into the tapering-off period which had actually begun. It was utterly impossible to succeed in both attempts. The government could ballyhoo the people about the need for carrying a heavier load and showing greater willingness to work hard and make sacrifices, or it could begin to adjust the war economy to the lighter load which the economy was going to be bearing henceforward; by no conceivable bit of agility could it hope to do both things at once. But it was going to try, just the same, and the result was the creation of the most violent internal strains —strains which shaped government policies and, in the end, helped to determine what the postwar world was going to be like.

The Kiplinger *Washington Letter* put its finger on the difficulty as early as December 4, 1943, when it warned its readers:

"Two different tunes are being sung by official Washington.

"One is that it is unpatriotic to think about the time of the end, for such thinking is bound to divert energies from war production, and every ounce of production lost may cost the lives of many men. Also, that peace rumors are enemy propaganda to undermine our war effort, and that the people should put them out of mind, lest the people relax.

"The other is that it is high time to think about reconversion, which must be undertaken within industry as soon as Germany is beaten, that it is past the time when reconversion plans should have been laid, that we must now hurry with plans to keep the internal economy healthy for the strain of the later time when we shall be fighting Japan alone.

"What the administration is *talking* is the first view, above.

"What the administration is *doing* is the second.

"Regardless of precise time of German war end, our government is now starting a frantic scramble toward plans for industry conversion from 'full' war production to 'semi' war production."

When Nelson wrote to the President in August calling for a start on reconversion planning, his anxiety had seemed just a trifle premature. By late autumn, however, such anxiety obviously was not premature in the least, and Nelson had gone to work without waiting for specific instructions. At the meeting of the top board of WPB on November 30, 1943, he had declared himself.

As manpower, manufacturing facilities, and materials became available in any given area, he told the Board, his policy would be to authorize the production of additional civilian goods, provided that this production did not interfere with the more urgent programs for munitions production. The materials situation, he pointed out, was steadily improving. Both aluminum and copper were in much easier supply—aluminum was so much easier that substantial cutbacks in production were being ordered—and cutbacks in military programs were expected to make the situation in these and other metals progressively easier in the next few months. In the near future, he said, he would bring the whole subject before the board for extended discussion.

The near future turned out to be the Board meeting of January 11—the same day the President went before Congress to assail disunity, bickering, and work stoppages and to demand a national service act. On that afternoon, in the cramped quarters which WPB was then using for its board meetings, Nelson proposed a limited relaxation in WPB's restrictions on building construction.

Those restrictions were practically air-tight. They prohibited practically all kinds of construction not directly essential to the prosecution of the war. All sorts of chinks had developed in the economy since those rules were adopted; a good many building needs were urgent, and if they could be met without interference with the war effort it would be wise to start meeting them. Therefore, Nelson said, WPB should modify the rules so that in any area where there existed materials and manpower which were not needed for war work, some of the more essential types of building could take place. These, he said, might include minor industrial improvements, the erection of railway safety and signal equipment, a few of the more critically needed flood control projects, sewage-disposal plants and water systems in cities overcrowded because of war conditions, perhaps certain farm-to-market roads, perhaps even school facilities in cities that needed them most.

This proposal was by no means a reconversion program. Nelson did not yet have a reconversion program to offer. All he really had was an understanding that the war emergency had piled so many unfilled needs on the economy that the process of reconversion would have to begin far in advance of the actual end of the war. The coming of peace was going to find the nation with more unfilled wants, and more money to spend on their satisfaction, than anybody had ever seen before. If an intelligent reconversion plan was to be developed and put into operation, some of those wants would have to be met before the war ended.

If that could not be done, no conceivable reconversion plan would work.

But the proposal to relax building restrictions could not be put across. The Army and Navy were bitterly opposed, not merely to any relaxation, but to any talk of relaxation. In vain Nelson argued that the only kind of construction he proposed for the present was the kind that could be done without interference with the war program; in the eyes of the military men even that kind of construction would be harmful, because it would make people think that the war was about over. The Armed Services were beating all of the drums for a labor draft, they were preparing the stay-at-homes for invasion by insisting on a grim and Spartan way of life on the home front—the unutterable grimness of casualty lists having, apparently, escaped their comprehension. This proposition of Nelson's was a step in the opposite direction. It might not harm war production itself, but it would certainly ruin the offensive on the psychological-warfare front. Government could go ahead with the psychological warfare, *or* it could begin doing something about reconversion; it could not, under any dispensation whatever, do both at once.

The Army did raise one point that struck Nelson as valid. After all, the invasion of Europe had not yet taken place, and nobody knew just what was going to happen when it did. Certainly Nelson's program did not have to be put into effect day after tomorrow. Wait and see, therefore: make no relaxation until the invasion has been launched and we can see how it is going; if there are a few public services that simply must have a little construction work done before that time, we can always fall back on a broader interpretation of what constitutes "construction essential to the war effort."

In the end, it was so agreed. The project was shelved until after D-day; then it could be re-examined.

So ended the first approach to reconversion; heated argument, winding up in a draw, with the decision postponed. But this did not end the argument about reconversion. The argument had barely begun. For the improvement in the war production situation was not taking place in secret, behind closed doors; it was right out in the open, where labor, management, and the general public could see it. It was useless to argue that every ounce of metal was vitally needed for war work when there were large-scale shutdowns of aluminum pot lines due to a surplus of aluminum. Manufacturers who learned, via the cancellation of their contracts, that they were no longer needed for war production, could not be kept from thinking that in such case they might as well use a bit of the surplus metal to make nonwar goods. Workers who had been paid off from war jobs were bound to feel that patriotism need not prevent them from working to produce goods for civilians. Both manufacturers and workers *knew* that the war production program had passed the peak.

The workers' viewpoint was underlined, early in December, in a memorandum drawn up by WPB's two labor vice chairmen. These functionaries had been acquired a year earlier, when Nelson agreed that labor leaders might possibly make acceptable officers for WPB; from the CIO he had drawn Clinton S. Golden, and from the AFL, Joseph Keenan, and to each he had given the title of vice chairman and a place at the WPB council table. The experiment had worked well and the two men had proved their personal fitness for high position; and now, in their joint memorandum, they were expressing concern about the effect of increasing military cutbacks:

"Shutdowns of mines, mills, and factories will reduce the rate of output of all operations by injuring the workers' morale; for the effort of all workers will be affected if they feel, rightly or wrongly, that the harder they work the sooner they will work themselves out of a job."

Therefore, the labor vice chairmen urged, WPB ought to get busy at once on concrete plans for increased production of civilian goods. Specifically, they suggested that the production of raw materials be continued at full blast, even though military needs declined, with the surplus stock-piled both as a reserve for military emergencies and as a means of quick expansion of civilian production; and they called for an expanded program to readapt manufacturing facilities to civilian use so that any surplus of labor, of materials, or of manufacturing capacity could be put to work as fast as it appeared.

If this expressed the workers' viewpoint, the Kiplinger letter in mid-December had spoken for management:

"Government propagandists, including high officials, have been scared into thinking that businessmen and workers might 'let down' on production if it became known that the peak of war production was so near at hand. So the officials did not reveal the truth, and said it was 'unpatriotic' to give any advance thought to the shift. Officials were not candid. Result is that the public generally is unprepared.

"White House has fumbled responsibility for making the plans. This means the President, Byrnes, Vinson, *et al*. They didn't trust WPB because they thought it contained too much 'business influence.' Same for the other agencies which had managed conversion of industry to war. So White House overlayered all these practical agencies with Baruch. He and his staff of thinkers are thinking, studying, deeply meditating. Meanwhile the practical agencies which know best how to get things done are champing at the bit, waiting for White House orders and Baruch."

For Baruch was back in the picture again. He had not become chairman of WPB, after all, but had formally been called in again by Byrnes—who, in turn, as director of a new Office of War Mobilization, was now recognized as "assistant President"—and Byrnes had made Baruch head of an Advisory Unit for War and Postwar Adjustment Policies, and Baruch and his staff were hard at work preparing a report on the reconversion problem. As had been the case with rubber, nothing in particular would be done until that report came out; presumably it would be accepted as a final definition of government policy and would set the pattern for the nation's preparedness for peace. After the January 11 meeting of WPB it was generally agreed that something definite might happen once the administration had the Baruch report to go on.

But if the administration, like the three gift-shop monkeys, was going to hear no evil, see no evil, and speak no evil on the subject of declining war production and the consequences thereof, the subject could not exactly be ignored altogether. The last man in town who could try to ignore it was Elmer Davis, head of OWI. It was his job to see to it that government told a clear, coherent story, and right at that moment the government seemed to be giving vent to a certain amount of double-talk; so he called a meeting of the heads of all war agencies in mid-January, to see if they could not agree on "general information policies planned by OWI to increase public understanding of war production and employment problems."

221

By experience and by conviction, Davis was a news man, and an uncompromising one. His concern was to find out exactly what the facts were and to use those facts in the telling of a straight story. He described the accomplishments of this meeting in the following words:

"On the topics generally termed, if somewhat inaccurately, cutbacks and reconversion, there has been, for the moment, a definite establishment of policy based on known facts—policy which may change in one direction or the other to conform to later developments, but which is the policy now. On such basis we should all be able to tell the same story."

This policy, he continued, included these points:

Government officials would avoid speculation as to the end of the war.

The probabilities as to economic developments, both after the war ended and before it ended, would be discussed "with great care."

All government officials would recognize the duties and responsibilities of other agencies and would not "discuss activities for which they are not responsible, or matters which overlap other agencies, without careful co-ordination and clearance."

Further, "all public expressions on production shifts should fully and accurately explain the status of public policy in terms of the facts as reported to OWI by the agencies concerned." These facts, Davis added, were that there was not going to be any big resumption of civilian production, that even minor shifts in production must be very carefully undertaken, that the minor shifts currently going on were "very small, almost inconsequential," that planning was under way to make possible a rapid shift to civilian production when military conditions permitted, but that unexpected military developments would of necessity make such planning very difficult, so that short-term shocks to the economy were to be expected.

In intent, this was excellent. The last thing Davis wanted was to lay down a propaganda line. He was simply pledging OWI to insist on the telling of a straight story—a story based on the facts and shaped by the government's official policy. The only trouble was that the facts and the government's official policy might presently begin to differ considerably; in that case, which guide would be followed? And just what was the government's official policy?

Was a national service act needed, for instance? The President had asked for one, and the President, of course, is the top policy-setter of them all. But he had asked for it in a very left-handed way: had asked for it, in fact, in such a manner that he clearly was not making it a matter of top policy. He had not sent a draft of the measure up to Capitol Hill, he had not pulled his party leaders in Congress together and urged them to fight for the legislation, he had applied no pressure anywhere. In recommending the law he had even admitted that it was not really essential, and he had specifically made his recommendation conditional on the passage of various other laws which were quite certain not to be passed. On paper, he had made the need for a labor draft a matter of central administration policy; actually, in terms of practical politics, he had done nothing of the kind.

Nor was his administration a unit as to the facts in the matter. The Army held firmly, vehemently, even violently, to the opinion that a labor draft was above all else essential; the War Production Board felt that it was not needed at all, although Nelson did not feel quite up to contradicting the President in public about it. The War Manpower Commission had not seen any need for a labor draft, although Chairman McNutt later gave the measure his endorsement with the wry comment that he was bound to go along with the boss. If OWI should try to bring about the telling of a uniform story on the need for a labor draft it would be in for a merry ride.

Similarly with the matter of cutbacks, war production, and reconversion. Davis had said, hopefully, that "we should all be able to tell the same story." But if such ability existed at the time he held his policy meeting it vanished immediately thereafter, never more to be seen by living man. No more violent differences of opinion between men ever existed on this earth than developed very shortly among responsible government officials about the respective significance and importance of cutbacks, war production programs, and the chances for increasing production for civilians. OWI was caught right in the middle of these differences. In carrying out its function of causing a coherent story to be told, it was presently to run into the necessity of deciding which official or set of officials should be upheld, publicity-wise, and which should not; for the different officials were about to begin clamoring for the public ear with stories which differed as night differs from day.

Thus OWI was committed to an admirable information program which could not possibly be put into effect. The organization did do its manful best. Four days after the policy meeting OWI set up an interagency information committee to "increase the flow of government information about production and unemployment problems"—which was fair enough, except that it meant, in practice, that the Army's theory about the critical, overshadowing nature of those problems was going to be embodied in the party line. Anyway, a standing committee composed of information men from the War and Navy Departments, WPB, the War Manpower Commission, and OWI was to meet weekly to make sure that everybody understood the news developments that were coming up in the different agencies, that important news got proper treatment, that gaps in information were filled adequately, and that where it seemed advisable news releases on emerging public policy might be "developed" and disseminated.

This contained additional pitfalls. Early in February James Brackett, a ranking OWI deputy, wrote to Vice-Chairman Donald Davis of WPB to express concern about a point which was bothering a good many people just then—a point which, indeed, was fundamental to the whole situation: namely, that Washington's appeals to worker and industry about the need for increased war production were getting completely fouled up, locally, by dramatic cutbacks in war factories. A city whose principal factory had just shut down, laying off thousands of workers, because the Army no longer needed what that factory was making, was not apt to be impressed by dire warnings from Washington about the need for harder work and a more sustained effort. Rationally enough, Brackett felt that the relationship of these cutbacks to the national picture had better be made just as clear as possible; and he suggested to Davis that WPB's Production Executive Committee—high Sanhedrin of the whole production program—permit an OWI representative to attend its meetings so that a proper story could be told.

"Various plans are being developed," he wrote, "for quite extensive use of radio and other media to tell the basic production story to as many people as possible. We shall be able to get considerable *national* understanding as to the facts of *national* peak production and the shifts under the peak. But this understanding will be continuously vitiated if similar understanding of the actual facts and meaning of the cutbacks cannot be disseminated. Not only is the area concerned disturbed, but the cutback is frequently given national publicity with obvious effects on national opinion."

But Brackett was bumping into the same thing Elmer Davis was about to bark his shins on. Davis had hoped that "we should all be able to tell the same story" when the underlying fact was that we simply did not all have the same story to tell. Brackett was hoping for dissemination of "the actual facts and meaning of the cutbacks" when those were exactly the points which an administration that was conducting psychological warfare was not going to publicize if it could possibly help it. The actual facts and meaning of the production situation, for instance, were that the load was definitely declining and that the nation had passed the point where a draft of labor might be necessary; but the minds and hearts of the men who were responsible for the cutbacks were devoted to the thesis that production was in a state of crisis, that the home front was on the point of going sour, and that a labor draft was needed to cure a situation of anarchy. In such a case, what price actual facts?

CHAPTER EIGHTEEN

Memo for General Grant

THIS was the high noon of the world's greatest democracy. The people had been asked for more than any people had ever given before, and—in mine and in factory, on the farm and in the forest, at home and in the training camps—they were doing all that had been asked of them. They were justifying a belief, a legend, and an inheritance; for this the immigrant ships had sailed west and the wagon trains had crossed the plains, forests had been cleared and cities had been built, traditions had been created out of death and faith and courage, strength had been drawn from the air and the soil of the richest, proudest land on earth. They were waging war on the seven seas and three continents, they had the power to say what the future would be like, and from now on—to be precise, after the winter of 1944 —the only question was whether the people's leaders would live up to them.

For it was up to the people's leaders to chart the way into the future. They had to look ahead to victory and decide how the great issue that would come with victory was to be met. The issue was simply this:

Do we try to pick up all of our peacetime affairs, after the war, exactly where we were before, in exactly the same old way, as if nothing at all had been changed?

Or do we, on the contrary, accept both change and the need for change, and use this tremendous effort which the people have made in such a way that the nation can adjust itself to the new world which is coming in out of the mist and the smoke?

This was the real problem which had been carefully avoided all through the early stages of the defense effort, which had been avoided again under the impact of war, and which was now being posed once more in connection with the approaching end of the war. This was the last chance to define what we had been fighting for, to face the tragedy of bloodshed and loss and human misery which the war had cost and find a straight answer to the question: Who benefits by all of this? Whether anyone realized it or not, this was what lay back of the attempt to grapple with the problems of reconversion.

In the beginning, almost everybody agreed that something had to be done quickly. Then there began to be doubts about that word "quickly." Then there was a grand row over exactly what it was that ought to be done, and over who should do it. And, finally, there was agreement-by-default to do nothing at all.

Failure, unredeemed and infinitely costly; due to nothing in particular, perhaps, except a lack of the faith that will move mountains—or a faith in the essential rightness and holy destiny of the people themselves, which after all is the same thing.

But it began brightly enough; began, very aptly, with an important report from Mr. Baruch.

Baruch felt that the situation was urgent. Long-awaited, his report on war and postwar adjustment policies was made public on February 18, 1944, and it called for action—for immediate action, to make possible a smooth and swift transition from war to a peacetime economy. To that end the armed services and the War Production Board were advised to begin immediate work on an "X-Day reconversion plan" which could be put into effect just as soon as Germany was defeated.

The report was exhaustive. It ran to 120 pages and it covered all of the fields in which reconversion operations ought to begin. It asserted that the general goal should be to restore healthy private enterprise in the American economy just as rapidly as possible after the war, and it insisted that this could not be done just by waiting for the war to end and then suddenly lopping off all of the wartime controls.

"The greatest danger that our nation faces," said the report, "not only in the transition period but also in the long-time future, is the tendency for people to become broken up into blocs and segments, each organized for the narrow interests of the moment."

Further, the report warned:

"Our concern over pressure groups is another reason why we have guided our recommendations so that once victory is won we can close the books on the war as quickly as possible. We have not wanted to leave the government after the war a jackpot of controls which invite every pressure group to hit it."

(Do you by chance remember what happened in 1945 and 1946: the great campaign to knock out price controls, the great campaign to end rationing, the great campaign to halt "government interference" with building, the great campaign to kill controls over materials, all of the great campaigns put on by blocs and pressure groups to the tune of full-page advertisements and frantic speeches in Congress?)

Official Washington went on to read the detailed recommendations of the Baruch report. In the main, they covered these points:

There should be a "work director" in the Office of War Mobilization, to handle employment problems of veterans and others.

A "financial kit" to make possible speedy termination of war contracts should be worked out, including provision for 100 per cent payment for all completed articles.

There should be a Surplus Property Administrator in the Office of War Mobilization, with a Surplus Property Board to give him guidance.

There was needed "a general tightening of the entire government war machine, both for mobilization and demobilization."

Needed war-powers legislation, such as that which provided for price controls, should be extended.

War contracts should be canceled as soon as the goods involved were no longer needed. (In other words, don't keep on making munitions just because we want to keep workers and factories busy.)

Small business should be protected—as far as may be practical, without interfering with the war—in the resumption of civilian production.

Nor was this resumption of civilian production a matter which could be put off any longer. In the X-Day plan which the services and WPB must work out, the report said, there would have to be a plan for estimating war-contract cancellations in advance so that the authorities would have a good picture of the industries which would be affected and the resources that would be released; and tentative choices of industries and plants to be freed should be made, to contribute both to greater war efficiency and to "the speediest resumption of civilian production and to an orderly change-over from war to peace." It was admitted that there were objections to present discussion of postwar planning; "but we conclude," said the report, "that the American people will face the facts courageously if the government deals frankly with them."

Thus the Baruch report; a blueprint for action, detailed on some points, vague on others, emphatic that reconversion ought to be planned and that it was high time to do something about it. All in all, it was an excellent and a useful document, and it at least gave the outlines for an effective program.

Byrnes got busy at once. Four days after the report was issued he held a press conference to announce that, as director of the Office of War Mobilization, he was naming William L. Clayton, then an Assistant Secretary of Commerce, as Surplus War Property Administrator, and Brigadier General Frank T. Hines, Veterans Administrator, as Director of Retraining and Re-employment. He was doing this without waiting for Congress to pass enabling legislation, Byrnes explained, because the situation was urgent; contract cancellations and the discharge of men from the armed forces were creating reconversion problems that had to be met at once. He pointed out that some 3,769 Army prime contracts had already been canceled, affecting at least ten times that number of sub-contracts, and he predicted that another two and one-half billion dollars in production cutbacks would be ordered before June 30. He added that he would instruct the agencies concerned to follow the other recommendations in the Baruch report, notably the suggestion that WPB and the armed services get together at once on the preparation of an X-Day reconversion plan.

The ball was in play now. Byrnes had made it clear that the war effort was shrinking, as far as industry was concerned, and shrinking fairly fast. Even in the midst of an all-out war, the cancellation of two and one-half billions in war contracts inside of four months is a sizable drop, creating a good deal of slack in the production mechanism. The existence of this slack was now officially recognized, and it was a matter of top government policy that direct action on reconversion should begin.

It was Nelson's responsibility to show how the slack might be taken up, and he proposed to increase the production of those nonmilitary goods which would be of direct aid to the war economy. There was a long list of such necessities, ranging from railroad equipment to spare parts for farm machinery, but the most urgently needed seemed to be goods for the mushrooming war manufacturing centers. There were hundreds of thousands of families which had shifted to new communities in order to work in war plants. These communities were seriously short on such basic services as commercial laundries, drug stores, restaurants, nursery centers, and public transportation. These shortages made it hard for the war plants to hold their workers. Excessive labor turnover was a serious problem in such factories; the only effective way to reduce it was to remove the causes; therefore, the production of such seemingly nonwarlike goods as equipment for stores, laundries, and restaurants would be of direct aid to war production. To be sure, it was a good deal simpler to sit back in Washington and denounce workers who moved out of congested, hard-to-live-in war centers as unpatriotic slackers; you could get a name, that way, as a determined, hard-hitting public official, the worker had been a handy target ever since the assault on the forty-hour-week law two years earlier, and if the whole process built up a backlog of festering ill will for the postwar period there was no need to worry about that just now. The trouble, however, was that that didn't reduce labor turnover. Therefore, Nelson figured, the first step was to use a little of the surplus in production capacity to produce goods which would enable the war economy to operate a little better.

Long-range, the problem was different. Essentially it was a matter of having the motor turning over so that the car would start moving as soon as peace came. It involved filling the pipe lines for certain key industries—the construction industry, for one —clearing the decks so that there could be a smooth resumption of civilian production when the time came, and above all arranging matters so that the end of the war would not mean a hot inflationary scramble in which the only values that mattered would be values that could be expressed in quick cash.

Now these short-range and long-range problems tied in together, and they could at least be approached in the same way. Find out exactly what goods the nation needed most, find out the quantities that were needed, figure the men, machines, and materials that would be required to make them, dovetail all of that in with the decline in war production, and you would have a program by which civilian production could be resumed in an orderly way. Then there would be no mad rush when peace returned, there would be no such folly as devoting resources to making evening bags and building new night clubs and race tracks when what the country had to have first was work clothing and new homes, and—last but not least—since the whole business would be carefully controlled it need not be allowed to interfere with war production at any point.

That, in any case, was the way Nelson saw it, and that was the way he presented it at a meeting of the top board of WPB late in February. He was careful to explain that for the immediate present he sought only a very minor revival of civilian production, limited to a few of the items that were most needed by the war economy. What he wanted most was agreement on the general policy.

Which was just what he did not get, then or thereafter. After careful and expert study, the administration had decreed that reconversion should begin at once, but it had forgotten to get the consent of the military. The armed services would have none of Nelson's policy. Patterson and Forrestal, of War and Navy, respectively, were emphatically opposed to the whole idea; they were seconded, with equal emphasis, by the important brass that attended the WPB meetings with them—Major General Lucius D. Clay, assistant chief of staff for material, Army Service Forces, and Admiral S. M. Robinson, the Navy's chief of procurement and material. They argued that there could be no relaxation whatever of the restrictions on the production of civilian goods; if there were, dangerous leakages of manpower and materials away from war production would occur—or, at the very least, the populace would begin to think the war was about over and would consequently relax. Restrictions should be made tighter, not looser.

The services simply were not open to argument, and their position—however much it might differ from top government policy, as laid down by Byrnes and Baruch—at least had the merit of extreme simplicity: there must be no interference with the war effort. Let Nelson and his staff try to show that the proposed policy would not create any interference, and the answer was still the same: there must be no interference with the war effort. If Nelson argued that the immediate increases in civilian production which he was asking for would actually help the war effort, he was still told, with military firmness, that there must be no interference. Neither facts nor logic made any impression. The reply was unvarying.

This went on all afternoon (or, to be more exact, it went on to the very end of the war) and the WPB meeting ended in a complete deadlock, with the proposed approach to reconversion left hanging in mid-air. The armed forces held their position with admirable tenacity.

Their position was not impregnable, however. While he appeared to be the last man in town likely to do such a thing, Nelson nevertheless had the authority to order the proposed policy into effect regardless of military objections, since all of the powers lodged in the War Production Board were vested in himself as chairman. On the following day, accordingly, the Army executed a flanking maneuver and carried the fight to the Production Executive Committee, an important WPB organism which was under the direction of Executive Vice-Chairman Charles E. Wilson.

. . . Matters of routine organization are of primary importance, and if you ever want to run the United States of America, never mind about the top jobs; take over the spots down at the operating level, and you'll really have your hands on the controls. The Production Executive Committee became a key factor in the whole reconversion struggle, not because anybody planned it that way but simply because the organization was set up as it was. A year earlier, after Eberstadt's abrupt departure from WPB, Nelson had made a slight mistake; he had almost completely divested himself of operating responsibilities. The entire mechanism by which WPB did its job he placed in Wilson's hands; he, Nelson, would make the policies, and Wilson would carry them into effect.

This hadn't looked like a mistake at the time. It was an effective working arrangement, in fact, and Wilson was an exceptionally capable executive. As an aid in meeting his responsibilities, Wilson had organized the Production Executive Committee, consisting primarily of representatives of WPB, Army, Navy, and Maritime Commission—an operating group, set up to get prompt action on problems that cut across agency lines, as most of the important production problems did. The Committee worked well and Wilson made it a highly useful instrument.

But the setup left Nelson vulnerable, and the services took advantage of it.

To begin with, in any government organization the operating man is apt to find himself in possession of an effective veto power over the policy man. A policy hangs in a void until somebody does something to put it into effect. In WPB, most of the important policies would have been more or less ineffective unless actions in line with them were taken by Wilson, and Wilson did his work through the Production Executive Committee. Up to the winter of 1944 Nelson and Wilson had worked well together and this little fact hadn't bothered anybody, but it was there just the same.

In addition, the Production Executive Committee had been set up to act, not to advise. The top board of WPB was purely advisory, but the PEC (as alphabet-minded Washington knew it) was different. It was not just a civilian board on which the Army and Navy had representation; it was a practical working group in which all hands enjoyed equal status, it tended to take formal votes on moot points and when it had voted the vote was binding. The services drew a great deal of water in PEC.

And as a final complication, the White House had to all intents and purposes taken Wilson out from under Nelson and made him independent.

Wilson had never wanted to come to Washington. Nelson got him only by inducing President Roosevelt to draft him, and Wilson was forever looking forward to the day when he could return to General Electric. In the late fall of 1943, Wilson concluded that the bigger part of his job was finished and that it was time for him to leave; accordingly, he wrote a letter of resignation and gave it to Nelson. The question of accepting or rejecting the resignation, however, was promptly and publicly taken out of Nelson's hands by Byrnes, who informed the nation that Wilson was indispensable and must stay. Early in January, Wilson was called to the White House and given a similar message by the President himself.

What this meant was perfectly clear, if anybody ever wanted to make anything of it. Nelson's chief aid, his operating man, the official without whose cooperation no Nelson policy could go into effect, was no longer answerable to Nelson at all. If the two

233

men should disagree on a matter of importance a completely impossible situation would result.

None of this had escaped attention over at the War Department.

At the meeting of the Production Executive Committee the armed services, with true military logic, passed from the defensive to the offensive. General Clay declared that "in view of present labor conditions"—the Army, remember, was insisting that a labor draft was needed above all else—"the proper approach is to set and hold to a level of civilian production," and suggested that the level already set for the first quarter of 1944 would be a proper base. If this were done, the general pointed out, the government would be relieved of "the necessity for judging the essentiality of individual programs." In plain English, what he was asking was that production levels be frozen where they then stood, military cutbacks or no, and that any argument about the actual need for greater production of any civilian goods be dismissed in advance as irrelevant.

The Production Executive Committee agreed with him and voted that production of civilian goods should be programmed "within the level of production of the first quarter of 1944."

As it happened, this decision didn't stick. It was discovered, shortly after the meeting, that allocations for increased second-quarter production of a few badly needed items had already been made and that it would be almost impossible to stop the slightly cumbersome bureaucratic machinery and scale them down. Besides, there was a doughty character named J. A. Krug to deal with. Krug, who was then program vice-chairman of WPB (later to become, successively, WPB chairman and Secretary of the Interior), pointed out that this matter of setting levels for the production of civilian goods was a responsibility of his own Requirements Committee and should be considered there, where such interested parties as the Smaller War Plants Corporation, the Office of Civilian Requirements, and the two WPB labor vice-chairmen could be heard. In the end the moderate increases already scheduled in the production of such goods as laundry machinery, dairy equipment, and bakery machinery were okayed by both Nelson and Wilson.

The important point, however, was that the Production Executive Committee had shown that it would follow the Army line on the reconversion issue. The cue for the Army was unmistakable: as far as possible, make the question of increasing civilian production a matter for PEC to handle, not WPB.

Now it might have been supposed that the Byrnes-Baruch office would be looking on impatiently and calling for action if the military men got in the way of reconversion planning, and that Nelson could expect something in the way of topside backing for his program. But Nelson was so far out of favor with Byrnes and Baruch that it wasn't even funny, and the newspapers were flatly stating that there was a bitter undercover contest between Nelson and Baruch for control of reconversion planning. Nelson had tried to get this smoothed over and had had no luck whatever.

Late in December Nelson had written Baruch a long letter, remarking that "for some time it has been clear that external forces were driving a wedge into our personal relationship," and that "the malice-mongers evidently are determined to break not only our friendship but also our working relationship." He also pointed out that publication of these stories was hurting morale in WPB; top officials were beginning to assume that if Baruch was on the warpath for Nelson's scalp (as the news stories insisted) WPB was a doomed agency and its attempt to work out a reconversion program was wasted effort, and they were in consequence beginning to show signs of wanting to resign and get back to their regular jobs. Nelson suggested, therefore, that Baruch do what he could—as, Nelson assured him, he himself would do—to prevent the publication of such stories.

This was very delicately phrased. Nelson knew a thing or two about the way stories of contests and rivalries in Washington get printed; on occasion, he himself had shown considerable deftness in the art of planting such stories where they would do the most good; and the natural assumption for him to draw would be that the stories in this case had been inspired by Baruch himself. What he was really saying, then, was that if Baruch would refrain from planting such stories he, Nelson, would likewise refrain, the stories would no longer be printed, and it might be possible for WPB to get on with the reconversion job without the handicap of a popular assumption that its efforts were being opposed by Baruch.

But this inspired tact didn't get anybody anywhere. Baruch's letter of reply was brief, not to say curt, and it was phrased with a delicate care fully equal to Nelson's. He still felt, Baruch wrote, that WPB must play a leading part in reconversion; and as for the matter of the wedge—well, he would not permit anything of a personal nature to interfere with the best interests of the country.

Events were shaping up, in other words, for a big storm and a rough night on the waters. And it was not just the personal fate of a few government officials that was involved; it was the postwar course of the American democracy that was at stake. The rift between Baruch and Nelson was one of the reasons why reconversion failed, but it was only *one* of the reasons; the ultimate break between Nelson and Wilson was one of the results—but *only* one. Nelson and Wilson were the men who got the bruises, but it was the country itself which collected the crippling scars.

In February of 1944, however, what seemed to be chiefly involved was the continuation of the ancient scrap between soldiers and civilians in government. The approach through the Production Executive Committee not having yielded immediate fruits, the military now undertook a second flank attack.

This came on February 27 in the form of an announcement from the Director of Selective Service, Brigadier General Lewis B. Hershey, that he had instructed all local draft boards to review occupational deferments for all men of military age, especially for men under twenty-six. This, he revealed, was done following receipt of a memorandum from the President declaring that the nation's manpower resources had been seriously depleted by overlenient deferments.

No more draft deferments for men under twenty-six for any reason whatever, and precious few deferments for men up to the early thirties: here was a stroke that was really calculated to give the boss of war production some uneasy moments. If the manpower shortage had not been much of a problem in war industries before, it was going to be a problem now; Selective Service was going to *make* it a problem. The big push for a labor draft, as a direct result of this Selective Service action, had now become an equally big push against any increase in civilian production. The whole reconversion issue had been brought into the line of fire of the heavy artillery that was operating on the psychological warfare front.

The first man to be embarrassed by this new decree was Paul McNutt, head of the War Manpower Commission, who discovered that his horse had been shot out from under him without warning.

McNutt, a husky, likable Democratic party stalwart, who had all of the qualifications needed to carry a man to the top in American politics except the habit of being lucky at the right moment, had not been consulted about this new policy. Indeed, its enunciation caught him squarely in the act of explaining publicly that no such policy was needed or contemplated. He was in the Middle West at the time, and when the Hershey announcement hit the news wires McNutt was holding a press conference in Des Moines, discussing the benefits that had been derived from occupational deferments. He had just said that without occupational deferments "it would not have been possible to do the magnificent production job the United States has accomplished," when the Hershey story broke over his silvery head. McNutt swallowed the rest of his press conference whole and returned to Washington to see what cooked.

The second man to be embarrassed was Nelson, who had had no more advance warning of the new policy than McNutt. If Nelson's embarrassment was less public than McNutt's it was no less profound. As nearly as the WPB industry men could figure it, the new policy would promptly pull some thirty thousand men out of the scientific and technological end of industry. Some of the biggest and most important of the war industries were brand new—synthetic rubber, for instance, and electronics—and of necessity most of their expert technicians were young men. In addition, there were other basic industries like mining and transportation in which a goodly sprinkling of husky young men was essential. By insisting that all of these young men should be hurried into the Army at once, the military men had shown that their complete incomprehension of how America thinks was balanced by an equally complete incomprehension of how America works.

Having considered the situation, WPB early in March formally notified the Joint Chiefs of Staff that the new manpower policy might easily cause shortages in the production of the most crucially needed war goods—synthetic rubber, high octane gasoline, radar, and so on. Back came the answer: We'll chance that,

237

we've got to have the men in the Army, the need for more soldiers is the main thing just now.

This tune changed greatly, later on, when the War Department began calling on God and man to witness that production deficiencies due to a shortage of manpower were hampering strategic planning and must be overcome at whatever cost; and at the end of 1944 the Truman Committee examined the situation and its new chairman, Senator Mead of New York, arose in the Senate to declare:

"The committee conducted a survey of the use to which the armed forces put certain highly trained experts drafted from technical war production jobs. By and large, the result of this survey was to show these men landed in clerical positions or in other places where their creative training and ability was wasted. By and large, there is no question that to a substantial degree the precipitous drafting of men from industry, in many cases some time before they were actually needed in the armed forces, has created temporary surpluses in the armed forces and corresponding shortages in war production."

All in all, it was an odd performance. A sweeping new policy on manpower was put through without consultation either with the official responsible for the nation's supply of labor or the official responsible for war production. The policy was adhered to (with minor modifications) in the face of sharp warnings that it might have a bad effect on war production; ten months later the most competent of Senate committees found that the new policy had not really been necessary and that it had hurt war production as predicted. Completely incredible, all of it: but it was fair notice that the military men were going to block what they considered premature action on reconversion no matter what they had to do.

As an antireconversion move, the draft policy was eminently successful. It not only raised manpower shortages in certain key industries, thus providing an excellent argument against any expansion of civilian production; it also helped to knock Nelson loose from part of his authority over production.

Some months earlier Nelson had ruled that contracts for the manufacture of needed items should not be placed in areas where there were labor shortages. This was aimed at the Army's pleasant habit of placing heavy new orders in areas that were already over-loaded with war work, when there were other places, not over-loaded, that could produce the desired articles just as well. A bit later Nelson extended the order to cover the manufacture of articles not bought by the government—i.e., goods made for the civilian market.

It was up to the War Manpower Commission to say whether or not a given area actually had a labor shortage. Accordingly, the Commission had systematically classified the nation's various production areas, grading them in four groupings ranging from Group I (manpower extremely tight) to Group IV (no man-power shortage exists or is anticipated). Now, with the new non-deferment policy, the Commission felt obliged to adopt a more restrictive policy on manpower. On March 9 it announced such a policy—a sliding scale arrangement which sought to channel all new civilian production into Group III or Group IV areas and which set up new barriers to prevent the placing of such work in Group II or Group I areas.

The Production Executive Committee warmly endorsed this action and decreed that there could be no resumption or expan-sion whatever of civilian production in any Group I area; in a Group II area it could take place under only the most extraor-dinary circumstances and by special permission.

What resulted from this was something tolerably close to the outright freeze on civilian production which the Army had demanded a fortnight earlier. A mechanism which had been set up to channel Army buying more intelligently was now being turned into a device to prevent increases in civilian production. The War Manpower Commission was being edged over into a position where it, and not the War Production Board, was apt to have the final say-so on any question of raising nonmilitary production. . . . It had been less than a month since the admin-istration decreed that the reconversion issue must be ignored no longer, but so far the Army was getting excellent results from its campaign to keep Nelson (or anyone else, for that matter) from doing anything about it.

. . . Perhaps U. S. Grant would have had a word for it. In the fall of 1863 Grant visited Chattanooga after the disastrous battle of Chickamauga, to inspect the badly beaten Federal Army. He found it in such poor shape that he removed its commander forthwith and appointed a new one; and the deposed general, before retiring northward, came to see him and submitted a plan which his staff had previously worked out for revictualing, reorganizing and generally reinspiring the starving and dispirited Army.

"He made some excellent suggestions," said Grant afterward. "My only wonder was that he had not carried them out."

So with reconversion. Excellent suggestions were made, and the only wonder was that they were not carried out. The need for planning and for action was clearly seen, and the ruinous consequences of ignoring this need were ably pointed out; all of the signals were given; and, in the end, no plan was put into effect. Reconversion, when it finally came, came like a thief in the night.

Not that everybody and his brother just sat on his hands. There were reports, conferences, committees and subcommittees to study, to make findings, to coordinate, and to activate, and there were special orders and directives; the records on these activities were more than enough to fill a five-foot shelf. Nor was this entirely without result. Measures for surplus property disposal were taken, and there was quick and effective action to enable contractors who were dropped from war work in mid-stride to get their money promptly without haggling. But the real job was not done.

And it can't all be blamed on the War Department. To be sure, the War Department did fight the reconversion program step by step, and in the end it had its way, but it couldn't have turned the trick unaided. The War Department had not yet taken over the government—not in the winter and spring of 1944. The power to overrule the military still existed; was enjoyed, not only by the administration as a whole, and not only by the Byrnes office which had called for the reconversion measures which the Army was opposing, but by the War Production Board itself, as far as the readjustment of industry to peacetime pursuits was concerned. The trouble was that when it became apparent that a reconversion plan could be put into effect only by winning a knock-down fight with the military, most of the men who should have been making the fight discovered that they didn't want to fight—not on that side, anyway.

For the administration, by now, had just about completed the deep sea change which began when the war started. It had become perfectly representative of the prewar, pre-world-revolutionary order, with all of its virtues and all of its faults, given to the most high-minded and well-intentioned efforts to avoid difficult problems by assuming that they did not exist. It was not possible for this stream to rise higher than its source. A transcendent democracy could not emerge from this situation because a transcendent democracy was not in it to begin with, and was, as a matter of fact, what frightened the good men of the administration above everything else. And when Nelson discovered, as presently he did, that he could fight effectively for reconversion only by making his reconversion program an active instrument for the kind of changes which democracy needed, he found himself battling among men who clung desperately to the conviction that nothing should be changed very much.

General Grant needn't have wondered. There were perfectly good reasons why the excellent suggestions were not carried out.

CHAPTER NINETEEN

The Mouse and the Elephant

THE BIG shots from Washington were inspecting the war factory in Connecticut, and the management had rolled out the red carpet. The visitors motored in from the airport and got out in front of the factory by twos and threes, chatting with their hosts and staring idly up at the front of the big building while the company officials, deftly and unobtrusively, got them sorted and lined up in the order of their importance. At last everything was ready and the party started for the factory entrance; first man in line was Charles E. Wilson, executive Vice-Chairman of the War Production Board.

At the gate was a grizzled watchman, stationed there to check visitors in and out and to bar the unworthy. He halted Wilson and said to him, "I knocked you out once."

Wilson looked at him, thought a minute, then grinned.

"Then you're Joe So-and-so," he said. "He's the only man who ever knocked me out."

The watchman nodded, the two men shook hands, and the visitors passed on inside. Wilson chuckled and turned to the company president at his side to ask, "Did you hear that?" He went on to explain; many years ago, when he was a young factory hand at Bridgeport with everything ahead of him, he had fancied himself as a semipro boxer, and often sparred with others like himself at smokers. One night he had fought Joe So-and-so and had indeed been put away. He had not seen Joe since. The two men had gone their separate ways, one was now a watchman at a factory gate, the other was president of General Electric and top production expediter for the U. S. Government; both were glad to recall the night, thirty-odd years before, when they had fought with their fists, and Wilson was pleased to shake hands with the only man who had ever knocked him unconscious.

A fighter, this Wilson, by instinct and by experience; direct action personified. Massive, powerful, abrupt, with a rasp to his voice like a top sergeant's, Wilson rather looked as if he had been hewn from a block of weathered hardwood with an adz.

He could address a group of war-workers in a steel mill or forge and, in the heat of exhorting them to greater effort, offer to throw off his coat and either pitch in and do the hard work alongside of them or beat the daylight out of the laggards, and he was obviously quite capable of it, physically and emotionally. He had drive and he knew how to impart it, as innumerable producers of munitions discovered during the war, and when he sought the solution to a problem his instinct was to put his head down and slug his way through; never mind weighing all of the subtleties and abstractions, make a decision and stick to it—even a bad decision is usually better than a good decision too long delayed. He was known as a liberal businessman, and when he came to the War Production Board his confidential assistant, for some months, was none other than Mordecai Ezekiel, one of the most noted of the New Deal theoreticians. (They *did* make an oddly matched pair, and the union was bound to dissolve sooner or later, but it did some useful work while it lasted.)

Wilson's emergence as top operating man in WPB had been a defeat for the Army, but it was a defeat the Army took in its stride. Wilson figured that he had been brought to Washington for just one thing—to speed the production of munitions—and while he was a fighter he also believed in cooperation; and the War Department people presently discovered that he was a man they could work with even though he did possess and exercise authority which they felt WPB should not have, and the Production Executive Committee setup, which was a voluntary sharing of that authority, pleased them mightily. It was not long before the military men liked Wilson just as strongly as they disliked Nelson. From the Army point of view, Wilson was the man who helped get things done, and Nelson was the man who was always arguing with them, needling them, and making decisions in favor of competing programs. Also, when a new problem came up Nelson liked to mull it over and take his time with it; Wilson could usually be depended on for a yes-or-no answer without delay.

At the same time it was Wilson rather than Nelson to whom most of WPB's officials looked for leadership. Divorced from direct operating chores, Nelson began to seem remote, almost aloof; Wilson ran the machine, and ran it most efficiently—it had been loose, cumbersome, almost disjointed, before he arrived, and

243

he had pulled it together. In addition, he struck the average business executive as a solider, not to say a safer, sort of person than Nelson. To be sure, he did have that reputation as a liberal, and in the fall of 1943 he made a notable speech warning against the emergence of fascist-type thinking among the higher ranks in big industry, but somehow he seemed to be a man who could be relied on not to go off the reservation. There was always a faint New Dealish flavor to Nelson; he flirted with dangerous ideas, relied heavily on the advice of men like Bob Nathan, kept on intimate terms with Leon Henderson, was known to think FDR a great man; nor could it be forgotten that he owed his present position to the prominent part he had taken in the revolt against Knudsen. He had saved the dollar-a-year system from extinction, to be sure, but after two years as chairman of WPB he did not command the instinctive loyalties of the dollar-a-year men. If there should ever be a showdown, most of the important people in WPB would be apt to line up with Wilson rather than with Nelson.

The showdown was rapidly approaching. Nelson and Wilson began to explore the ways in which civilian production might be increased. They had different ideas about the steps that were immediately practical and about the way in which those steps should be taken; relatively minor differences, which ordinarily could have been ironed out. But even to touch this subject of increasing civilian production was to raise the most explosive questions about economic and industrial democracy. Minor differences as to method and practicality quickly grew to symbolize the very great differences which existed as to the fundamental issues. Without in the least intending to, Nelson and Wilson presently got into a fight that could not be compromised —a fight which, in the end, blew both men out of Washington, completely deflated the War Production Board and left the door wide open for full military control of the economy.

And the Nelson-Wilson fight, which was regarded as the central factor in the situation, was really only a by-product. The time had come for a fateful decision, but it was not to be merely a decision whether this man or that man would be top dog. It had roots that went far back—say, to the covered wagons moving west, to the privateers swinging into the English channel, to Valley Forge, to the Mayflower Compact, to whatever you choose that goes deep to the heart and origin of the American dream.

. . . There are many values to our democratic life; values we have worked for, dreamed of, prayed for, and on not a few occasions died for. Do we, in this spring of 1944, as we move forward to victory in our greatest war, create a situation in which those values can be brought closer to reality, so that to us and to all men can be given the courage and the hope for the terrible years ahead? This, and nothing less, was the deep central issue that was coming up for decision, and it was to be settled by the way in which men handled the prosaic business of determining when and how various factories were to return to ordinary peacetime routines. And this decision was going to be determined, ultimately, by all of the things that had been done in connection with arming democracy for the war—the chances accepted and the chances missed, the issues squarely faced and the issues weakly side-stepped, the final sum of choices made and attitudes created since the wheels of the arsenal of democracy first began to turn. The struggle over the decision was to be singularly undramatic, except for the single, misinterpreted episode of the tragic clash between Nelson and Wilson. There was to be no fire bell in the night to awaken people and call them to meet a crisis. The currents we had already set moving were to carry us through. *The fault, dear Brutus, lies not in our stars.* . . .

The approach to the reconversion problem brought Nelson and Wilson, plus dollar-a-year-land generally, up against the key element in the situation: speedy reconversion would mean a rising level of civilian production well in advance of the time when all war production was ended.

That was very likely to give an advantage to small producers and to independent producers—to the people who "didn't belong to the club," as Searls had put it in another connection—and a disadvantage to the established industrial giants. The war economy had been based upon big industry, and big industry would carry the load as long as any trace of the war economy remained; when the tapering-off process began the little fellows would inevitably be released first and the big fellows last. Therefore a policy of increasing production for civilians as fast as plants were available could easily mean a direct threat to established patterns of industry. Producers who were no longer needed in war work would find the way open to get a long head start in the race for peacetime markets while the established producers were still making goods for the Army and Navy; and those peacetime markets already loomed as the largest, most profitable markets any producers on earth had ever seen.

The War Department was insisting that nobody at all be allowed to resume peacetime operations until such time as war production had dropped to a mere trickle. The industrial thinking represented in WPB did not agree with this viewpoint, but to make a successful fight against it WPB would have to agree on a reconversion plan; and when the attempt to work out such a plan was made it quickly became clear that *how* reconversion was started and controlled was going to be of very great importance—of so much importance that powerful elements were apt to side with the War Department and prefer no reconversion at all to accepting reconversion of the wrong kind. There was no room for a middle-of-the-road position; devising and executing a reconversion plan would either make big industry more secure than ever or give big industry the scare of its life.

Originally, Nelson had simply proposed that the nation's over-all level of production be held fairly close to its wartime peak, with civilian production rising as war production dropped. Nobody outside of the War Department had any particular quarrel with that; the fun started when people began trying to figure exactly how this rise in civilian production would take place.

Developing his plan, Nelson proposed that the increased production of civilian goods be *programmed*—a bit of WPB jargon which meant that each increase would be carefully planned and charted by government, with WPB picking the manufacturers who would be permitted to produce, providing them with raw materials, and fixing the varieties and quantities of goods that might be made. So far, Nelson was right in line with industry thinking. The next step, however, was to decide what officials in WPB were to do this job.

Nelson simply followed his organization chart on that one. As WPB was constituted, all of this charting and planning would be done by an organization called (aptly enough) the Program Bureau, which operated under the Program Vice-Chairman. And right there was where the shoe began to pinch.

For the Program Vice-Chairman then was tough Cap Krug, a government career man out of TVA, who was thought to be addicted to various New Deal ideas; and the Program Bureau contained what survived in WPB of the original New Deal planning group, symbolized by the now-departed Nathan and still infected with his thinking. So presently the dollar-a-year men realized to their horror that the Nelson plan really meant control of industry, during the all-important transition period, by New Deal planners and theorists; more control, carrying more far-reaching consequences, than the New Deal itself had dared to contemplate during its palmiest days.

The dollar-a-year men were not going to have that at any price. They wanted increased production of civilian goods and they wanted programming, but they wanted the job handled by the right people and they were perfectly frank about it. It was just at this time that Charles Kohlhepp, head of the Program Bureau, got a memo from one of his aides who had been out in the WPB industry divisions taking soundings; and the memo warned Kohlhepp bluntly that "members of industry divisions and members of industry were emphatic in declaring that the process of reconversion was not going to be guided by 'professors and planners.'" The memo added that "the industry people simply would not stand for their playing an influential part in the process."

One consideration should guide all reconversion planning, as the dollar-a-year men saw it; the old competitive patterns in industry must be preserved intact. When the last traces of the war economy evaporated, each industrialist must be able to pick up exactly where he had left off. If he had had 20 per cent of the market for his particular product, prewar, then he should have exactly 20 per cent of it in the reconversion period. WPB should do its programming in such a way that all new manufacturers would be kept out of any given industry until all of the prewar manufacturers had resumed production, and as production was resumed in any industry all of the early starters should be limited to quotas based on their prewar production.

As this attitude was noised abroad it created a bit of a stir; for what the industrialists were really saying was that the interests of the old-line producers should outweigh every other consideration in the resumption of production—that these interests

247

should be protected no matter how great the country's need for new goods might be, that the industrial base must not be broadened by bringing in new producers, providing more jobs and increasing competition. Early in March Senator Francis J. Maloney of Connecticut wrote to Nelson to ask him if this was going to be WPB's official attitude.

Nelson replied immediately that it was not. To do as the industrialists wished, he said, would "do irreparable injury to the free enterprise system in the United States"; when the time came to increase civilian production there should be no restrictions on the entrance of new businesses into established industries, "even though the effect on competitive situations may be painful." He added, "I do not believe that you can have a democracy and at the same time forbid new competition," and he concluded with the assurance that "there will be no deviation from this main policy as long as I have responsibility for the board's activities."

This was clear enough—and extremely unwelcome to the majority of the industrialists in WPB, whose support Nelson lost from that moment. Being violently opposed to Nelson's proposal, the dollar-a-year men began to realize that they had warm allies over in the War Department, who were also violently opposed. The reasons for the opposition were different; the Army simply opposed reconversion as such, while the industrialists wanted reconversion but opposed the kind Nelson was insisting on. But the common ground of general antagonism to what Nelson was trying to do was broad enough to form ranks on, and the ranks formed swiftly—thus demonstrating, neither for the first nor for the last time in American history, the extreme ease with which industry and the military can make book together when the heat is on.

Having formed ranks, they brought forth a counter proposal: Let there be a reconversion plan, with programming and all the rest—but let it be guided and controlled by the Production Executive Committee. As General Clay put it at a Committee meeting, the Committee should "undertake the responsibility of determining policies to govern the character, timing, and extent of any expansion or resumption of production for civilian use consistent with the maintenance of military programs at peak efficiency." This would freeze out the Program Bureau theorists completely; to all intents and purposes, the way in which peacetime production was resumed would be determined by the industrialists and the military men working together. With such sponsorship reconversion might be mortally slow in starting, but it assuredly would not contain anything to worry the industrialists.

The War Production Board was now at an impasse, with most of its top officials somewhat sketchily committed to two quite incompatible desires—to resist the Army so as to bring about reconversion, and to connive with the Army to keep reconversion properly conservative. It was revealing its own tragic inadequacy; by the very nature of its organization, WPB was neither emotionally nor intellectually able to cope with a problem as delicate and complex as the reconversion issue. But the cleavage which resulted was immediately interpreted, vastly oversimplified, as a personal fight between Nelson and Wilson.

The personal fight was there all right, by now, even though it wasn't as important as Washington supposed. Nelson and Wilson were having a difference of opinion out in public, and all of the pressures which centered around the basic issues were acting on each man in such a way as to turn the difference of opinion into a regular row.

Wilson favored the PEC proposal. As the man in charge of WPB operations, it was natural for him to assume that he would be responsible for the operation of reconversion programming, and the Production Executive Committee was the instrument through which he operated; and in supporting the PEC plan he was simply agreeing with all of the officials who worked most closely with him and looked to him for leadership. Yet Wilson began to discover that he was coming in for severe criticism, and he could easily be pardoned for thinking that there was no justice.

He had supported Nelson's plan up to this point, had done his best to convince the Army that providing necessary community services for war workers (who were quitting the jobs because such services were lacking) did not come under the head of needlessly pampering the civilian economy, and he had strongly endorsed Nelson's letter to Senator Maloney. But current news stories were depicting his present position as an attempt by himself, with Army backing, to take WPB away from Nelson. Worse yet, the fact that big industry had a dollars-and-cents reason for licking Nelson's plan was being linked with Wilson's own peacetime position as head of one of the nation's largest corporations —so that Wilson, who prided himself on his reputation as a progressive business leader, was finding himself pictured as a leader and spokesman for corporate greed. Bitterly resentful, he concluded that these critical stories were being planted by Nelson's own staff, and this conclusion did not make him any fonder of Nelson personally.

On the other hand, Nelson was beginning to feel much as a ship captain might feel whose crew was beginning to mutiny in favor of the first mate. The Army appeared to be supporting Wilson just as it had previously supported Eberstadt, and most of WPB was definitely in Wilson's corner; but if the affair came to a climax Nelson couldn't fire Wilson, as he had fired Eberstadt, partly because WPB would fall apart if he did and partly because both the President and Byrnes had publicly said that Wilson was irreplaceable. Technically, Nelson had the power to put his own plan into effect regardless of objections; actually, there was grave doubt that he could make any such decision stick. He was stymied because his principal lieutenant held better cards than he did. So, for a time, nothing at all happened. Nelson played a waiting game, and the longer this game was played the wider and more personal became the breach between himself and Wilson.

In spite of the obstacles Nelson might have gone ahead with his plan if he had been fully satisfied with it, but he wasn't. It was all very well to say that any increase in civilian production would be carefully programmed with the public interest in mind; as a practical matter, this plan was overelaborate and probably unworkable. If running the war economy had shown anything, it had shown that the American industrial machine is almost infinitely complex. It had been hard enough to work out a scheduling process for war production, where the requirements were clear and relatively precise—so many tanks, so many destroyers, so many rifles, so many shells, and so on. To try to do the same thing for civilian goods in the reconversion period would be a planner's nightmare.

The men in the Program Bureau began jumbling together figures on bobby pins and sewer pipes, air brakes and frying pans, alarm clocks and diapers, kitchen stoves and ten-penny nails and pickaxes and rayon slips and desk lamps, and had sober second thoughts. To try to work out exact quotas for several thousand items as heterogeneous as these, and to determine just when which factories should make how much of each, with due regard for the raw materials each producer would need, and all of this at a time when production levels were supposed to go up at an increasing rate—this looked like the direct road to complete confusion. Something a great deal simpler was needed—something that involved far fewer controls and restrictions and much less centralized planning, something that would approach the great problem of reconversion by turning loose the overwhelming energy and vitality residing in the American industrial system.

In the end, Nelson abandoned his original plan completely and took an entirely new tack. If it was impossible for government to plan and supervise every detail of the new production, why not turn the whole job over to industry—which, traditionally at least, was passionately anxious to have production carried on with a minimum of controls? Why shouldn't the proper use of idle machines and surplus materials be industry's responsibility all the way through, with government acting only to make certain that the new production did not interfere with war work? Why not end the bitter argument about who was to do the programming by having no programming at all? In place of *telling* industry to produce, why not simply *let* industry produce? There had been a great deal of talk about free enterprise, in which there was alleged to be great virtue: perhaps the solution was to take this talk at its face value and rely on free enterprise for quick reconversion.

The more Nelson pondered the matter the more he realized that this offered the only handy way to cut through the existing web of WPB restrictions on civilian production. That web was almost inconceivably intricate. There were on the books many hundreds of official orders prohibiting or limiting the production of almost every imaginable kind of peacetime product, and putting similar prohibitions or limitations on the uses that might be made of raw materials. Untangling these orders, bit by bit and step by step, so as to allow the production of, say, baby carriages, or to permit the use of copper in the manufacture of window screens, would be incomprehensibly arduous. Upwards of a dozen separate orders might have to be amended, revised, or annulled, and when this was all done it would probably be found that there existed two or three additional orders which had somehow been overlooked but which would have to be fixed before the prospective baby carriage manufacturer or window screen maker could actually start work. Nelson had had his experts begin an elaborate study of all the orders, away back in September, so that when the time came to relax controls somebody would have an intelligent idea of just which controls should come off first; but the study was not yet completed, and some sort of short cut was urgently needed. It would be ever so much simpler if manufacturers could just be authorized to produce regardless of the limitation orders, provided certain conditions designed to safeguard war production were met.

By no one was this approach welcomed more than by Maury Maverick, who saw in it a final chance to recapture some of the values which had been given up when the country went to war. Maverick was now chairman of the Smaller War Plants Corporation, a semi-independent agency dimly responsible to WPB, set up by act of Congress early in the war when Congress discovered that the small businessman was not likely to get much consideration from the big-league operators who were running WPB. Maverick's job made him, ex officio, a vice-chairman of WPB, where he got an intimate glimpse of how the economy was being run and intensely disliked what he saw—and disliked, for that matter, most of the people who were running it.

He had good reason to be concerned about the situation of the small businessman, and in mid-April, 1944, he went before a Senate committee to explain why.

Cutbacks in military orders, Maverick testified, were hitting the small producers hard. The Army might say all it pleased about the sheer impossibility of permitting any rise in the level of civilian production, but independent manufacturers were finding that there was less and less war work for them and if they could not presently get something else to do they would begin to go broke in large numbers. The total of unfilled orders in small plants had declined by 36 per cent between September, 1943, and February, 1944. This, said Maverick, was happening partly because the big contractors, seeing the over-all drop in the level of war production, were pulling in their subcontracts (chief source of activity for the little fellows) and were doing the work in their own plants, and partly because the armed services were concentrating the new orders still further in the hands of the large producers.

But the little fellow couldn't get new, nonwar work, to speak of, Maverick continued, because the Production Executive Committee and the War Manpower Commission had hearkened to the Army's talk of a manpower shortage and were decreeing, in effect, that manpower was too precious to be used for any civilian production. This, said Maverick, bristling angrily in the witness chair, was a complete departure from the method that had been used to solve all previous shortages.

"Not so long ago steel was awfully tight," he said. "But did anybody suggest that no steel at all should go to nonmilitary programs? Of course not. Neither the Army nor the Navy ever made such a suggestion. Everyone recognized that a certain amount had to go to nonmilitary purposes for the success of the war effort. Now that they say labor is tight they adopt a type of procedure which no one ever suggested when materials were tight.

"The real difference is this: the materials problem was worked out on a detailed program-by-program, plant-by-plant basis, involving a lot of work. Now that labor is supposed to be tight, they merely issue an ill-digested one-page rule that cuts little plants down as if they were attacked by a national prairie fire."

Both in WPB meetings and in public, Maverick bluntly declared that the opposition to Nelson's plan was motivated by nothing more lofty than a desire to save the postwar business opportunities for the big manufacturers. When the dollar-a-year men urged that during the reconversion period the production of civilian goods be limited to firms which had produced such goods before the war, and argued that this was simply a matter of fairness to the manufacturers, Maverick scornfully said that he had seen that dodge used before—had seen it down south, where the white folks liked to keep the colored folks from voting; this was nothing but the old "grandfather clause," and by no other term would Maverick refer to it, then or thereafter. Probably it was due to Maverick, as much as to anyone, that the long dispute over reconversion did not stay up on a lofty plane where it could be settled with dignity and without heat. Maverick believed this fight was for keeps and that the in-fighting was going to be dirty, and he waded stoutly in to contribute his share and, if possible, contribute it first. When Wilson complained that Nelson's people were inspiring newspaper stories impugning his motives, he almost certainly had Maverick chiefly in mind. If he didn't he probably should have.

Maverick was very active in helping to work out the reconversion plan on which Nelson finally decided to base his big fight. During the winter, various minor officials in WPB had been calling attention to the increasing quantities of raw materials which were now available. Maverick promptly suggested that these materials would be most welcome to the small manufacturers and urged that some way be found to permit their use. Nelson matched this suggestion with his own plans for cutting across the intricate network of limitation orders, and at last—about the time the invasion of Europe took place—settled on a new formula, the formula which was to become *the* reconversion plan.

This formula had four points:

1. It would lift all restrictions on the use of aluminum and magnesium.

2. It would permit manufacturers to place "unrated orders" for the machine tools they would need when they reconverted to peacetime work. (The "unrated" meant that the orders could be placed at once but could not be filled until the manufacturer with whom they were placed had no more military or other priority orders unfilled.)

3. It would allow a manufacturer to use just enough engineering time and critical materials to make one experimental model of whatever product he proposed to put on the postwar market.

4. By far the most important of all—the tail that was going to wag the rest of the dog—was that it would empower the field officers of WPB to authorize any local producer to make practically any peacetime product he chose, regardless of any and all existing restrictive orders, provided the producer was no longer needed in war work, provided the needed labor and materials were readily available, and provided that the whole job could be done without interfering with war production.

This last proposition came to be known as the Spot Authorization Plan; "spot," because the WPB official on the spot would determine, from his knowledge of local conditions, whether or not a given manufacturer could get into production. It looked mild enough on paper, and probably would have been mild enough in actual effect, since the permissive factor was hedged about with abundant restrictions. But to all of the people who did not want early reconversion, and to all of the people who did not want impious hands laid on the status quo, it looked like the thin edge of the wedge. As, in point of fact, it really was.

For this was the exact opposite of planned production. This was the enacting clause to Nelson's pledge that new competition would not be forbidden "even though the effects on competitive situations may be painful." It was even the opposite to what the business community had most complained of in the New Deal, for it took the controls almost entirely out of Washington and, in effect, placed the country's chief reliance for reconversion on the energy of some hundreds of thousands of independent businessmen. This, in other words, was taking the free enterprise system at face value on a nation-wide scale; any producer might make anything on earth he wished to make just as soon as the war situation permitted, the decision as to timing would not lie in bureaucratic Washington but would be made by officials accessible in his own community, and his success or failure—his contribution to the nation's supply of goods, his impact on the general competitive situation—would depend, ultimately, on his own enterprise, his own ability to make the most of the opportunities offered by the easing of wartime pressures. This was *really* free enterprise—not the we-point-with-pride kind that is used to justify a price-fixing agreement between giant corporations, but the down-to-earth kind that means a better life for the ordinary human being.

The immediate tangible effect of this plan would probably have been rather small. It would not have resulted in any huge volume of production before the end of the German war; could not have done so, since its whole operation was keyed to the pace of war production. Nelson himself—who, to his own amazement, was finding himself pictured as a New Deal Samson applying blind strength to the twin pillars of the temple—used to insist that big industry was scared over nothing. Suppose, he would say, the little fellow who owns a little shop gets out of war work and starts to make consumer goods; suppose he makes —oh, say electric refrigerators; suppose he makes and sells them for a good two years before the regular manufacturers of electric refrigerators can get back into business; is he, in the end, going to do them any real harm? Won't the industrial giants, with their experience, their resources, and their sales organizations, be able to regain their markets quickly enough, once the war ends, if they are on their toes?

. . . Free enterprise again; and rumblings, far off, in the background: On their toes? With the greatest sellers' market in all history coming up, they've got to be on their toes yet? . . . As somebody once remarked, there was nothing much to be afraid of but fear itself, but as things turned out that seemed to be enough. For although this program involved a very slow and gradual approach to reconversion, it did mean one thing clearly enough: neither War Department officials nor prominent-industrialists-on-loan would have very much to say about the when or the how of reconversion. This plan contained a seed which, if it were once planted, would sprout and grow in a completely unregimented way.

The elephant is the largest of land mammals, and has strength and durability beyond all other creatures, but it is scared to death of the little mouse. This plan was an authentic mouse, loosed among the elephantine herds of business big shots in and about WPB, and the trumpetings that went up to heaven were enough to knock the leaves off all the trees.

Nelson delayed formal presentation of his plan until after the invasion of Europe had established itself as a success. Then he brought it forth, at a meeting of the top board of WPB. When the dust had settled enough to enable him to count noses among his own vice chairmen, he found exactly three who were willing to go along with him—the unwavering Maverick, chuckling sardonically amid the turmoil, and the two labor vice-chairmen, Clint Golden and Joe Keenan. All the rest were opposed. The last semblance of harmony between Nelson and his vice-chairmen had vanished, never to be seen again.

But the basis for the opposition had changed. Nobody could publicly oppose spot authorization, unrestricted use of light metals, and advance ordering of machine tools on the simple ground that these measures would be harmful to big business. If the plan was to be fought—and it was, if any virtue remained in Israel—it could only be fought on the ground that it would be a peril to war production. Which finally and irrevocably bound the opposition to the War Department view.

Nelson found this out when he got ready to announce his program to the public. When he had a press release prepared the massed vice chairmen were bitterly opposed to its issuance, or at least to its issuance in the form Nelson proposed. He figured that the big idea was to tell people about the new program; to them, the important thing was to declare solemnly that the war situation was so crucial that there could not be any reconversion for a long, long time. If that could be done, to the extent of a couple of pages of impassioned prose—if the plan could be properly deprecated in advance, so to speak—then, they agreed, it might be all right to mention that this program did exist, on paper, in an anemic and ghost-like sort of way.

This row lasted for some twenty-four hours, with all hands seeking a formula and not finding one—and with the real issue, of course, being Nelson's insistence that the program be announced and the vice-chairmen's insistence that it not be announced. In sheer desperation the ball was finally passed to the WPB Information Division, which was instructed to find some way of saying the thing and making both sides happy.

If this was to be a war of words, and enemies domestic and foreign were to be whipped by sheer power of rhetoric, the information men could feel right at home; the formula, accordingly, was quickly found—the problem, after all, being no worse than the one which confronts a newspaper rewrite man when one of the publisher's particular pets is taken in sin by the police and the sad details have to be printed with due regard both for the public's lust for news and for the victim's influence in the front office. . . . What finally came out, then, agreeable to both sides, was the solemn statement that the invasion of Europe made it imperative for government, labor, and industry to get war production up to schedule and keep it there *and* to make prompt and adequate preparation for expanded civilian production so that everybody could get on with the war "secure in the knowledge that reconversion is being properly planned and prepared for." From that point it was easy enough to give a detailed description of the Nelson program, coupled with the statement that "restrictions which are not essential to war pro-

257

duction and which hamper industry's preparations for the reconversion period need to be lifted at once."

But if this satisfied the vice-chairmen, for the moment, it certainly did not satisfy the War Department. The extent to which
the Nelson program threatened established practices and favored
positions in industry was something that could be left for the
industrialists to worry about; its threat to the War Department's
determined drive to put over a labor draft and convict the populace of anarchic complacency was something that could not be
ignored for a moment. The details of the plan were unimportant;
if any reconversion plan at all were put into operation, Army
control over the economy would be doomed and military men
would be reduced to the function of running the Army and
fighting the war. The effect of the spot authorization system on
war production might, as Nelson insisted, be utterly infinitesimal;
its effect on public psychology was apt to be very great.

And public psychology was what mattered. Here we were,
once more, back where we started. The whole reconversion program—the whole effort to do something, in advance of the war's
end, that would enable the nation to go into the transition period
relieved of the intolerable pressures built up by a war economy
—was to be fought and was ultimately to be beaten on the ground
that it would have a bad psychological effect. Government by
public relations was about to go into its final, culminating stage,
guided by those masters of public relations, the generals and the
admirals. Decisions that would shape postwar years and postwar
policies were to be made on the old, familiar, disastrous basis of:
What will people think?

CHAPTER TWENTY

Great Beast

ACROSS the ocean there were those who held that the people
were a swinish multitude with no face, born to be ruled
with whips and lies, a multitude whose fears, blind appe-
tites, and infinite credulities were the only forces anyone need
take into account. They built a society on this belief and they
armed it for conquest, and they boasted that because all other
beliefs about people were delusions, and therefore weak, they
would control the earth for the next thousand years. And so
there was a great war, testing (as it had been written) whether
any nation so conceived and so dedicated could long endure.

This belief was the source of evil and despair and it had to be
beaten down by force of arms. The people provided the strength
that was needed, and the men who directed the use of that
strength were cool and shrewd, and great victories were won.
But the faith for which those victories were won was weakened,
and the people were betrayed, because those who led the people
were afraid to trust them. For the truth was that the leaders
of the people had some share in the belief that the people were
fighting to destroy.

Not that anyone ever put it that way. No disbelief in democracy was ever avowed. But when the time came to stake everything on the belief that the people were something more than
an embodiment of unreasoning desires and passions, the government failed to bet that way. It refrained from taking steps which
it had already said must be taken, because it was afraid that if it
took them the people would be too stupid and greedy to behave
properly. To make the people behave properly the government
scolded them and tried to frighten them and hid the truth from
them, for it was believed that the truth would not be understood and that the people would not support the war unless they
were scolded.

So the anonymously eminent personage had referred to a strike
whose effect on war production was absolute zero as "the damnedest crime ever committed against America." So the Secretary of

259

War denounced the people for a state of anarchy, and the War Department sternly demanded a manpower draft to make the people do what they were already doing voluntarily. So occupational deferments were canceled just when the man who knew most about them was explaining how essential they were. And so the Army was just about as alarmed by Nelson's reconversion plan as it would have been by the appearance of a Nazi panzer division on the highway between Baltimore and Washington, and took strong measures to defeat it.

For whatever else it might have meant, this reconversion plan definitely meant good-bye to all of the scolding and the double-talk. It proposed that the government act as if the people were old enough to know the score—that it entrust them with the knowledge that their industrial economy was doing more than enough to win the war, and that it act on that fact without being frightened by the assumption that the people would thereupon conclude that the war was over.

The Army had to beat the Nelson plan, even if the heavens and the earth were moved, because the Army distrusted the people. In the WPB meetings where the plan was endlessly argued, the Army was perfectly frank about it. Nelson's plan specified that the only expansion of civilian production that would be permitted would be production that did not in any way interfere with war work; the Army replied that even that kind of production would interfere, because it would create the wrong psychological effect.

The Army thesis ran about like this:

Do anything whatever to expand civilian production, do anything even to pave the way for some future expansion, and you'll make people think the crisis is past. If they think that, they'll relax. If they relax, then the workers will leave war plants to look for jobs with a peacetime future and managements will refuse to take new contracts and won't push so hard on the war work they still have, and as a result the whole war production program will fall flat. It's not that these orders would of themselves do any particular harm; it's the psychological effect that would be ruinous. We can't let people think that the war is nearly over because if they do they won't work hard enough.

The military men had been bumping into what people thought all through the winter and spring of 1944, and they didn't especially like it. A sample case is to be found in their experience with the Brewster Corporation, where the Navy, in mid-May, had suddenly found it necessary to cancel a contract for the production of fighter airplanes. The Brewster workers reacted with unexpected vigor. Like all other war workers, they had been needled for months about the great urgency of the production situation and the overwhelming need for more planes, and had been told unceasingly that they must work hard and "not let our boys down." Now, without the slightest warning, they reported for work on a May morning to find that their whole program had been canceled and the entire factory was to be closed because the planes they had been making were no longer needed. So they staged a brief but angry "sit-in" strike, declaring that they would remain in the factory until more war work was provided.

This singular strike, aimed at forcing a continuance of work rather than a stoppage, had been copied in other plants where there were similar unexpected cutbacks, and the psychological effect (as the Army might have put it) was most unfortunate. Just when the military men were demanding a labor draft to prevent workers from leaving war jobs, the workers were going on strike to prevent their war jobs from leaving them. The expression, "cutback jitters," referring to the state of mind among workers who suspected that their factory's war contract was about to be canceled without warning, passed into common currency. Something had to be done, and done quickly.

Justice Byrnes, as boss of the Office of War Mobilization, took a long look at WPB and sent Executive Vice-Chairman Wilson a directive instructing him and his Production Executive Committee to take general charge of the cutback problem and to "adopt uniform policies for the future cancellation of contracts." This was deeply unwelcome to Nelson, for cutbacks were at the heart of the reconversion problem and this action gave the Committee exactly what it had been asking for and what Nelson had been denying it—a big measure of responsibility for reconversion policy. However, Nelson by this time knew better than to expect any help from the Byrnes office—and, anyway, the cutback jitters were spreading and somebody had to check them, so PEC set up a large interagency staff and told it to work out some means for getting new military work promptly into factories whose old contracts had died.

The staff went to work at once and labored prodigiously until well on in the autumn, but it did not cure the cutback jitters because they weren't to be cured that way. The official theory was that more than enough war work existed to keep everybody busy all the time, and that all that was needed was a way to dovetail new jobs with old jobs. Unfortunately, that just was not the case. No amount of effort could conceal the fact that, over the long pull, new requirements were not being given to the nation's war production machine as fast as the old requirements were being met. That was why the administration, six months earlier, had ordered a quick study of reconversion possibilities; that was why Baruch and Byrnes had called on the Army and WPB to get together on a reconversion plan; that was why Nelson had finally brought out his four-point program.

But that was the one fact the Army was unwilling to see discussed in public, because it obviously made the labor draft and the psychological warfare campaign completely unnecessary. So the Army simply ignored it and talked vigorously about something else. It argued that war production was disastrously behind schedule; that it was behind schedule because the unpatriotic workers, deluded by hopes of an early peace, were quitting war jobs and looking for an easier way to make a living, and that Nelson's plan would make them quit even faster by confirming their hopes and encouraging their reprehensible desires. The inevitable result, the Army said, would be reduction of munitions output to a level that would endanger military operations overseas.

In the end the Army succeeded in committing the entire administration to this argument. It won complete dominance over the civilian end of the government, and, winning it, destroyed all hope for reconversion.

Now it was just this matter of war workers quitting their jobs that Nelson's plan was designed to cure. Nelson's idea was that cutback jitters would cease if workers saw that peacetime production was going to increase as fast as war production fell; for if a factory could begin making civilian goods as soon as its war contract was canceled, uneasy workers would not feel that they had to protect themselves by quitting ahead of time in order to look for jobs that would last. The spot authorization plan would help war production rather than hinder it, therefore; would mean fewer workers leaving war jobs, not more.

It is deeply significant that this argument was supported firmly by the two top labor men in WPB, Keenan and Golden, who were practically unique, among all the high officials who were worrying about the worker's psychology, in that they knew something about it first-hand. In July they sent a joint memo to the other WPB vice-chairmen, asserting that the Nelson program would help worker morale and would prevent the letdown which the Army was so anxiously predicting. They added, acidly, that "The duty of the WPB to the military is to assure that war production requirements are met. So long as this duty is performed, the military are not in any position to oppose action by the WPB for the benefit of the civilian economy." This was true as gospel but somewhat irrelevant, since the Army by now was getting things well under control.

When he announced his program, Nelson had said that it would go into effect on July 1. About a week before that fateful date, however, Nelson fell ill of double pneumonia and went into a hospital—leaving Wilson in charge of everything right at the moment when all of the War Department and most of WPB were going on the warpath.

As Nelson's chief deputy, Wilson found himself responsible for putting Nelson's program into operation. But it was bitterly opposed by all of the officials in WPB with whom Wilson worked most closely and in whom he had the most confidence. It was even more bitterly opposed by the Production Executive Committee—which met on June 28 and voted solidly that "the entire question of the resumption of civilian and peacetime production" ought to be reopened and considered anew at the next board meeting of WPB. This of course put the Committee, an operating subsidiary of the War Production Board, in the position of trying to dictate policy to the parent organization, and Wilson could not go for it. He pointed out that the arguments which were being raised against the Nelson plan had all been raised, and heard by Nelson, at WPB meetings prior to Nelson's illness. He, Wilson, had been instructed to issue the orders; there was no new element in the situation that would justify him in reversing the Chairman.

There was. however, as it happened, a little matter of the cumbersome routine common to all government organizations. Getting the orders drafted properly took longer than had been expected, and it developed that they would not actually be ready for issuance until some days after July 1. The next WPB board meeting did, therefore, do as PEC urged and review the entire situation. With Nelson away, the members of the Board accepted the Army viewpoint in toto and voted unanimously that "the issuance of the proposed orders at the present time would interfere with war production." It recommended, therefore, that their issuance be postponed until Nelson was on his feet again.

Again Wilson refused to accept the vote as binding. The most he could do, he told the board, was visit Nelson in the hospital and tell him how the board felt. A few days later he did so, but Nelson's mind was made up at last. The orders were to be issued, he told Wilson, just as soon as bureaucratic routine permitted.

Whereupon the Army wheeled up its heaviest artillery and opened fire.

Under date of July 7, Nelson got an official letter from the Joint Chiefs of Staff, signed by Admiral William D. Leahy, Chief of Staff to the President. This letter was released to the press upon transmission, and it got front-page play in the papers of July 9. It read:

"We are disturbed over the existing lag in war production which, if it continues, may necessitate revision in strategic plans which could prolong the war.

"In view of the major offensive operations under way on every front, it is essential at this time that there be no relaxation in war production and that deficits in deliveries be made up at the earliest possible date.

"The issuance of orders at this time which will affect our ability to produce war materials is not consistent with the all-out prosecution of the war."

This was really an appeal to the public, of course, not to Nelson—for letters from the military chieftains to the boss of war production were not ordinarily released to the press. The Army was reaching over the head of a civilian official in government, trying to panic the public into opposition to that official's policies.

And the letter itself was pure double-talk which simply would not stand analysis. Of course there must be "no relaxation" in war production; of course deficits in deliveries must be made up promptly; of course orders that would "affect our ability to produce war materials" should not be issued. There never had been any argument on those platitudes; Nelson himself would accept them, and did accept them, as quickly as the most ardent general in the Army. And as to "the existing lag in war production": that sentence could have been written, and would have been fully as pertinent, timely, and significant, on any week end from the day after Pearl Harbor to the spring of 1945, simply because there was *always* a lag somewhere in the infinitely complex war production program which would have dire consequences if it were not overcome. That was inherent in the very nature of industrial warfare, which is forever in a state of apparent crisis; you can always put your finger on some spot in the production picture and say, "There will be merry hell to pay if this isn't fixed." The situation in the early summer of 1944 was no worse in that respect than it had been all along, which is to say that there were grave production problems to be solved and that they were being solved just as they always had been solved before. The Army could, if it chose, make the situation look like a production crisis, just as a newspaper can at any time create the appearance of a crime wave by giving front-page publicity to every entry on the police blotters; and it was exactly that kind of trick which this letter was trying to play.

If there was one man in Washington who knew the facts on matters of production it was Senator Truman, who had been watching affairs with full information and coolly competent judgment. On the very day Nelson got his letter from the Joint Chiefs of Staff, Truman issued a statement demanding action on reconversion, declaring that "the time for discussion is past" and adding:

"It [the reconversion program] has been opposed by some selfish business groups that want to see their competitors kept idle until they finish their war contracts. It also has been opposed by Army and Navy representatives who want to create a surplus of manpower with the hope that the consequent pressure on unemployed workers would result in some of them shifting to occupations or areas in which there is still a manpower shortage."

Simultaneously, the Truman Committee served notice on Wilson that if WPB did not speedily issue a statement announcing that the orders were going to be put into effect, the committee would immediately begin public hearings on the whole business "to obtain a public record for future action."

This was a bit rough on Wilson, what with the Chairman still away, the Army increasing its opposition to the hated orders, and the industry phalanx in WPB as determined as ever in its opposition. Wilson himself had grave doubts about the Nelson orders—the doubts of an intensely practical man who was getting gray hairs meeting production problems out on the firing line, and whose instinct it was to concentrate on the job at hand to the exclusion of all else. But although he could not support Nelson's program, he refused to overrule Nelson while Nelson was still absent; as a slugger, it was his nature to slug a man who was on his feet facing him, not a man who had left him in charge and retired to a sick bed.

What, under all of these cruel circumstances, could the opponents of reconversion do? Appeal to Caesar, maybe?

Done! The whole business was now brought to the attention of Justice Byrnes. Byrnes conferred with Nelson by telephone, counseling delay; a bit later, it was announced that the four orders would be issued, but that they would be issued on a staggered basis—aluminum and magnesium order on July 15, experimental model order on July 22, order on machine tools July 29, and spot authorization on August 15. A breathing spell had been gained, at least; possibly something could be done with it?

Possibly; beginning with a renewed effort to educate the public. The Army went to unheard-of lengths to convince people that there was a critical war production shortage, and developed a virtuosity of technique that was nothing short of admirable—or, at least, amazing. There was, as a sample, the time a high general in the supply end of the War Department held an off-the-record conference with a group of business paper editors to expound on the desperate nature of the production situation. One of the reporters who covered the War Production Board heard about it, and a bit later went around to ask the General what the story was. The General dwelt at length on production shortages, on the tremendous need for supplies in Europe, on the serious drop in the general output of war goods; and, as a final kicker, said impressively that the annual rate of war production now, in August, was a good two and one-half billions below the rate that obtained in the previous November. (Down two and one-half billions: obviously, a production crisis of an alarming nature!)

The reporter, who had been around quite a while, thought that one over a bit and then said:

"But, General, isn't it true that that was a *planned* reduction? Weren't the programs reduced by around two and one-half billions, beginning the first of the year?"

The General looked at him for a long moment, then smiled a faint, glacial smile, like a croupier motioning to a punter to rake in his winnings.

"Oh," said the General. "You remembered that, did you?"

That was a typical sample. The general level of production *was* down below the November level because it had been put down; but the technique was to emphasize the fact that it was down, to omit all reference to the cutbacks, and then to imply that the drop was entirely due to a lamentable failure by workers, by manufacturers, and by the civilians-in-government who had charge of such matters. After which, of course, it was easy to argue that this was no time to begin unlimited production of goods for stay-at-homes.

A parallel tack was also given a heavy workout. The armies in France were advancing. As they advanced, across a land in which railroads had been systematically destroyed, the supply problem became acute. Miracles of transportation were performed, but even so it was not possible to bring munitions to the front quite as fast as they were being used. Hence there were shortages on the firing lines—tragic, heart-rending shortages, paid for in American lives. The War Department publicized these shortages extensively—and then, in the same breath, bore down on the production lag at home, leaving the plain implication that the shortages at the front were caused by a letdown in the factories at home —which simply and flatly was not true.

This technique reached its final perfect flowering in a press conference held in the Pentagon Building by Under-Secretary of War Patterson. Patterson presented a baker's dozen of GI's just back from the fighting front in France. These lads, shy before the reporters and the cameramen, told their stories one by one: desperate fighting, not enough shells or grenades at hand, ammunition strictly rationed, chances missed and lives lost because of that rationing. "It's tough to see your buddies get killed and not be able to stop it." It was a harrowing picture they painted, and God knows they were telling the truth; but the clear, obvious, intended implication of the whole performance—though nowhere touched on by the soldiers themselves—was that this tragic state of affairs existed because of a failure in production back home.

The Truman Committee kept itself informed on such points, and some months later—in December—Senator Mead told the Senate that there had been "a misconception of the problem" in regard to supplies at the front.

"Insufficient production in the United States has not up to this time been the cause of shortages of weapons and ammunition at the front," he declared. "Any shortage has been due, up to now, solely to transportation problems overseas."

The Senator then referred to "certain news stories concerning actual shortages of ammunition in the hands of our fighting men" which implied that production failures at home were the cause. Such implications, he had been assured, were not intended, and in any case they were not well founded.

Senator Mead may well have been assured that the implications were not intended, but the assurances are a tale to be told to the Marines. The implications were unquestionably intended. Those infantrymen didn't just happen to wander back to the Pentagon Building under their own steam; they were brought back, and their press conference was arranged for them by top brass, and there is not under the all-seeing heavens any imaginable reason why this was done except to convey precisely the implication Senator Mead complained of. The press conference may not have speeded the fabulous Red Ball express very much, but it was a useful item in the Army's program of psychological warfare against the people back home.

It was right at this time that the Kiplinger news letter remarked that "the cries of the military men sound much like propaganda. They don't fib, but they do pick and play up bad spots to make a scare. The implication, the impression, the effect, is close to misrepresentation."

Close enough; practically a bull's eye, you might say. . . .

And now the luckless Office of War Information came stumbling into action.

On August 10 Nelson got a letter from Edward Klauber, Acting Director of OWI in the temporary absence of Elmer Davis, enclosing an elaborate "plan and program on production information" which was about to be sprung on the public and in which Nelson's hearty co-operation was earnestly invited. Nelson, who had just returned to his desk, rumbled and snorted as he read it like one of Bill Jeffers' freight locomotives taking an eighty-car train over the continental divide.

For OWI was making the Army line the official information policy of the government. It held that the production situation "is crucial and may grow more so," and it had mapped out an elaborate publicity campaign to "buttress the emotional appeal to patriotism"—which is about as elegant a way of saying "propaganda" as you could easily find. OWI was proposing an intensive use of radio, motion pictures and the daily press to prove that while reconversion would of course be planned and calculated in due time and with full wisdom there could be nothing like actual reconversion at the moment; that management and labor alike should forget about the prospect of working to produce civilian goods; that war workers should stay on their jobs in spite of hell or high water (which, after all, was just what the unhappy Brewster workers had tried to do), and that the production crisis deserved the exclusive attention of the nation.

The prospectus was not short. It went on to relate that beginning August 14 (by coincidence, one day before the all-important spot authorization plan was due to go into effect) OWI would devote to this campaign a full 25 per cent of its radio time, with sixty-second blurbs on the basic theme being heard "on sixty-five radio shows weekly, both daytime and evening, on all four networks." Top generals and admirals would broadcast on the desperate need for more production; movie stars and war correspondents who had been overseas would speak on the same theme; Nelson himself was urged to speak. Indeed, in its ineffable ignorance of what was really going on OWI pointed out that "Mr. Nelson's appearance on such a broadcast would be important since he could make clear the fact that there is no incompatibility between these controls"—the controls demanded by the Army to make reconversion impossible—"and everyone's plans and desires for early reconversion."

Then came the part that really made Nelson fume. Formulas

would be developed for special radio dramatizations, and network dramatists would be asked to write scripts involving battle-front situations and describing "fictional military situations where the success of our arms was perhaps jeopardized for lack of materials at issue." This, it was pointed out, would "add to the general backdrop of urgency."

. . . In November, 1944—by which time the Army was making more noise than ever about the "desperate" production situation, even though Nelson had been officially beheaded and the reconversion plan was safely embalmed—one of the ablest of the WPB officials, Hiland G. Batcheller, Chief of Operations, made a careful analysis of the production situation, and the analysis is worth glancing at here, ahead of time. Batcheller found that 60 per cent of all war production programs were fully up to schedule and that 40 per cent were behind to a greater or lesser degree. But two-thirds of the lagging programs were behind schedule either because the schedules had been increased so sharply and abruptly that no conceivable amount of production could get them on the target promptly, or because of the introduction of new models or changes in design. Only about one-fifth of the deficiencies were due to labor shortages, and these labor shortages were definitely not due to the psychological causes which were all the Army would talk about—and which, it must be borne in mind, were the entire justification for the great OWI propaganda campaign. On the contrary, Batcheller said, these labor shortages had very tangible physical causes—bad housing, inadequate transportation, lack of proper community facilities, and so on: the very points which both Nelson and Wilson had emphasized, early in the year, as matters which could be remedied by judicious expansion of civilian production. On the whole, Batcheller concluded, the important production problems were the same ones that had been cropping up since the beginning of the war, and they would be solved exactly as they had been solved before. . . .

But of this kind of knowledge OWI was completely innocent, then and thereafter. It was paying for a defect in its basic organization. The original Horton information division had lived with the agencies it served, had grown into them, knew at all times exactly what they were thinking and doing, had accurate first-hand knowledge about the facts in each one of them. But

OWI had been superimposed over a whole network of independent information groups. It supplied policy control, but it lacked direct access to the facts. It was now preparing to put on a great propaganda campaign about a production crisis, but of its own knowledge it could not say whether such a crisis existed—could not say and had no means of finding out. It blithely sent off its prospectus to Nelson and invited him to participate, completely unable to grasp the idea that the whole campaign was designed to defeat his reconversion policy.

By a wonderful accident, Nelson got two messages from OWI on the same day. One was the letter from Klauber, enclosing the prospectus; the other was a message from OWI's London office, routed to Nelson via OWI's Psychological Warfare Desk. This message plaintively called for a statement by Nelson that could be used overseas to refute the claim that American war production was lagging. The London office pointed out that "claims of failing production might have a tendency to stiffen enemy resistance, raise enemy combat morale, and by prolonging the war bring about the loss of American lives"; could Mr. Nelson, therefore, at his early convenience, sponsor a statement for overseas use which would show that production really was in good shape?

Apparently the great campaign to discourage Americans by showing that they were weakly failing to put forth their best efforts had unlooked-for results overseas. In the hands of the clumsy—which is certainly where it reposed in the summer of 1944—psychological warfare on the home front can be a two-edged weapon.

It was the Klauber prospectus that got Nelson's attention. He stormed angrily, writing Klauber that the intention of the OWI program "seems to be to create the impression of a war production crisis which does not exist" and declaring that if it were put into effect "I shall be obliged to take strong measures to offset its unfortunate consequences on the public mind." This did induce OWI to drop its weird plan for broadcasting playlets showing American soldiers being beaten in battle because the workers back home were slacking on the job, but it accomplished nothing else. The propaganda drive was to go ahead, with or without Nelson's co-operation. Rather to his amazement, Nelson got a cordial reply from Klauber expressing delight "to know that

271

you and I are in precise agreement on nearly everything that is in your letter," and pointing out that "on the basic question of a production crisis I know you will be fair enough to realize that the determination does not lie with me."

Which was just the point. OWI was about to enforce a party line, but it had no voice in determining what the party line was to be. It was taking its cue from the Byrnes office, which—having originally set in motion the machinery to provide a reconversion program—was now in the act of agreeing with the Army that the reconversion program should be made inoperative.

The administration had got itself into a fine fix. It had set up a powerful information agency—designed, not to give the people a straight pitch at all times on everything that was going on, but to "end confusion" by showing that there was complete unity on all matters of importance. Now a matter of supreme importance had arisen and the government was decidedly not a unit, and the people needed nothing so much as they needed a clear, detailed elaboration of all the facts. But instead of this the people were about to get an impassioned campaign designed to show that there was a grave production crisis for which they themselves were responsible—even though the agency which was to conduct this campaign was admitting that it lacked the authority to decide whether such a crisis actually existed. This, finally, was what came of the administration's decision to junk an information mechanism based squarely on the people's need for unretouched facts and to adopt one based on the government's need to create a desired impression.

Not, all things considered, a minor matter.

To repeat it once more: what was at stake here was not just a question of personalities involving a dispute between two men named Nelson and Wilson. This was a matter of saying how the country was going to come out of the war and how its future was going to be shaped, of determining whether civilians or military men decided national policy, of trying to bring the nation out of the war in a better state of preparation for the unpredictable than it had gone in, of equipping democracy for the long peacetime pull. And when this came up for settlement, in the summer of 1944, its handling was determined by a deep, all-pervasive fear and mistrust of the people's ability to do the right thing in the light of all the facts. From first to last, the one solid argument against the reconversion program was that it would have the wrong psychological effect—which can be translated only as "the dumb clucks aren't to be trusted."

Sixty-five radio shows a week on all four networks "to buttress an emotional appeal to patriotism"; dramatic skits to establish "a general backdrop of urgency," backed up by speeches from generals, admirals, and movie stars; stay-on-the-job appeals dinned into people's ears unceasingly: don't look for other work because you aren't going to find it; if you don't snap out of it we'll lose the war; the determination doesn't lie with me, I just beat the drum . . . and exactly whose war is this, anyhow? where is the strength to win it coming from? whose ideals and dreams of a better life are hanging in the balance these days?

Distinct in the shadows, dapper ghost of an ill-born aristocrat who fought against Thomas Jefferson:

Your people, sir, is a great beast.

CHAPTER TWENTY-ONE

Return of the Hollow Men

BY THE middle of August the important question seemed to be: Who runs WPB from now on—Nelson, or Wilson? The one safe bet seemed to be that the two men could not, in view of everything, go on pulling together in double harness much longer. The split in WPB had become too wide and too well advertised, and personal feelings had been too much aroused. It had become a gag and a wisecrack, right then, that the longest distance in Washington was the short walk across the waiting room from the door of Nelson's office to the door of Wilson's. Sixty feet, perhaps, altogether—a gap nobody could bridge.

Accordingly, both the War Production Board and all the interested bystanders sat back and gaped when it suddenly became known that Nelson was going to go to China.

This was to be a special mission, purpose stated rather vaguely. The President needed to have a top industrialist and war production expert visit China to determine how China's industrial potential could be strengthened for better use against the Japs, and also to figure out some sort of long-range industrial program which, in the postwar period, would enable China to survive and prosper. As an industrialist and war production expert Nelson easily qualified, and he sincerely wanted to make the trip. Wholly aside from the fact that he had some definite ideas about improving the situation in China, the situation in WPB now was such that a brief absence from Washington, for any purpose whatever, looked extremely good to him.

So as to the mission itself there was no argument; Nelson wanted to go, and the assignment was a natural. What everyone wanted to know was: If he goes, is he ever coming back? In his absence the Number Two man would of course take charge of WPB; and the Number Two man, as nobody could help remembering, was Wilson, with whom Nelson was at swords' points over deep and basic matters of policy. Wilson had recently had one experience of sitting in for the absent

Chairman and trying to steer the Chairman's course at a time when it was under violent fire; the course was still the same and the fire was getting hotter than ever. How would it work this time, with Nelson removed to China instead of just to a hospital room in Washington?

However Nelson and Wilson themselves may have felt about it, the rival forces in and out of WPB drew their conclusions quite speedily. The Wilson camp was elated and the Nelson camp was dejected. It couldn't just be by chance that Nelson was going all the way to China at a time when the tension between himself and Wilson was something you could twang like a banjo string; this looked exactly like presidential intervention in favor of the no-reconversion group. The technique of kicking a discredited official upstairs was familiar, and China seemed to be an ominous destination anyway—Mr. Wallace, it was easy to recall, had gone on an extensive mission to China not long before the President had moved to unload him from the Vice-Presidency. The interoffice buzzing that had been going on for weeks in the top, medium, and low levels of WPB—to the serious interference, occasionally, of the routine work of getting on with the war—now reached a pitch that could be heard all over town.

Which led up to the final showdown. On a drowsy Sunday morning Sterling Green of the Associated Press, contemplating the fact that he would have to write, for the Monday morning papers, a story rounding up the week-end developments, if any, on the general reconversion situation, meditated on Nelson's impending departure for China and decided to find out, once and for all, whether it really meant what it seemed to mean. (No use asking Nelson himself: he was spreading sweetness and light, insisting that the assignment was entirely welcome, even denying that there were any real differences of opinion between himself and Wilson on reconversion. Their only argument, he was saying, was simply over the question of timing. This was true enough, in a way, but since the question of timing was precisely the point that mattered, the explanation was not quite as soothing as it sounded.) So Green, running down his list of WPB officials who were intimate enough with Nelson to know what was really going on, finally called one of them and put the question to him point-blank: Did this trip to China actually mean that Nelson was being eased out of WPB and that his reconversion program was thereby being scuttled?

The Nelson man at the other end of the wire was bitter, explicit, and slightly vulgar.

"It certainly does," he said with feeling. "Nelson is being kicked right square in the groin."

Green wrote his story, modifying the blunt quotation to "kicked in the teeth," and the yarn hit the front pages Monday morning.

That did it. Here was what amounted to official confirmation for all of the contrasting hopes and fears. Nelson was being kicked in the teeth, the reconversion program was going to be kicked in an even more painful and crippling manner, the Army point of view was going to prevail, and if big industry, as alleged, was all for the Army viewpoint, then big industry had won the battle of Gettysburg and the little fellow was on the road to Appomattox. All in all, then—to your tents, O Israel, the redcoats are coming and the dam has bust, this is the year of the big wind and there is foul play at the crossroads, and nothing short of the trumpet of the Archangel Gabriel will ever restore peace and harmony again.

The uproar that followed was heard everywhere, and most especially in the White House. Senator Truman, who had already spoken the mind of himself and his committee about the reconversion program, communicated his feeling to the President. So did Senator Murray of Montana, who was head of an active committee on small business and who felt that Nelson's reconversion program offered the small businessman his only hope. So did the CIO and the AFL, who did not like the Army campaign for a labor draft and a pool of unemployed workers, and whose presidents hastened to espouse Nelson's cause. A backfire was built up which, if it might not have the effect of saving either Nelson's job or his program, was at least going to make it impossible for Wilson to take his place. For this fight—a fight, at bottom, over the kind of philosophy that ought to prevail in getting the country out of the war and into the peace—was by now 100 per cent personalized. The various groups and forces which wanted something done about reconversion and dreaded Army control had to have a hero, and the only possible candidate was Nelson; not the hero they might have chosen, perhaps, not a knight in shining armor fighting from first ditch to last for unsullied Jeffersonian democracy, but nevertheless a man who was fighting their fight and whom they had to support. Having a hero, they had to have a villain, for the hero always fights a villain; and since the man the hero was fighting seemed to be chiefly Wilson, why—Q.E.D.

This was about as completely unjust as a thing could easily be, since Wilson was simply an honest, patriotic, and high-principled man trying to do his best in an uncommonly difficult and intricate situation, and since he actually wasn't the man Nelson was fighting at all; circumstances had just put him in the line of fire, and there was no good way for him to get out of it. It is worth noting that when the President proposed to make Wilson the acting chairman of WPB during Nelson's absence, Nelson consented readily. But the whole business was way out of any man's control by now, and the great Nelson-Wilson fight was all anybody was looking at.

But the real fight had already been lost, and the fundamental issue had been settled, even though the point almost universally escaped notice. The country was *not* going to start its preparations for the momentous peacetime adjustments that lay ahead until the military men gave their consent, and that was that. If this meant binding the harness of what-used-to-be on an economy which, in the process of winning the greatest of all wars, had already burst all the old bounds, why, it meant that and there was no use shadow-boxing about it. Nelson might stay, Nelson might go, Wilson might replace him, or the job might go to Joe Doakes—as far as the fundamental problem was concerned it all made no difference. Step by step, from the first careful move for the defeat of the Axis down to now, all of the chances to bring democracy out of the war with a conscious rebirth of its revolutionary strength had been missed; had been missed, in the last analysis, because it was precisely the revolutionary strength of democracy that was most frightening to the men who had the decisions to make. The reconversion program was an attempt to salvage something from the lost opportunities —the *last* attempt, for the duration of the war; and by the time Nelson had agreed to go to China the program was plucking at the coverlet and babbling of green fields. The showdown came too late.

Thus: the reconversion program had gone into effect, as scheduled, on August 15—had gone into effect but not into operation, because its wings had been neatly clipped by a special directive from the Byrnes office.

On August 4, well in advance of the issuance date for the spot authorization order, Byrnes had decreed that the War Manpower Commission should take special steps to provide labor for war factories. As part of this operation, he ordered that in loose labor areas—the regions where workers were unemployed because of lack of war work, and where it had been anticipated that the spot authorization plan would actually provide some production —no increase in civilian production could be permitted, unless the local representative of WMC would certify, in writing, that labor was available for such production "without interference with local and interregional labor recruiting efforts."

This order, which took final authority over any increase in civilian production out of the hands of WPB and gave it to the War Manpower Commission, was an even tighter curb than it appeared to be. It required a local WMC official to put himself irrevocably on the spot whenever he gave an okay for increased civilian production. He would have to go on record, formally and in writing, that there was no chance to recruit for other war jobs, either locally or anywhere in the United States, any of the labor which the new production might employ. In actual practice, no bureaucrat in his sober mind would be in the least likely to commit himself in that manner; it would infallibly fly back and hit him in the face if at any time the region for which he was responsible failed to provide its quota of recruits for war work. In addition, the Commission as a whole now had a keen vested interest in preventing any increase in civilian production; for, to the extent that it permitted such production to increase, the Commission would become the direct target for the War Department's wrath whenever the War Department felt moved to complain—which, judging by past performance, would be approximately every day in the week.

The victory for a reconversion program was therefore more than a little hollow, and it quickly got even hollower. The order lifting restrictions on the use of light metals was hedged about with qualifying amendments so that it became, in effect, a substitution order, stimulating the use of light metals in place of scarcer materials on production that was going to take place anyway, but doing very little more. The permission to make experimental models of postwar items looked much less lustrous when the Army began threatening that any manufacturer who took advantage of it might get all of his occupational deferments canceled en bloc; and the provision for placing "unrated" orders for machine tools was restricted until, by the end of the year, it had been made virtually inoperative.

As a final blow, it developed—on the very day the spot authorization plan went into effect—that there was not, unfortunately, going to be any steel for the reserve pool which was supposed to be set up for the use of manufacturers who were authorized to make civilian goods. A man who qualified under the plan might, just conceivably, get permission to produce, but he would not be able to get any steel to produce with.

This determination, which came down from the Requirements Committee on the basis of supply estimates furnished by the WPB Steel Division, drew an angry protest from Maury Maverick, who announced that something almighty queer was going on. One of his aides, John Blair, had submitted a report which Maverick found highly interesting: the Steel Division, Blair pointed out, in its regular quarterly forecasts of steel supplies, had consistently overestimated the amount of steel that would be available, all through the first two years of the war—when steel was "in tight supply," as the jargon had it, and there was no question of using any of it for any nonwar purpose. But beginning with the start of 1944, Blair continued, the Steel Division had suddenly gone to the other extreme, and now all of its forecasts were sharply underestimating the quantity that would be produced. This had the effect of preventing allotments to nonwar production, which was carried on largely by the little manufacturers; it also, at this moment, prevented the setting up of a steel reserve for use under the spot authorization plan, whose beneficiaries, again, would be little manufacturers. Maverick protested with heat and vigor, but for the moment at least he got nowhere.

So the reconversion plan was stalled, on dead center, and any man with eyes to see might foretell that it was going to remain stalled. But that did not take any of the edge off of the great Nelson-Wilson showdown, whether the showdown be considered purely as a spectacle or as a visitation sent to try the souls of the two men most intimately involved. The headlines had made a personal duel out of it, and as a personal duel it was going to come to its climax; and, like all such matters in the official family at the capital, it was finally going to come up to Mr. Big himself for settlement.

. . . Pity, for a moment, the harassed President. He had recently returned from a tour of the Pacific. He was sitting at the steering wheel in the greatest of all wars, and decisions on everything from fundamental military strategy to the creation of a new postwar international society were up to him. A presidential election campaign was just getting into its swing, and he had to win it for the sake of the things he was fighting for just as Lincoln had had to win in 1864; was to win it, in the end, principally by demonstrating that the wear and tear of twelve years in the White House had left him physically capable of riding bare-headed through a pelting autumn rain. He was handling domestic problems, as any president in his position would be bound to handle them, through deputies; and now his deputies could not agree, and it was up to him to say who was right and who was wrong. Divided counsels were coming to him. Assistant President Byrnes, backed by Elder Statesman Baruch and by trusted military leaders, was telling him that Nelson was wrong and would have to go; balancing this group there was Harry Hopkins—thick-and-thin Hopkins, ignoring the approach of death just as the President was ignoring it—urging support for Nelson and for Nelson's program, with labor leaders, New Deal senators, and Vice-Presidential Nominee Truman crying Amen to him. Nelson—Wilson, Wilson—Nelson, this is too intricate for any man to pick up cold—do we stop on the road to Armageddon to get to the bottom of a personal row, and must the commander-in-chief of half the world decide whether the time is at hand to let the shop on the corner make a few electric flatirons? All of the lines lead to the White House in the end, and it is up to the man in the White House to give the decisions, and before very long we are going to Yalta, and is there any way on earth to get the gasoline and the shells up to Patton's far-ranging divisions a little bit faster? Decide it, decide it one way or the other, just so that it gets off the books; this is the Valley of

Decision, Mr. President, and the Valley of the Shadow lies just eight months ahead. . . .

So the showdown came. August 24; and all top and middle ranks in WPB are summoned to a meeting in the bleak auditorium of the Social Security Building, where matters of weight are to be imparted. Meeting is set for 10:30 A.M.; postponed, at the last minute, by myriad telephone calls, until just after lunch. (The boss is at the White House.) Lunch time comes and goes, the auditorium fills, and presently Nelson and Wilson stride in together and take seats facing the men who work for them.

All in all, a singular meeting, not devoid of drama. For the last time they are all together; the 500 business executives, the names of whose peacetime affiliations read like American industry's blue book, and the two men who have guided their diverse efforts to the target, the two men who have had under their control more sheer physical power than any men in the history of the planet—power immeasurable and incalculable, power which grows as it is used, power which poses its own problems until finally it becomes, as it is now, almost independent, ready with blind momentum to take charge of the destiny of the nation which rules the world. They have done their individual best, the men in this room; it is no use looking for bad men or for villains; these men were brought together to solve today's problems, and nobody warned them that they were to hammer out the shape of tomorrow. The room grows silent and the two leaders sit grimly facing the audience, silent, tense, like a pair of iron-clads with steam up.

Then Nelson gets up and stands at the little rostrum made and provided for addresses to WPB convocations; an absurd little thing of wood, looking oddly like an ecclesiastical pulpit. (Nelson once remarked, ruefully: Isn't this a hell of a congregation they've made me rabbi of?) He tells the crowd what everybody already knows—that he is leaving in a few days for China on a presidential mission, that during his absence someone of course will have to act as chairman, and he bespeaks loyalty and support for this unnamed someone. He touches on current disagreements over matters of reconversion policy, repeats his statement that they are not disagreements over principle but are concerned simply with the matter of timing, regrets that the publicity attending them has brought unjust criticism on various officials

281

who follow another light than his, and he eulogizes Charlie Wilson
. . . "Charlie has my complete confidence, there is no real quarrel
between us, he is a grand person and I trust him implicitly. I
think he has something he would like to say to you."

Nelson sat down. So far, the script was about what had been
expected. Every word Nelson had said was exactly what he
would be saying if he were preparing to hand the reins over to
Wilson; every word carefully weighed so as to make Nelson's
personal defeat look like no defeat for the program he stood for.
No reporters were present, to be sure, but WPB leaked like a
sieve, those days, and the gist of this meeting would appear in
tomorrow morning's papers just as surely as there were little
green apples.

Wilson got up, a big block of a man, poised on the edge of
some internal explosion. He spoke angrily about undercover foes,
rumor mongers and character assassins; during recent weeks he
had been under sharp criticism in the press and on the radio, a
man from big business charged with playing big business's game,
the vice-chairmen who sided with him had been criticized likewise, and Wilson—who had not been born yesterday—was fairly
clear on the point that a great deal of this criticism had originally
been inspired by people right within WPB. He said as much, now,
glancing about the auditorium under thundercloud eyebrows; it
seemed almost likely that he would stride down the aisle at any
moment and have at his critics personally. This back-biting, Wilson said, had created a completely impossible situation in WPB;
if he took over, in Nelson's absence, everything that he did and
everything that he said would be measured against the critics'
yardstick and he would find himself denounced for cutting the
throat of an absent chief. Therefore—and now it came—he was
getting out. He had given the President his resignation and had
insisted on its acceptance. He was leaving WPB and government
service now, pronto, at once, and he would be out of there just
as soon as he could straighten up his desk and remove his personal
effects.

Curtain. Sensation. End of meeting. No press release was issued,
and none was needed. The reporters had all of it, just as soon as
the audience came boiling out of the doors. Nelson and Wilson
walked out, found themselves in the same elevator, rode up to
the fifth floor without exchanging a glance or a word. The press

room typewriters began to clack madly; Nelson had won, Wilson had lost, the President had voted for the quick-reconversion plan, the battle of the century was over, Nelson had come out on top once more, this acutely personalized row had been settled for keeps.

. . . Or had it? Nelson was due to leave for China within forty-eight hours. Acting Chairman, in his absence, was to be J. A. Krug—the Cap Krug who had fought the civilians' fight during the preceding winter, who had found Army and industry division opposition too much for him, and who had left to take a commission in the Navy; Krug was back now, by presidential edict, to take over for the departing Chairman, and as far as any man could see the military had taken a big licking. But was it all precisely as it seemed to be? Nelson was warned, privately, that it was not.

This matter of his trip to China, now; if it was to be a short trip, keeping him out of Washington for just a few weeks, he could return and sit back of his old desk and pick up where he left off, and his victory would be real. But suppose his trip to China lasted longer than just a few weeks? Things happened fast in WPB, nobody could remain a chairman in absentia for very long, the acting chairman would become the permanent chairman by sheer force of daily circumstances; Krug was nobody's shadow-man, he could not be expected to continue indefinitely to be just a fill-in, sooner or later he would have to block out his own policies and make his own decisions. Wilson had gone, but Nelson was also going; the big question—*if* this was all a matter of personalities—was: Is he coming back at all?

Washington gossip travels fast. Within hours the grapevine brought to Nelson the word that both Nelson and Wilson had lost—Wilson dramatically, Nelson undramatically. The trip to China was going to take much longer than Nelson had supposed, and his union with WPB was henceforth to be a union in name only.

Cautiously, Nelson did some checking. The picture was not entirely clear, but it seemed to be encouraging; Byrnes and the military were still insisting that Nelson was through, but Hopkins was insisting that Nelson was not through. The final decision, it seemed, had not yet been made, but Hopkins was confident that everything would be all right; the big hurdle had been passed, and it seemed in order to make the trip as planned. So Nelson went to China. The plug was pulled before he even got out there. At the next White House press conference a reporter asked the President, casually, if Mr. Nelson would return to the chairmanship of WPB when he finished this mission; equally casual, the President replied that he didn't know yet, that the China job was complicated, that all in all he would have to see. That was tipoff enough for anybody. Nelson was Out.

He did return from China, eventually. He went back to his desk in WPB and stayed there just long enough to draft and transmit to the White House his formal letter of resignation. Then he took on a special assignment as assistant to the President —to work out sundry details connected with his China mission. Of that China mission, no more was ever heard by mortal man. Nelson lingered for a while in a quiet office in the antiquated State Department Building, and at last—after the manner of Washington's discrowned czars—slipped off into the shadows.

And what, in the end, was all of this about, anyway?

Not at all about what it seemed to be about: a this-man-or-that man row to demonstrate anew the clumsiness of New Deal administrative practices. The Nelson-Wilson contest, which looked so important at the time, was unreal, however much personal feeling may have been temporarily created; was simply a long, blurred shadow, cast on the wall by something that burned out of sight somewhere; a symptom of much, a cause of nothing, a symbol to be read or misread.

The war was still fluid, but it had reached the point where it was not to remain fluid much longer. Day-to-day actions and decisions made in the interest of winning the war would go on working after peace had come; would set the mold in which the postwar world would harden. Now the shape the postwar world might take was a matter of very great importance, not merely to a considerable number of people who had paid with their blood for the whole business and who were going to have to live in the postwar world after it had been created, but to a smaller and more influential number of people who had a direct and acute concern with the vested interests and establishments of the prewar world, which might conceivably get crushed if a new world were created. Whatever happened, this war must not be recognized as part of a world revolution, and when the enemy had been beaten, what was left by the armies, the bombs, and the hung-by-the-heels Caesars must be put back into the same old forms. The gin party in the corner apartment would be suppressed, as Mr. Knudsen had urged so long ago, and peace would descend on the neighborhood again; and the kingdom, the power, and the enduring glory would be preserved by patriotism plus 8 per cent, with option to purchase. This was not so much a matter of conscious decision as of habits of mind, ancient conservatisms unable to face change, all of the inertias bred by satisfaction with the Things that Were.

Some years before the President had remarked that much would be expected of those to whom much had been given, and he had spoken of a generation whose lips were touched with fire; but the President had to work through people and institutions, and the war had not given him people or institutions ready to contemplate the creation of a new order.

This China mission, for example.

Nelson thought it was real. The President thought it was real. It started out, in fact to *be* real. . . . Picture the moderately enlightened man of business studying an oriental world floundering in political and economic chaos; home place of half the people on earth, all of them desperately in need of the goods the modern world could make, but able to pay for those goods much less than the modern world could afford to accept. Here had grown up the Japanese end of the Axis, sweat-shopping feverishly to turn out shoddy to meet this need; Japan, not a part of the modern world but a travesty on it, pure medievalism blending serfdom with the mechanics of mass production. Japan's ability to pose as a world power, to launch armies and navies and air fleets at the western bosses of the oriental world, had been based squarely on this industry, which had rested upon the fact that only Japan could serve this infinitely hungry, infinitely poverty-stricken market. Japan was being crushed now, but her destruction would solve nothing; after the war the oriental world would look for goods with a new desperation, a feverish new insistence, its demands would have to be met no matter what—and the westerners could not supply the goods, because no western nation could produce them at a price the orientals could afford to pay.

But if they chose the westerns could equip China so that

China, in time, could provide the goods. Therefore, said the man of business, let's act now so that China can move into Japan's place, after the war, as workshop and supply house for the Far East. Never mind about equipping China as a center for heavy industry; much simpler and infinitely quicker to enable her to become a producer of inexpensive consumer goods, and to modernize her transportation and distribution system. Thus Chinese industrial prosperity can begin on a solid basis, the heavy industries can follow later, the great economic vacuum of the orient can be filled. Peace, perhaps, in the Far East—and something is set in motion that will slowly but steadily reduce the hopeless poverty of hundreds of millions of people, something that may yet mean stability, order, and a chance for a nonviolent transition, east of Suez, from the old era to the new.

Thus Nelson, and the tentative plan he evolved on his way to the Far East. Beyond doubt his idea was oversimple and over-hopeful; but its real defect was that it rested on an implicit acceptance of the inevitability of profound change in the oriental world. The plan was politely spoken of, on Nelson's return, as it got progressively more and more desiccated on its dreary shuttle around government offices. When Nelson finally left government service, some time after Roosevelt's death, he could only say that he did not know what the fate of his plan had been. It had no fate. It simply hung in suspension. Presumably it is still hanging there.

All of which, come to think of it, was very much like Nelson's experience on his other foreign mission, his trip to Russia, which took place in 1943. He came back from Russia highly excited about a plan he had worked out in conversations with the commissars: a plan for postwar trade whereby Russia and the United States, over a period of two decades or more, would ex-change goods for mutual benefit. He had a long list, itemized by Stalin himself, of the heavy goods Russia would need after the war—railroad equipment, heavy machinery, dynamos, generators, structural steel, road-building machinery, and so on; a list of needs which would have taken all of the surplus production of American industry, working at top capacity, for a full genera-tion. On the other hand there were the goods America needed— raw materials of all kinds, from manganese to petroleum, from lumber to copper to lead to zinc; things America had used with prodigal abandon during the war, materials in which she had seriously depleted her reserves, materials her industrial power was based on, materials that could be obtained by trade with Russia.

Nelson expounded on all of this one evening, shortly after his return from Russia, at a little party given by Blair Moody, Washington correspondent for the *Detroit News*, and kindled the enthusiasm of a group of reporters and columnists. This program —Nelson explained, teetering slowly on his heels before a fireplace, highball in his hand, his big bland face beaming like a harvest moon as he talked—this program needn't even involve state trading of the ordinary kind. It could mean cash money for American producers—for the heavy industry boys, on whose fate American prosperity traditionally rests—and it meant getting back, for the nation as a whole, many of the irreplaceable raw materials that had been consumed during the war. What would we ever do with those quantities of materials that would be imported under this plan? Why, stock-pile them, of course—freeze them, park them in the middle of Nevada if necessary until they were needed; make a national reserve out of them, not to be touched except by act of Congress and direction of the President —but in any case get them, and insure our own industrial prosperity in the process.

Of course, Nelson added, this meant taking it for granted that there would be close co-operation between Russia and America during the postwar years. In effect, he said, it would mean a quarter of a century of friendly competition between an enlightened capitalism and an enlightened communism—and both isms, he felt, could do with a bit of enlightenment—to see which could do the most for its people.

When he stopped explaining, at last, the late Raymond Clapper grinned at him.

"Don, there's only one thing wrong with that program of yours," he said. "It just makes too damn much sense."

It just made too damn much sense. It was predicated on the simple-minded assumption that America and Russia need not be irreconcilable rivals for world dominion, that somehow a new and more hopeful world order could be brought out of the war. And its fate foreshadowed the fate of the China plan. It went astray somewhere in the upper plateaus of government, buried under a heap of memoranda, damned by faint praise and smothered by impeccably-stated howevers, neverthelesses, and it-must-be-borne-in-mind's.

Two projects, then, for Russia and for China, lost in the dim twilight on the outer marches; of a piece with the plan for reconversion-according-to-what-we-need; pointed toward a new era and a new world at a time when the look and smell of these had grown frightening. In the eyes of all the world the President was the apostle of a new era and a new world, but he was served by large numbers of officials who had different ideas. The hollow men were taking over.

CHAPTER TWENTY-TWO

The Stork Does Not Bring Babies

I T WAS downhill all the way after Nelson got fired. Not because Nelson himself was such an important person; there
were no important persons, come to think of it, in those days,
except for the endless files of young men who went silently to
their deaths, uncomplaining, infinitely heroic, across the background of the stage, proving once again in mud and dust and
agony that the last thing the race really cares for is the profit that
can be weighed and written down in the ledgers and turned into
spot cash, proving that the values that are died for are the values
that will never make sense to the calculating and the grasping.
These were The People, on the march to something that had been
glimpsed beyond the horizon ever since the fire blazed in the
burning bush in Asia—the little people, as condescending folk
like to call them, the little people who are not little at all, whose
patient endurance justifies whatever hopes humanity is entitled
to, who prove in every generation, in a language that cannot
lie, that this race is held down by nothing at all but the blindness
and the selfishness of the men who think they lead it.

Not the little people: the *big* people, the great people, the
deathless people—winning a new chance for themselves and for
those who come after them, eternally sold out by those who
have Something to Gain, always transcending their leadership,
always writing "You were right!" in letters of blood across the
record of what men soever have been willing to trust them and
brave enough to struggle for them.

And the firing of Nelson marked a defeat for the people. This
red-faced stout man, who came up from a mail order house and
who did his imperfect best amid the Washington spotlights for
three years and more, did manage to stand for something and
when he went down it went down too. The pattern had become
fixed, and it was a pattern shaped by those who do not trust the
people; a pattern by which we have lived ever since.

Witness an outburst by Maury Maverick, who was called to
the telephone, one November day in 1944, when a functionary

in the office of the WPB chairman phoned to remind him that there was to be a meeting of the Production Executive Committee on the following day. Was there anything Mr. Maverick wished to communicate to that meeting?

Ill-tempered, profane, and given to tall talk, Maverick ground the telephone receiver into his ear, hitched his chair forward, and let fly.

"You know what they're doing to me, don't you?" he rasped. "They started on the roof, and they took rubber hoses and beat me, on top of the roof, and then they threw me down that chute—you know—and then they threw me down the steps to the third floor, and then they kicked me, on that escalator, and I got a leg cut off and both of my ears. Then they laid me down on the floor, and if it hadn't been for sulfa drugs and penicillin and injections of blood transfusion I'd have expired. Of course, they gave me sulfa drugs and penicillin, and I got in the center of the Cross and said twelve Hail Mary's, and God preserved my life. But that's all. I just came out with my life. So I don't know what the hell I could talk to them about."

There were times when you had to know Maverick fairly well to understand exactly what he was driving at. What he was trying to say here was that as watchdog for the interests of small business he had found himself completely and permanently stymied by the industrialists and the Army brass who made up the Production Executive Committee; that every attempt to provide work for small business or to get on with the reconversion program was being thwarted, and that even as stout‚ a battler as Maverick—who could hear far-off bugles in the wind, and who was never frightened of anything—felt that further combat was useless.

All such matters were being handled by PEC now, and the Army was having its way all across the board. Krug was running WPB, and Krug had been known as a "Nelson man," but Krug came in to find the lines drawn too tight for breaking. The issue had been settled, the Byrnes office held the controls and was backing the War Department on every point, and Nelson's exile was an object lesson in what happened to men who tried to swim against the current.

Increasingly stringent restrictions had been put on the original reconversion program until by now it was inoperative. Spot authorization had been virtually suspended, and increases in the programmed type of civilian production had been barred. Psychological warfare was reaching a new high, one degree short of plain hysteria. All that anyone ever heard about was the heavy rise that was taking place in the "critical" war production programs. Completely unpublicized were the steady reductions in the noncritical programs, which were pushing more and more of the little manufacturers out of war work and were making more and more workers wonder what tomorrow's job was going to look like. There was no way for the little fellows to get back in, once they got out, in most cases, since the critical programs—heavy trucks, heavy ammunition, heavy tires, and so on—simply did not involve items that could be made in the smaller plants, and since, as Maverick had pointed out six months earlier, the big war contractors were increasingly canceling their subcontracts and pulling the little fellows' work into their own factories.

It was a bad day, altogether, for the small manufacturer, and Maverick's feeling that it was useless to make any more appeals to the authorities was quite understandable. The administration had now reached the point where it would neither say nor do anything that might in any way contradict the Army's frantic assertions that production was in a state of crisis, that there was a desperate shortage of manpower, and that the home front was letting the fighting man down.

. . . One collateral effect of this drive on the public psychology may be worth a brief passing glance. The Army, at that moment, was feverishly pushing the construction of new plants and tools for heavy ammunition. Three years had passed since Pearl Harbor, and it might seem a bit late in the day to be building new factories to make the Army's basic, primary item of firepower; it had to be done, however, because there had been a drastic cutback in the heavy ammunition program a year earlier, and plants and machinery which had been making heavy ammunition had, with wartime liberality, simply been scrapped. Now the fighting in Europe was lasting longer than the Army had anticipated—not the overoptimistic civilians; the *Army*—and it was chewing up more and more munitions; and if the campaign to flog civilians into a greater production effort happened to divert attention from the miscalculations of the military, at a moment when those miscalculations might be very embarrassing if pointed to—well, what of it?*

Then, in December, came the Battle of the Bulge.

If the War Department had been worried about the production situation before, this tragic military setback pushed anxiety right up through the roof. Justice Byrnes—now Director of War Mobilization and Reconversion, by act of Congress—had called in General Lucius Clay early in November as his Deputy Director for War Programs, to co-ordinate the work of all agencies in order to assure the meeting of war production schedules; and if there had been any lingering doubt that WPB and all the other war agencies were going to do exactly what the Army wanted, it now vanished utterly. Byrnes laid down a new draft policy, designed to freeze all workers in their war jobs and make nonwar workers take war jobs under threat of being drafted into the Army. (Like the tightened policy on draft deferment announced early in 1944, this policy was promulgated without advance discussion with either the War Manpower Commission or the War Production Board, the two agencies which might be supposed to be most concerned; WPB, in fact, was at that very moment circulating, though it dared not publicize, the Batcheller survey showing that only a minor part of the production deficiencies were in any way caused by manpower shortages; but the soldiers said this new step was necessary, and that was all that mattered any more.) Various food products which had been taken off rationing were abruptly put back on, there was renewed talk of prohibiting the publication of comic strips (just how this would help the soldiers on the Rhine was obscure, but the idea was a fetish of Mr. Patterson's), and all the race tracks were ordered closed. There seemed to exist no very clear authority for the race track action; if it were to be enforced, the enforcing would have to come from WMC, which could set the tracks'

* Note Colonel Robert S. Allen's assertion, in his outspoken book, *Lucky Forward* (pages 189-190), that military operations in Europe in the fall of 1944 were badly hampered by lack of replacement troops, the War Department having decided in mid-summer that war in Europe would end in November and that shipment of replacements should therefore be reduced. At the exact moment when that decision was made, the Department at home was sternly preventing reconversion on the ground that the end of the war was far off and a letdown at home might postpone victory or even invite defeat!

manpower ceilings at zero, or from WPB, which might make it impossible for the tracks to get any supplies; but nobody seemed inclined to make an issue of it, and the tracks closed.

In addition, the Byrnes office decreed a curfew, or early closing, for night clubs, bars, and such-like, as a measure to save electric power for war purposes. This one turned out to be faintly embarrassing, for a moment or two. When the curfew was announced the reporters came around to WPB to get estimates on the amount of electric power (or of coal, used to generate electricity) that would be saved by this order, and we had to confess that none would be saved, to speak of, since the shutdown would take place around midnight when practically everybody else was using no electricity at all. WPB's Office of War Utilities, which had been in charge of the power situation throughout the war and which had done a bang-up job from the moment Cap Krug organized it, had not even bothered to draw up estimates, having figured that there was no conceivable need for any such step.

But the Office of War Utilities just didn't get the idea. What was being done was not being done because it would help to win the war; it was being done—by all but open admission—to make the public realize that there was a war on, to impose "sacrifices" on the people at home, to arouse public emotion and to help shape public psychology. It was government by public relations carried to its logical and cockeyed extreme. The underlying reason for it, originally, had been to bring about the passage of a national service act (which was still being demanded, in shrill tones, although even the generals were beginning to see that such a law couldn't be passed); a little later, it had served to make completely impossible any action on reconversion; but it had got past that now, it was being pursued as an end in itself, it carried its own gratifications, the military was feeling its oats, and the military was in the saddle.

One thing leads to another. If he was barred, by decisions made before he took office, from actually doing anything about reconversion, Krug figured there was no particular law to keep him from at least thinking about it, and he had his WPB organization working hard to lay out a program for the relaxation and removal of controls after VE-Day.

After VE-Day; nothing could happen before Germany surrendered, there was no use arguing about that any longer, the war economy would have to go full steam ahead up to the very hour of German collapse. But there would be a period—a long period, by Army calculation; a year or more, certainly—between the time of Germany's surrender and the final defeat of Japan, and it was obvious to practically everybody that in that period a much lower rate of war production would be needed. During that period, then, if it were planned intelligently, various controls could be removed entirely and many others could be modified. Civilian production could be brought up progressively, different pipe lines could be filled, and there might after all be a smooth transition from war to peace; might at any rate be a transition that was planned as a transition and not a mere scramble to get the lid off.

Krug's experts had been at work on this all fall. The big idea was to find out how much of a drop in war orders there would be after Germany surrendered. Early in 1944 General Levin H. Campbell, chief of Army Ordnance, had confided to a couple of Nelson's aides (who were sent over to discuss reconversion prospects) that this cut would be very sharp indeed, almost great enough to permit a return to normal civilian production. The General had, in fact, been of the opinion that there could and should be substantial reconversion long before Germany's surrender, had agreed that stocks of munitions were gratifyingly large, and had seemed willing to go farther than Maverick himself in proposing quick relaxation of controls. He had wound up by predicting that "when Germany surrenders the military program can be cut to about one-fifth of its present size and can be handled out of existing stock and arsenals."

But Campbell wasn't top man in the War Department, by a long shot—he'd be bottom man, probably, on duty in Kiska or somewhere, if his superiors ever found out that he had talked to Nelson's people that way—and his estimate was far from being the official one. By the fall of 1944, after much trouble in getting any sort of firm statements on the matter, the WPB statisticians finally obtained a guarded admission that it would be tolerably safe for them to figure on a cut of somewhere around 40 per cent in the war production program within the year after Germany's surrender. This was a far cry from General Campbell's prediction of an 80 per cent drop, and it wasn't too definite in any case, but at least it was something to work on and the WPB experts worked on it. Take the controls off as rapidly as sible after Germany quits, without endangering the war gram, don't keep any control over industry that is not needed to insure war production, don't use the controls to bring about social or economic reform, make remaining war needs the sole consideration—that was the platform, and on that policy the plans were laid.

Which was fair enough, except that the picture immediately began to change. In December the War Department sent over word that the 40 per cent drop was no longer a sound basis for figuring. The Armies that would invade Japan were to be completely re-equipped and rearmed; the required level of war production after VE-Day would be much higher than anyone had supposed; it looked now as if a drop of only about 20 per cent, during the first year after Germany quit, was the most that could be anticipated; Germany wasn't beaten yet anyhow, all kinds of stuff might be needed for the next winter's * fighting on the Rhine and in the mountains; the whole business was under thorough study, and WPB would be notified in due time.

Due time seemed to be some distance away. December passed, and January, and February, and still WPB could not learn what the VE-Day drop would be. Meanwhile, spurred by the tragedy of the Bulge, Army statements of requirements began to grow fabulous. Enormous orders for items such as boots, shoes, and textile goods began to pour in, and by spring it suddenly appeared that there would be less for the civilian economy to operate on, in the summer and fall of 1945, than at any previous stage in the war. WPB's Civilian Supply people found themselves wondering whether there would be any leather at all for civilian shoes during the coming year (there plainly would not be, if the new Army requirements were accepted at face value) and whether the Army's overwhelming new demands for textiles would leave any overalls or work gloves for the very factory workers who were being ordered so sternly to stick to their jobs.

The spring of 1945: the Rhine had been crossed and left behind, the Ruhr had been taken, the enormous Russian drive toward Vienna and Berlin was in high gear, all of the sands

* Next winter—i.e., the winter of 1945-46!

were visibly running out, the war was rumbling to final victory with a roar no one could mistake. This was the winter of 1864-65 all over again, with Lee hopelessly pinned at Petersburg and Sherman starting up through the Carolinas and nothing in the cards anywhere to prevent the inevitable. What sort of figuring was going on, anyhow? What kind of logic was it, which said that it was precisely now that the heaviest load of the entire war should be imposed on the civilian economy—that it would take four-fifths as much war production to defeat crippled, isolated, navyless Japan as it took at the very peak of the war effort against both Japan and Germany?

Military logic, to be sure; whose shadow still lies long across the land. And the trouble with this logic is not simply the fact that money was wasted and civilians were inconvenienced. War is waste from beginning to end, the side that can be the most wasteful is the side that wins, and the men who do the fighting must have more of everything than they can possibly use. In view of the fantastic sums spent on this war, any excess which was spent needlessly in the spring of 1945 is not worth quibbling about. Nor did the civilians actually suffer. There was enough to eat, people were clothed and housed, they got to and from their jobs, there were necessities and even luxuries to be had, nobody has any very serious squawk coming there. War is one long snafu anyhow, and there is no point in protesting the fact.

The real trouble is that this blindly arrogant military policy— accepted by the administration without protest, and permitted to stick—was the final, most effective move in the government's long retreat from democracy. The people were winning their war, but they were not to be trusted with their own victory.

For it was fear—fear, and nothing else, certain to leave a great heritage of fear—that lay back of the whole performance.

Fear of the people, who were not believed to be smart enough, or loyal enough, or decent enough, or patriotic enough, to do all of the things that needed to be done, unless someone stood over them with a speaking trumpet in one hand and a whip in the other.

The people are on the march, and they are not marching toward the past. But it is in the past that all our certainties lie, it is in the past that all privileges are rooted, it is only in the future that beacon fires, lit by the flames of this war, may yet give light for the people to find their way unaided. Therefore, archdeacons of the night, speak loudly!

More than a year earlier, at the very beginning of 1944, important brass spoke angrily of crimes against America and of a state of anarchy, and demanded a labor draft to compel the people to win their own war. A little later, nobody was to be allowed to prepare for peace, or even to talk about it, lest that cause the heedless and irresponsible people to relax ahead of time, and great plans were laid to create a suitable "backdrop of urgency." Now —with the staff officers overseas betting whether Patton, Montgomery, or some Russian would be the first Allied soldier to enter Berlin—this fear that the stupid people would still lose the war reached an all-time high. After Germany surrendered (it was argued) nobody would do any war work, the war plants would all stand idle because the people would be clamoring senselessly for new autos and iceboxes and radios, and the war with Japan would not get won because no stay-at-homes would realize that there was still fighting to be done—the soldiers and sailors who were fighting the Japs being, apparently, all orphans without kith, kin, or connections.

From the winning of their independence the people had not been so profoundly mistrusted by their own servants—or snarled at so bitterly, or cut off so abruptly from the ideals they had followed.

Behold, now, how all of this worked out. As a citizen, you are still paying for it.

The great scare campaign had made it certain that nothing could be done, either by government or by business, in the direction of reconversion until after the defeat of Germany. Germany eventually collapsed amid its own ruins, and the European half of the war ended, and the time came to start the intricate process of readjustment; the time, at least, to begin doing the things which would make orderly readjustment possible. But then, as the wise-cracking naval officer remarked, the Japs treacherously surrendered. Instead of a long tapering-off period, the basis of all the plans, there was no tapering-off period at all. By the middle of August the war was simply over, gone, done with, finished. It was time to readjust to peace, and the plans for readjustment were still being made.

So we got, at last, in its finest flowering, exactly what the

Baruch report had so piously prayed we would not get—a situation in which all the pressure groups in the land moved up to try to hit the jackpot.

These pressures were like nothing anyone had ever seen. A greater weight of buying power was massed behind them than any economist had ever dreamed of, and it came hand in hand with a dire shortage of every conceivable kind of goods, from bacon to box cars, from automobiles to houses, from movie projectors to roller skates to machine tools to children's clothing to manicure sets. Demands for basic necessities mingled with demands for extreme luxuries; the economy was going to soak up everything that wasn't nailed down, the great gold rush was on, the market place was hotter than any market place had been since the first cave man swapped a bear skin for a stone axe. The event that everyone had foreseen and dreaded—a mad, uncontrollable scramble, a complete chaos of irresistible economic forces—was taking place with a vengeance.

Amid this, what chance was there for a sad remnant of a War Production Board (presently rechristened Civilian Production Administration) to stem the tide? Particularly, a War Production Board that had lost its independence twelve months earlier and had gone soaring and skittering through the skies as tail to the military kite? There were still controls to administer; there were still ways of guiding the furious, unleashed energies into proper channels, so that some of the necessities might at least be produced ahead of the luxuries. . . . But these controls and these ways existed on paper and in theory, and no mortal man at this stage of the game could be expected to stand up against the pressures. To the luckless men in the Social Security Building, after Japan surrendered, the voice of industry was a savage, overwhelming shout: Get the hell out of the way! They got, there being nothing else they could possibly be expected to do. The controls came off and the scramble became official.

Stand a row of dominos on end, push the first domino over, and before long the domino at the end of the line falls down. When the industry controls came off, price control was doomed. Technically, of course, it could still be continued; actually, as everybody could see, trying to retain price control in the frantic period of readjustment after controls over production had been abandoned was on a par with King Canute's venture in commanding the ocean tides to obey him. Price control *had* to die; under the setup, with everyone invited to shoot for the jackpot, there was no way on God's green earth to save it, even if anyone had tried—and the way things were, with free enterprise looking more and more like a nation-wide Donnybrook, it was as much as a man's life was worth even to try, so nobody in particular did try aside from Chester Bowles, and would you look at what happened to *him?*

So the lid really came off, and one thing continued to lead to another. Having been assured by high authority all through the war that it was selfish, anarchic and never to be trusted, labor began to demand its share, and there were strikes and rumors of strikes all across the land. (At the height of this, a curious phenomenon: the Secretary of Commerce, who chanced to be Henry Wallace, released an analytical report indicating that the auto industry, what with all of this and that, including past and present profit levels, could afford to grant a wage increase without boosting the price of automobiles—and set the editorial writers clucking distractedly from New York to California. . . . So *that's* what comes of putting him in as Secretary of Commerce; profit levels have nothing to do with it, higher wages always mean higher prices, if the cost of living goes up it's all labor's fault, if we don't produce enough to satisfy the demand that's labor's fault too, labor just doesn't work as hard as it ought to. Cluck cluck.) As with labor, so with everybody else. The farmer needed protection, too; needed, also, products like farm machinery, more electric power and power facilities, more wire fencing, incubators, and so on, if anyone could find time to make them for him, but never mind about that, the controls are off, supply and demand will work themselves out eventually.

Eventually. Meanwhile, we need houses. Somehow those building industry pipe lines, which looked so significant back in the fall of 1943, never did get filled, and the unsatisfied demand for housing is like something nobody ever imagined. There will be a vast government housing program, then, to relieve this congestion and provide homes for veterans and other folk. But it takes controls to put through a housing program at a time like this; controls, and an administration tough enough to use them. But we are committed to an era of no controls, and it's probably un-American for government to put restraints on the building industry, and something seems to have happened to building costs anyway. So we will have this housing program but we won't do much with it because the pressures are too great; hang your clothes on a hickory limb, dear daughter, but don't go near the water.

Spiraling prices, spiraling costs, spiraling wages, and the dollar buys just about half as much as it bought before the war; a nice inflationary boom, bringing with it divers unlooked-for by-products.

The by-product, for instance, of confusion and disunity, given to us just at the time when clarity of purpose and consciousness of unity were of all things the things most needed. All the little problems that had been side-stepped during the war had not, thereby, been removed from the scene; they were popping up now all over the place, and if they were not being settled they were at least getting a great deal of attention. As a sample, there was the fundamental problem of fitting labor into the general democratic scheme of things and making it a full-fledged, responsible member of the family. This one had been dodged, and we had had a labor-management committee system sold to the anxious chant of this-isn't-it. Now, somehow, in the postwar years, there seemed to be an ominous gulf between capital and labor; businessmen complained that labor didn't have any sense of responsibility and labor leaders protested that management was not to be trusted—and the fundamental industries like coal, steel, automobiles, and railroad transportation were torn by bitter strikes, with further increase to the inflationary pressures. In the midst of which the administration—a new administration, not recognizably New Deal or old deal, but obviously composed of Pharaohs who knew not Joseph—stood irresolute, the bewildered storm center of a world it had never made, groping blindly for a light that should have been lit much earlier, when there was fire in men's hearts.

But that was only part of it.

We have learned, by now—learned the hard way, if there ever was a hard way—that such a thing as national isolation simply does not exist, and that what may happen to the most powerful and wealthy nation on earth is inescapably tied in with what the other nations may be and do. Through 1946 and 1947 a bankrupt world tried desperately to recover; but the one great emporium where it could get the goods it needed for recovery, the great economic power to which the rest of the world's trade and finance are inexorably keyed, was off on a swirl of inflated prices. Great Britain borrowed three billions and more, to get a stake—and found the stake evaporating before it could be effective, because of that inflation. Every country in Europe whose government sought to restore something resembling normal trade and prosperity, as an alternative to rising communism, found its task made harder because of that price spiral. The task was made harder, and the time was made shorter; and, simultaneously, the very price inflation which brought that about created new pressures to keep America from extending more aid. Everybody in America was shooting at the jackpot, which meant that recovery and stability abroad were going to be delayed; and that very delay was beginning to generate pressures of its own, to which a dismayed American government could not avoid being extremely sensitive.

At home, the administration fumbled and stammered, seeking to be all things to all men and becoming, at times, nothing at all to anybody. Nothing was clear anywhere, except that the good old days of the 1920's were coming back, and there was no way to prevent this because there did not exist—had not been forged in the heat of war—a program to command the allegiance of the majority which had voted against the good old days so many years earlier. Confusion, disunity, every man for himself, every pressure has its way *except* the pressure of the inarticulate people who want peace, homes, food and clothing at prices they can afford to pay, some promise of security in their jobs and in their persons, some visible and tangible sign that the war had really meant something; here, brought forth at the end of the people's war, which the people had won, was the sure recipe for the rise of reaction. The times were made to order for the men who knew exactly what they wanted—which was not entirely accidental, since it was the men who knew exactly what they wanted who had helped make them that way.

So a strange and wonderful sight began to appear in 1947. Back toward the top, ready to take charge of the peace and, if by chance such could not be avoided, of the Next War, came trooping the very elements and persons who had been discredited in democracy's great struggle for survival. (Progressive symbol in the Department of State: first the Secretary of State was the man who had insisted, before Pearl Harbor, that we had enough aluminum, enough steel, enough rubber; then he was the man who had enabled the military to prevent reconversion; and finally he was the soldier who had damned labor's crime against America.)

Vested conservatism, which had not seen the need for crushing Hitler, which had proved its own incompetence when the attempt to crush Hitler was finally made, and which had so narrowly escaped being permanently dispossessed in the stormy days after Pearl Harbor—here it came, back again, nothing learned and nothing forgotten, confident of its own abilities and determined on its own survival, bent upon remaking the earth in the image of the past, so full of beans that it made a bewildered administration, at times, look New Dealish in spite of itself. In the spring of 1942 it had been possible for Senator O'Mahoney to chant "They were wrong . . . wrong . . . wrong" at the high priests of conservatism and nobody had argued with him, because all men could see that they had been tragically and disastrously wrong. But here they were again, the brave old dollar-a-year crowd minus the dollar a year, ready to take charge of the nation's destiny in time of crisis: and isn't this about where we came in?

It may be that this constitutes a rather large chicken to come out of so small an egg. After all, let's be reasonable. Confusion and reaction at home, recovery overseas desperately handicapped, rebirth of ardent reaction on the domestic scene; all of this, then, coming out of the military's panic distrust of the people?

All of this. It did not happen by chance, and the soldiers were not the only ones to distrust the people, and reaction of every kind was certain to benefit if that distrust were allowed to become dominant. It could all have been foreseen at the time. Was foreseen, as a matter of fact, by a few.

From first to last—from Nelson's dismissal down to VE-Day— the one steady and unavailing fight for an adequate, democratic approach to reconversion, an approach that would rest on confidence in the people rather than on distrust, was made, significantly enough, by three men—by Maverick, the unrepentant New Dealer from Texas, and by Joe Keenan and Clint Golden, the two labor leaders who had been given vice-chairmanships in

WPB. The details of what would happen if the soldiers had their way were not clear, but the general scope and significance of the consequences were clear enough for these men to see. They knew very well what the final results would be if the military gained full control; they fought and they were over-ridden, but they knew very definitely what the fight was all about.

It is just possible, all things considered, that some of the men on the other side of the fence knew, too. After all, in WPB and in the War Department, there were quite a few men who knew that the stork doesn't really bring babies.

CHAPTER TWENTY-THREE

A Quart of Milk

YOU COULD begin to see it that April morning in 1945, when the body of Franklin Roosevelt was brought north for the formal services at the White House. The troops lined the curb all the way along Pennsylvania avenue—tanned, somber, in full battle kit, standing guard along the historic highway where so many pageants have passed to symbolize stages in the progress of the great American dream. Jefferson had gone along that avenue when the dream was young, riding informally on horseback, scorning pomp as unfitting in a people's republic; Lincoln, escorted by jingling cavalrymen, with rebellion across the river and the threat of assassination lurking in the alleys; Grant, unemotional in his triumph, leading an army with smoke-stained banners; Wilson, sick and broken leader of a lost cause, riding off to the shadows with a bitter heart and with a vision that foresaw the future.

And now Roosevelt, not the least of the servants and leaders of democracy, while the rifles came up to the final salute and the bayonets flashed in the sun, and the impassive faces looked out from under the rims of the helmets; Roosevelt, who had called these boys together and clad them in the garb of soldiers, who had bidden them prepare to face the ultimate for a cause greater than themselves. The planes sped by overhead, flying low, filling the air with the deep roar of their passing, the planes he had called into being, the planes that would not have been there at all if he had not seen the need for them, the great planes whose targets he had chosen. The people stood silent on the pavements, one hundred thousand of them, two hundred thousand, half a million, a multitude beyond counting, men and women whose lives and whose work these last few years had been shaped by this man's bidding.

This in Washington: and beyond the seas the Axis was crumbling fast. Berlin was going down in its own lurid Nibelungen fires under the hammering of the Russian guns, and in the Pacific the Japanese were beginning their hopeless last stand;

and the men who had built the Axis, who had boasted that they rode the wave of the future and were the architects of the world's next thousand years, had this brief moment to exult in the death of their greatest enemy before their world collapsed upon them and they vanished in the ruins of everything they had planned. . . . Wandering stars, to whom is reserved the blackness of darkness forever.

Roosevelt was dead, but his death was about to be swallowed up in victory. But the victory had to mean something; had to be a victory of the spirit, and not just a victory of the strong arm and the mailed fist. And there was in the air, on the morning of that funeral procession, the shape and the beginning of fear. The man who had made the victory, and who had known beyond all other men why the victory was necessary, was gone. Who would interpret the victory now?

History is not altogether at the mercy of the nearest accident. The forces that were to bend the future and interpret the victory had been building up all through the war years, and they were due to have their effect whether one man lived or died. But the President had been the symbol of hope, the man who had said there was nothing to fear except fear itself, the leader matchless in finding expedients, the man who knew how to improvise and who could always find a new resort. With him there it was easy to trust that things somehow were going to work out all right. Without him, it was necessary to look at things as they actually were.

Perhaps that is why the wild rejoicing of VJ-Day, when it finally came, had in it more than a touch of hysteria—as if the people were using it, not merely to mark their release from what had been happening, but also to keep from thinking about what might happen in the future. (VJ-Day: day of triumph and victory and the end of the long trail, but given no great name out of the heart and the imagination, known only by a colorless alphabetical symbol borrowed from the jargon of the general staff.) Under the shouting and the cheering and the laughter there was a nameless and indefinable unease. The worst enemies the democracy had ever faced had been crushed to earth, but we kept on looking nervously over our shoulders.

Indeed, the strangest thing about the entire war was our reaction to it after we had won it. America did the most colossal job in history and came out of it with an inferiority complex and a deep sense of fear.

Colossal: not just a Hollywood word, but an adjective to be taken literally.

To begin with, America called more than ten million young men to arms—rather disillusioned young men, for the most part, heirs to a decade of national self-doubt, called up without benefit of flag-waving or the drums that quicken the heartbeat, reluctantly mustering to do what they knew would be a hard, mean, and distasteful job for an end that nobody, from first to last, ever put into clear English for them. These men went out, met the hopped-up enthusiasts of Japan and the cold professionals of Germany on their own ground, and beat them at their own game. If anyone had had any doubts on the point, they proved without heroics that the fiber of Valley Forge and Gettysburg was as strong as it ever was. The commonest report from our correspondents overseas was that not one American soldier in fifty could tell what he was fighting for, but somehow that seemed to make no difference. These civilians in uniform were soldiers in the grand tradition, ready to do anything on earth their country asked them to do even though their country didn't bother to make clear to them precisely why it was asking them to do it.

Back of the men in uniform there was the rest of the country: industrial America, with its mines and its factories and its farms, the economic muscle that had to support the direct military effort.

There is not much use in citing figures, because the figures are all so astronomical that they cease to mean very much; so many billion dollars worth of this, so many million tons of that, merchant ships and warships and airplanes and tanks and guns, wheat and steel and electricity and oil and coal and rubber, gigantic new industries created, goods produced in volume beyond the wildest dreams of the most optimistic. . . . Say that we performed the equivalent of building two Panama Canals every month, with a fat surplus to boot; that's an understatement, it still doesn't begin to express it all, the total is simply beyond the compass of one's understanding. The faith that can move mountains may have been lacking but the mountains got moved; in terms of sheer physical effort, America did the greatest job in the history of the human race. Here was displayed a strength greater even than cocky Americans in the old days of unlimited self-confidence had supposed; strength greater than any nation on earth had ever had before, strength to which nothing—literally nothing, in the physical sense—was any longer impossible.

All of this, furthermore, was the incredible capstone to something more than a decade in which the nation had learned to doubt its own abilities and to mistrust its own destiny. The unimaginable triumph of the war years followed right on the heels of the long depression of the 1930's, when the horizon closed in and there seemed to be nothing on the skyline that Americans could ever reach. This unimaginable upsurge of national power and vitality proved that the pessimists were wrong and that even the optimists had been too gloomy. It set the stage for a postwar release of human energy and confidence such as the world never saw before.

But the release hasn't taken place. Instead, there has been self-doubt and fear.

The end of the war did not leave us on a high mountain top, looking ahead to a limitless vista, with horizon lying beyond horizon to the end of time. Instead it left us in a mysterious valley, cloaked by an eerie fog and swept by confused alarms. We came out of the war timorous, uncertain, confused, not quite clear just what it was that we had done and everlastingly perplexed as to exactly what we ought to do next. We had won the war but we had done nothing more than that, and we began to see that a good deal more than that was urgently required.

For it was not—to repeat once more—just a war we had been fighting. It was a world revolution, and because we refused to recognize it as such the war turned out to be just one stage in the revolution . . . with more to come. A world revolution: one of the great turning points in human progress, a breaking-up of the old tables, a swallowing of old formulas, an overwhelming, fire-stained demand that human institutions be readapted to meet the eternal needs of human beings. A full quarter-century earlier, a statesman had remarked that humanity had struck its tents and was on the march; the march was still going on, a march of inarticulate folk who could not say just where they were going or just what they wanted, but who were deeply determined that there must somehow on this earth be more security and more happiness for more people. It was a joke and a jest, with us, and an evidence of ineffable dreaminess, when an American mused that one object of the war was to provide the Hottentot with access to a quart of milk every day. A joke indeed, and isn't the man impossible? But just whom was our Pilate's-jest a joke *on*, anyway?

We had been put in the position of fighting for the preservation of the status quo; the status quo at home, where reaction had found its voice again, and, by logical extension, the status quo abroad as well. Our unlimited strength had been applied to the attainment of strictly limited objectives, military objectives—which meant that we came out of the war to find that the real issues had not yet been settled. The big operators who made the working decisions had decided that nothing very substantial was going to be changed. The war ended, and things were changed to the very roots of human society, with more changes coming, despite our decree that change must stop. Therefore—unease, perplexity, fear.

Fear, to be specific, of communism.

As a matter of settled national policy, we are not going to permit the world to go communist. Well and good; there is in communism something deeply alien to the dream that we have dreamed, there is a threat and a menace in it, we are going to oppose it, limit it, check it, beat it down; we are going to have a showdown, and we are going to end this present danger.

So far, fine: but what are we going to do it with?

With words, of course; we have command over no end of them. With dollars, too; we have, if not an absolutely limitless stock, at least a prodigious quantity of them, and we will use them without stint (within, of course, the bounds of a proper government economy). And, finally, with men and guns and planes and all the rest of the paraphernalia of force.

And the only trouble is that we can't possibly do it that way. Not while we're scared, we can't. Not while what's really biting us is the fear of change at home.

For if we have in fact come to the final contest between communism and democracy, the first point to recognize is that it is a contest which takes place beyond the reach of words and dollars and guns, because it is a contest that takes place in men's minds and hearts. We are currently finding our allies, not in the things that appeal to minds and hearts, but in the men who have guns to shoot and ramparts to hold and bits of the old order to defend; bit by bit, almost as if we had planned it that way from the beginning, we are allying ourselves with all of the forces of the status quo in all the corners of the earth; when it was precisely those forces that created communism in the first place.

The people are on the march, and the one absolute certainty about it all is that they are not going to wind up back where they started. If, as we say, they are going to choose between communism and democracy, they are not going to base their choice on what democracy says or on how far democracy's guns can shoot, or even on the destructive power of democracy's bombs. They are going to base it on what democracy is, and they are going to decide what democracy is by what it does, by what it offers them in terms they can get their teeth into. It is not going to be a carefully reasoned choice; it will be a choice made with the blood and muscles and stomach—strictly a process of judging trees by their fruits.

Communism is a revolutionary force. *So is democracy*—an older, greater, stronger force, if it is once recognized for what it is and practiced that way. For democracy is The People—not just the important people, not just the cultured people, not just the people who own things and manage things and control things, but *all* the people, up, down, and across, all the time and everywhere: the people, with the strength they cannot understand and the dreams they cannot express and the destiny that goes beyond the circuit of all the wheeling stars. Democracy is not just a set of rules for conducting political affairs, a certain way of casting votes, or a formula for electing and removing office-holders. It is a way of life, and the people who follow it recognize it because they know that in everything that happens they themselves are both the source of strength and the authority which says how that strength shall be used.

Fine words, beyond doubt. Meaning just what, in relation to the war we fought?

Meaning, first of all, the chances we missed: the chances to bring democracy out of the war as a great revolutionary force that knew its own strength, knew why it was strong and knew exactly what its great power was going to mean.

Look back, once more, at the chances that were missed; missed, because of the fear of change that kept our war from being a people's war.

The full energies of the small business system—the businesses of the little producers, the *people's* businesses—were not expanded, called upon to become greater and to fuse their strength, turned into a basic and enduring part of the American economy. The way to do it was clear enough, the values that would grow out of it were obvious enough, the pressing need for it in terms of fighting the war itself was exceedingly obvious; but it would have meant far-reaching change in the economic order, and instead of doing it we bedizened a handful of railway cars in patriotic colors and sent them out, like a troupe of performing elephants in pink pantalettes, to make a show and to distract attention.

Labor was not moved up to partnership with ownership in the great war industries. The opportunity was there, the need was there, and one-half of the study and effort that went into, say, the perfecting of the Controlled Materials Plan would have produced an efficient working arrangement. But here was another pattern for lasting change, if there ever was such a pattern, and it was laid away to gather dust with the unthinkables.

The dollar-a-year system was not replaced by a form of control that would put direction of the industrial effort closer to the hands of the people. Not only was the opportunity for this present; it was such an open, pressing, clamorous opportunity that acceptance of it was to be avoided only by a frantic struggle; but the struggle was made, and in the end it was successful and the opportunity was evaded.

The base for closely knit control of the American economy was not shifted by a new system to handle patent rights and to direct wartime scientific and technological research into new channels. It was solemnly decided that the war effort must not be used to bring about social or economic reform, and to him that hath shall be given the fruits of a billion dollars worth of research; the attempt to shift the base was made, and made valiantly, but it failed. (Leading to the question: If democracy, fighting for its life, is not just then concerned with social and economic reform, is there anything easily definable that it is concerned with?)

Adequate preparation for reconversion was not made. Here

again the specter of change stalked across the moorlands, frightening good men; and because of that fright we followed the one course of all courses most certain to bring us out of the war unready for peace, confused about the values for which we fought and unadjusted to the demands of a changing world.

And through it all, running like a dominant thread, the people were not trusted with the facts or relied on to display that intelligence, sanity, and innate decency of spirit upon which democracy in all of its guises finally rests. Scold the people, cajole the people, deceive the people, whip them into line, make them realize there is a war on even if it takes all four radio networks and a five-star general denouncing a breakdown in morale; do anything and everything about it, even to the length of putting final reliance on outworn public relations techniques—but *don't* get down to letting the people know exactly what the score is because the good Lord only knows how they'll act if they do. In a very real sense, our government spent the war years looking desperately for some safe middle ground between Hitler and Abraham Lincoln. Unfortunately, there isn't any such place.

For the point of the whole story is that in this world revolution we had, and we still have, one reliance and only one: complete, 200-proof democracy, taken straight.

During the war it looked like too stiff a dose, and we backed away from it. It was a people's war; the people were doing the working and the fighting and the dying and in the end they would have to pay all the bills, but we never let ourselves build a war effort that would bring us into the peace with a dynamic, this-is-democracy-in-action program to excite the imaginations and grip the hearts of all the people everywhere. We retreated from democracy because democracy means Change—if it means anything worth the life of one drafted sharecropper; and the simple, paralyzing fear of change, born of the fact that the men to whom change would mean loss sat in the drivers' seats, took us to Pearl Harbor unready for war and to VJ-Day unready for peace.

Because we retreated during the war—because we did not, in the very process of winning the war, take the opportunity to give modern democracy a new meaning, a new vigor, a triumphant and eternally hopeful awareness of its own everlasting vitality—we are today in the exceedingly curious position of being at once the strongest and the most nervous nation on earth. We won an overwhelming victory and we have not the least notion what to do with it. And so, in a world where more profound, far-reaching, and lasting changes are taking place than at any time since the breakup of the Roman empire, we can think of nothing better to do than to strike hands with those men, in whatever quarter of the earth, who are struggling for a season against all change. We are afraid of communism, and with right good reason, but we are also afraid to use the irresistible weapon of democracy which lies ready to our hands. Instead we are relying on words, dollars, and guns, and none of them will turn the trick for us.

Get back, just for a moment, to the lowly Hottentot and his daily quart of milk. It was a ridiculous joke, of course, to suggest that getting that quart of milk for him might be one of the objects of the war, and so we didn't fight the war that way. But he still hasn't got his quart of milk; and just suppose (for the sake of exercising the imagination) that he finally comes to feel that by embracing communism, or by permitting the communists to embrace him, he will in fact get that quart of milk. (Ridiculous of him to feel that way, of course; but that's what the communists are telling him, and we're not telling him anything.) What do we do then? Persuade him out of that embrace with guns and bombs and the deep terror of atomic rays? But maybe that quart of milk is the only argument on this living earth that will really move him.

Isn't it, perhaps, up to us after all to see to it that democracy does mean a quart of milk to the hungry Hottentot?

Carry it a step farther.

Let the Hottentot represent all of the people on earth who desperately need much more of everything than they have ever had—and remember that those people outnumber all other kinds of people by many, many millions.

Let the quart of milk represent all of the goods and services that this miraculous, mechanized, scientific, mass-production age is able to provide—and remember that now, for the first time in all history, it is possible for men to produce more than enough of everything to go around.

Then work out the equation for yourself.

What chance does democracy have to win the world away

from communism unless it does clearly, recognizably and in actual daily practice mean more milk for the Hottentot?

And if democracy does mean that, how can democracy possibly lose?

Democracy, then, means more than just the bill of rights, secret ballots, and one-man-is-as-good-as-another?

Infinitely more. It means, when you come right down to it, The People, and nothing else.

The people; and the fact that every human institution, whether it be a corner grocery store or the presidency, a steel corporation or a congress, a labor union or a stock exchange, justifies its existence *only* if it serves the people's needs—first, last and all the time—better than any substitute institution could serve them, and if it is always directly responsive to their full, conscious control. It means capitalism when capitalism meets that definition—not otherwise; in the same way, it means any other ism provided the ism in question can pass that test. It means outer darkness and the strong pangs of dissolution for all men and all institutions who stand in the people's way, or lie to the people and mislead them, or levy unjust toll on that which of right belongs to the people (which is the earth, and the fullness thereof), or get between the people and the full exercise of the people's rights and powers.

It means all of these things and many more besides.

And, just incidentally, it means the end of all fear.